Religion in a Liberal State

The place and significance of religion in public life has become increasingly contested and legally regulated. Fudged compromises of the past are giving way to a desire for clear lines and moral principles. This book brings the disciplines of law, sociology, politics and theology into conversation with one another to shed light on the questions thrown up by 'religion in a liberal state'. It discusses practical problems in a British context, such as the accommodation of religious dress, discrimination against sexual minorities and state support for historic religions; considers legal frameworks of equality and human rights; and elucidates leading ideas of neutrality, pluralism, secularism and public reason. Fundamentally, it asks what it means to be liberal in a world in which religious diversity is becoming more present and more problematic.

GAVIN D'COSTA is Professor of Catholic Theology at the University of Bristol.

MALCOLM EVANS is Professor of Public International Law at the University of Bristol.

TARIQ MODOOD is Professor of Sociology, Politics and Public Policy, and Director of the Centre for the Study of Ethnicity and Citizenship at the University of Bristol.

JULIAN RIVERS is Professor of Jurisprudence at the University of Bristol Law School.

Religion in a Liberal State

Edited by

GAVIN D'COSTA
MALCOLM EVANS
TARIQ MODOOD
AND
JULIAN RIVERS

University of Bristol

CAMBRIDGE
UNIVERSITY PRESS

CAMBRIDGE
UNIVERSITY PRESS

University Printing House, Cambridge CB2 8BS, United Kingdom

Published in the United States of America by Cambridge University Press, New York

Cambridge University Press is part of the University of Cambridge.

It furthers the University's mission by disseminating knowledge in the pursuit of education, learning and research at the highest international levels of excellence.

www.cambridge.org
Information on this title: www.cambridge.org/9781107650077

© Cambridge University Press 2013

First published 2013

A catalogue record for this publication is available from the British Library

Library of Congress Cataloguing in Publication data
Religion in a liberal state / edited by Gavin D'Costa, Malcolm Evans,
Tariq Modood and Julian Rivers.
    pages   cm
Includes bibliographical references and index.
ISBN 978-1-107-04203-2 (hardback) – ISBN 978-1-107-65007-7 (pbk.)
1. Religion and law.   2. Secularism–Social aspects.   3. Liberalism–Religious
aspects.   4. Religion and law–Great Britain.   I. D'Costa, Gavin, 1958– editor of
compilation.   II. Evans, Malcolm D. (Malcolm David), 1959– editor of
compilation.   III. Modood, Tariq, editor of compilation.   IV. Rivers, Julian, editor
of compilation.
K3280.R4297   2013
306.6–dc23   2013009519

ISBN 978-1-107-04203-2 Hardback
ISBN 978-1-107-65007-7 Paperback

Contents

Contributors

VEIT BADER is Emeritus Professor of Sociology and of Social and Political Philosophy at the University of Amsterdam.

GAVIN D'COSTA is Professor of Catholic Theology at the University of Bristol.

MALCOLM EVANS is Professor of Public International Law at the University of Bristol.

CÉCILE LABORDE is Professor of Political Theory at University College London.

IAN LEIGH is Professor of Law at the University of Durham.

DEREK MCGHEE is Professor of Sociology at the University of Southampton.

MALEIHA MALIK is Professor of Law at King's College London.

JOHN MILBANK is Professor in Religion, Politics and Ethics at the University of Nottingham.

TARIQ MODOOD is Professor of Sociology, Politics and Public Policy, and Director of the Centre for the Study of Ethnicity and Citizenship, at the University of Bristol.

JOHN PERRY is Lecturer in Theological Ethics at the University of St Andrews, and McDonald Post-Doctoral Fellow for Christian Ethics and Public Life at the University of Oxford.

RAYMOND PLANT is Professor of Jurisprudence and Political Philosophy at King's College London. He was created Baron Plant of Highfield in 1992.

JULIAN RIVERS is Professor of Jurisprudence at the University of Bristol.

LINDA WOODHEAD is Professor of Sociology of Religion at Lancaster University.

Acknowledgements

In bringing this volume together, we have incurred a number of debts of gratitude. To the executors of Dr Derek Zutshi's bequest, and in particular Mr Patrick Zutshi, for their enthusiastic support of this project; to Laura Serratrice and Alison Dawson for their help in establishing the lectures and symposium; to Aleksandra Lewicki for practical help in running the event; to Emma Harris for assistance in preparing the manuscript for publication; and finally to our fellow participants and contributors for their willingness to continue conversing across those unhelpful disciplinary boundaries.

Introduction

It is now a truism to observe that over the last decade religion has reasserted its presence in public consciousness. One must still question just how broad or how deep this reassertion is. Perhaps the secularization thesis – and its contemporary reversal – were only ever plausible in the contexts of Northern European liberal democracies. Perhaps, with hindsight, these societies had only ever experienced a temporary lull in the 'furiosity' of their religions (Berger, 1999). Perhaps the religion which is now reasserting itself is a set of peripheral concerns bound to come into conflict with surrounding culture and even masking, or responding to, a general decline (Bruce, 2011). Or perhaps surrounding cultures are themselves changing in ways which make religious beliefs and practices more unusual and more awkward to accommodate. But as all these questions suggest, the public presence of religion is widely perceived to represent a growing problem, which, however one might explain, receives concrete expression in increased political contestation and even litigation.

There are other more general and familiar trends which suggest that 'the problem of religion' is new, or at least has new dimensions. The first of these is globalization. Globalization in its technological manifestation enables real-time awareness of movements and events across the world, as well as networks of the like-minded, who might be mere mavericks at home. It is easy to forget that the Internet started being widely used only from the late 1990s. Globalization brings with it a strengthened awareness of diversity, which in turn is reflected in politicization as different options for the public and collective expression of religions vie for adherents. The sacred canopy has become a contest of importunate umbrella salesmen. Politicization in its turn feeds juridification, as disputants seek solutions by reference to legal norms and processes in desperate recourse to the only remainder of society's 'crumbling cement' (Habermas, 1999).

1

The 'problem of religion' is particularly acute for liberalism. Liberalism emerged as a solution to the religious conflicts of sixteenth- and seventeenth-century Europe. And while the liberal solution may for some have been initially about compromise, over time it came to aspire to universality, neutrality and cosmopolitanism. Moreover, by and large, it worked. Or so, at least, it seemed. Yet the re-emergence of problematic religion, religion which has not remained content with the social and political spaces allocated to it in classic liberal solutions, has nourished and been nourished by a loss of confidence in liberalism's universality. Rationalism has given way to pragmatic and parochial consensus on the part of 'decent peoples' (Rawls, 1999) who need only – and can only – agree on minimal procedures.

Not surprisingly, the revival of religion, and revival of worries about religion, also find expression in the academy as the religious dimensions of disciplines have moved from the periphery towards centre stage. What for a while was recherché has become research once again. This has been welcome news to those of us sitting for some time on that particular periphery. Yet, located as we are in our own disciplines, we have become increasingly aware that the academic revival of religious studies (in the broadest sense) has largely been carried out in a series of parallel debates. And wary as we have been that interdisciplinarity risks the fate of the jack of all trades, we have also become convinced that plausible solutions to the 'problem of religion' require at least these parallel lines to cross.

The editors of this volume were therefore grateful for the opportunity presented by a substantial bequest given to the University of Bristol in 2007 to attempt to break through the disciplinary boundaries. Our mandate was to conduct academic events which would contribute (among other objects) to 'the promotion of religious tolerance and understanding' and consider 'the reasons for and possible solutions of then-current conflicts with a religious factor'. What emerged was a lecture by Professor the Lord Plant of Highfield on 'Religion in a Liberal State' embedded within an interdisciplinary symposium. Two papers from each of the fields of law, sociology, political science and theology and religious studies were commissioned to reflect on the questions and themes raised in Plant's lecture. Along with the lecture itself, these were discussed and revised, both during the symposium and subsequently, until what has emerged in this book is a multi-faceted series of reflections focused on the same fundamental question: what is the proper place of religion in a liberal state?

Inevitably, the principal backdrop for our conversation was the United Kingdom. In common with many 'Western' liberal democracies, the United Kingdom is characterized by a threefold diversity: a significant, albeit shrinking, legacy of nominal Christianity with an active core, often outside older denominations; a growing body of those professing atheism or at least agnosticism, engaging in little or no formal religious practice; and a wide range of world religions and new religious movements, of which Islam is increasingly dominant. Raymond Plant takes as his starting point the basic aspiration of liberalism to transcend such diversity in the name of a just and humane political order, but observes that recent legislative changes such as the Human Rights Act 1998 and the equalities legislation of the last decade have changed the nature of the liberal solution from one of ethos to one of rules. This not only has the effect of unsettling the fudged compromises of the past, it raises a fundamental problem of justification: why should a religious believer give up the reason for their existence in the name of an impartial order?

Plant reviews – and rejects – several possible liberal answers to this question. Liberalism is a way of coping with the fact of pluralism – but then so is fascism; liberalism is a matter of existential choice – but where then is its claim to transcend other religious existential choices?; liberalism is based on an overlapping consensus of comprehensive doctrines – but only if those comprehensive doctrines are held in a 'liberal' way, which it is not rational to expect; or liberalism represents a thick moral position of its own – but then why should it be authoritative over other moral conceptions? Only one liberal answer holds out more promise: liberalism is rooted, as it was for Locke, in some kind of natural-law theory. Plant goes on to demonstrate that apparently neutral concepts such as 'coercion' are irretrievably rooted in moral values, and then draws on the work of Alan Gewirth and John Finnis to posit a universal 'natural-law' grounding for such values. This in turn leads him to reject the recent political and legal turn towards religion as identity and reaffirm difference-blind solutions to problems such as hate speech.

The chapters which follow Plant's essay reinforce and probe his thesis, digging with increasing depth into the foundations of liberalism's treatment of religion. The lawyers provide further evidence for the difficulties Plant identifies with recent legal changes. Ian Leigh analyses developments in the case-law of the European Court of Human Rights and points out a growing tendency to require a policy of state secularism. This has developed out of a requirement of state neutrality, which itself represented a judicial response to cases in which states intervened with partiality in the affairs of competing religious factions. But neutrality has the effect of rendering problematic mild forms of religious establishment hitherto deemed compatible with the Convention's protection of individual rights to religious liberty and equality. Thus the function of the Convention has shifted from the protection of basic rights as side-constraints on otherwise unregulated state action, to the foundation of a pan-European constitutional ethos. The problem with 'neutrality' is that it is open to a range of conceptions, which Leigh identifies and explores. By contrast, Maleiha Malik focuses on problems created by domestic equality laws, drawing attention to both legislative and judicial unwillingness to resolve the limits of the accommodation of difference. These have been particularly acute where religious believers have come into conflict with the new acceptance of same-sex partnerships. Thus while the stakes are raised for participants, solutions are evaded. Malik suggests that the way forward is to eschew the rigid boundaries to which law aspires and look for negotiated settlements. In short, she commends a return to what Plant terms the 'fudged compromises' of the past.

There is implicit in these critiques a rejection of a certain conception of secularism, namely one which consists in the exclusion of religious expression and religious justifications from public life. This contestation around secularism is reflected first in the chapters by sociologists Linda Woodhead and Derek McGhee. Woodhead argues that secularism is straightforwardly illiberal where, for example, it is used to justify bans on religious clothing, state surveillance of people holding dangerous beliefs and the dismissal of employees who refuse to take on new duties on grounds of conscience. Rather, religion is integral to the foundations and development of liberalism and liberalism benefits from religious critique and opposition. In any case Britain is neither secular nor religious but betrays the very dialectic that is necessary to the survival of liberalism. Religion overlaps the public sphere in all sorts of complex ways. She therefore rejects the implicit framing of much current debate. Religion is not the problem; intolerance and illiberalism are.

What Woodhead takes as the characteristic 'non-secularism' of the British state, McGhee prefers to characterize as a 'moderate secularism'. His principal concern is to question whether Habermas's more recent proposals in respect of the place of religion in public life, along with the suggestions of others interested in 'public reason' such as Rawls, Audi and Baggini, are capable of meeting the requirements of moderate secularism. Basing himself upon Modood's characterization of moderate secularism in terms of the inclusion of religious identities and organizations in public life, challenging the supposed neutrality of secularism and softening the public–private divide, McGhee notes the opening up of new public spaces for the participation of 'poly-glottal' citizens and the translation of religious concerns into secular. However, he charges Habermas with a failure to understand the 'multiple subject positions' which religiously committed citizens may adopt, along with the 'intersectional nature' of all identities. Ultimately he suspects that Habermas has not managed to escape from Raymond Plant's charge that liberalism requires religious people to hold their beliefs in a liberal way.

Later in the volume, Milbank will also contest Habermas's implicit understanding of human nature and identity, but the following two chapters continue probing the theme of secularism. The political theorists Cécile Laborde and Veit Bader are also, respectively, more and less comfortable with the language of secularism. Laborde defends secularism (shorn of anti-religious sentiment) against the charges that it marginalizes, excludes, neglects or even attacks religion. However, she concedes that liberalism does require believers to accept that politics will largely be conducted in a secular mode and that freedom of conscience – which lies at the centre of secularism's conception of religion – relies on only a thin theory of the good. What is at stake in the secular ideal is the need for all people to respect the conscience of others by submitting to the disciplines of public discourse. This is entirely compatible with forms of interaction between religions and the states, such as the public funding of chaplaincies in public institutions.

Bader is interested in the foundations of a liberal-democratic constitutionalism which emphasizes the priority of rules and institutions over theories. But as well as rejecting an 'exclusivist secularism' based either on a comprehensive ethics or a foundational rationality, he considers at length a series of arguments that liberal-democratic constitutionalism must have religious foundations, which in turn impacts on the place of religion in public life. These arguments, which are barely heard in the United Kingdom, have been most fully developed in the context of the German constitution. In their conservative formulation they defend the dominant position of the Christian churches in education and social welfare; in their postmodern formulation they insist on the impossibility of neutrality and the inevitability of a structured toleration. Against such views, Bader argues that Liberal-Democratic Constitutionalism has no unique founding conditions – whether religious or otherwise. It simply requires personal virtues of moderation and self-restraint in the freedom of political communication and the exercise of political self-determination. This is most suitably expressed in a range of forms of associative governance.

Bader's essay paves the way for two theological perspectives. However, neither of the theologians John Milbank and John Perry seeks to ground their vision of the possibilities of politics in Christian foundationalism. Rather, in different ways both challenge what they take to be the way the underlying problem of the religion–politics relation is constructed and offer third ways. For both, the Enlightenment contrast between faith and reason gives rise to a characteristic form of liberalism: one which seeks to draw boundaries between private faith and public reason. Both reject this fundamental presupposition of what Perry calls 'Johannine' liberalism – that of the two Johns, Locke and Rawls. The collapse of consensus around these boundaries is precisely the problem, which repeated attempts to draw the lines here, or there, will not solve. Milbank looks for a solution in the Humean notion of 'sympathy' and suggests an urgent need to recreate a community of sympathy out of concrete discussions about who we are. In not-unrelated fashion, John Perry re-emphasizes the role of rhetoric and decorum in public speech, thus focusing attention on the virtues that make an open public process of identity-formation possible. Here too there is an idea of civility in operation which depends on a respect for the other's capacity for deliberation and action.

Through all these contributions, and in the course of our conversations, a number of overlapping themes emerge in the face of current difficulties. The first – in line with points made by the editors in other contexts (D'Costa, 2009; Evans, 2009; Levey and Modood, 2009; Modood, 2010; Rivers, 2010) – is that 'secularism' is not automatically a guarantor of 'liberalism', but must be carefully articulated and qualified if it is to do that work. The same can be said of other similar concepts that claim to transcend difference, both negative (e.g. coercion) and positive (e.g. neutrality). Whether one seeks to retain the secular label, appropriately defined, or disavow it in the name of liberal democracy or some other value, slippage in the direction of hostility to religion must be avoided. Both religious people and secularists may be illiberal.

The second theme is that an older commitment to freedom of conscience has been at least partially eclipsed by more recent ideas of neutrality and equality, and may need recovering. Freedom of conscience is not simply one human right among many. It is a fundamental and necessary value-commitment which grounds the structuring of public spaces within which difference can be negotiated. Although it is epistemologically more ambitious than some attempts to ground liberalism – and Plant indicates some of the ways in which that ambition may be fulfilled – it is more robust. At the same time it is legally more modest, representing protected limits to state action while eschewing grander, and less concrete, principles of constitutional design. Closer attention to freedom of conscience may well suggest that a brake needs to be placed both on the vigorous pursuit of secular neutrality as a required habit of the heart of every citizen, as well as on policies which treat religions as matters of fixed identity which must be protected and accommodated at all costs. The recent judgment of the Grand Chamber of the European Court of Human Rights in the case of *Lautsi v. Italy* (judgment of 18 March 2011) suggests that the need for such restraint is now being recognized.

The third theme is that new structural contexts for 'being liberal' still need to be developed if the challenges of religion in a liberal society are to be met. In spite of all the concerns, it is noticeable that many of the essays display an optimism in the genuinely productive capacity of respectful discourse to resolve problems which at first manifest themselves as the product of fundamental ideological conflict. It may even be possible to hope for the creation of new forms of community out of the crucible of pluralism. The rejection of passive resignation in the face of difference alongside public action to seek new forms of reconciliation is perhaps the most enduring moral legacy of liberalism. And it is in the light of such a hope that this record of our conversation is offered to a wider audience.

References

Berger, P., ed. 1999. *The Desecularization of the World: Resurgent Religion and World Politics*. Washington, DC: Ethics and Public Policy Center.

Bruce, S. 2011. *Secularization: In Defence of an Unfashionable Theory*. Oxford University Press, 2011.

D'Costa, G. 2009. *Christianity and World Religions: Disputed Questions in the Theology of Religions*. Oxford: Wiley-Blackwell.

Evans, M. 2009. 'Human Rights and the Freedom of Religion', in M. Ipgrave, ed., *Justice and Rights: Christian and Muslim Perspectives*. Washington, DC: Georgetown University Press, 109–16.

Habermas, J. 1999 '*Between Facts and Norms*: An Author's Reflections', *Denver Law Review*, 76, 4, 937–42.

Levey, G. B. and Modood, T., eds. 2009. *Secularism, Religion and Multicultural Citizenship*. Cambridge University Press.

Modood, T. 2010. 'Moderate Secularism, Religion as Identity and Respect for Religion', *Political Quarterly*, 81, 1, 4–14.

Rawls, J. 1999. *The Law of Peoples*. Cambridge, MA: Harvard University Press.

Rivers, J. 2010. *The Law of Organized Religions: Between Establishment and Secularism*. Oxford University Press.

1 Religion in a liberal state

RAYMOND PLANT

The role of religion in liberal societies raises deep questions about the moral basis and legitimacy of liberalism. This is because the legal and regulatory requirements of a liberal political order in many respects challenge religious practices and the ways in which religious beliefs are manifested. In the view of many religious people, it challenges their beliefs as well because of the internal connection between their beliefs and the way they seek to manifest and practise those beliefs. What is it that gives liberalism such authority and why are its beliefs and values so privileged?

The challenge, however, is not just to the basis of the authority of the liberal state, but also to religion within it and in particular whether a religion seeking a role in a liberal society can do so only if it is a *liberalized* form of that religion. If this is so, then it may be that being part of a liberal political order will have radical effects on the integrity of the beliefs held by those who espouse them by requiring that such beliefs should be held in a liberal way as a precondition of playing a part in the liberal order.

These are not just abstract, academic questions in normative jurisprudence and political philosophy but are also of current political importance and controversy. They have developed as an important part of the public agenda in Western societies at the moment. I give just a few examples of this:

1 the debate in France about whether to ban the veil worn by Muslim women in public places – a law which has now been passed;
2 debates in the UK arising out of the Equality Act 2010 about the rights of religious organizations to discriminate in recruitment in favour of those with sympathy for and in some cases belief in the doctrines and practices taught by that religion;

This chapter formed the first Zutshi–Smith lecture at the University of Bristol.

3 the decision of Roman Catholic adoption agencies to close down
   rather than offer children for adoption by gay and lesbian couples
   as the law requires them to do;
4 controversies over the wearing of religious symbols in both
   public-sector workplaces such as schools and hospitals and indeed
   private-sector organizations such as British Airways;
5 the disciplining of a nurse who offered to pray for a patient in her
   care in hospital;
6 the requirement that rooms in guest-houses which are also private homes to be available to gay and lesbian couples even if such
   relationships are against the religious beliefs of those offering the
   accommodation;
7 the role and function of faith schools in a liberal-democratic order
   when such schools are largely publicly funded;
8 the very categorical dismissal by Laws LJ of an appeal by an
   employee of Relate who was dismissed because he would not on
   principle offer counselling to gay couples on the grounds of his
   religious beliefs – a judgment which led Lord Carey to claim that
   Christians were in fact being forced out of the public realm because
   they were prevented from acting on their conscientious convictions.
   Pope Benedict XVI made a similar claim during his visit to Spain
   when he argued that in Western societies equalities and rights legislation is making it more and more difficult for the Roman Catholic
   Church to articulate its moral objections to homosexuality.

There has also very recently been an interesting development in France
on an issue which is at the heart of the problem I am trying to raise.
In *Le Monde* (12 May 2010) it was reported that Eric Besson, then
minister for immigration, integration and national identity, announced
that imams planning to officiate in France would have to attend one
of two designated public universities to learn how to articulate their
Islamic beliefs in a way compatible with French political values and
republican culture. This raises the question about the legitimacy of this
sort of role for government and the privilege which it claims in relation to other sorts of beliefs.

   These issues are likely to become more rather than less prevalent
as third-sector bodies including faith communities take a greater and
greater role in the provision of public services as part of Big Society
programmes and the scaling back of the role of the state as the provider

of services to citizens. The problems have become more obvious in recent years and it is arguable that this is the result of a transition from seeing liberal democracy as an *ethos* to seeing it as a matter of explicit *rules and principles*, which can be seen as embodied in *laws* such as the Human Rights Act 1998 and the Equality Act 2010. I will now explore this point in a little more detail.

Liberal democracy: from ethos to rules

An ethos is a matter of practice and habit and as such, in such a context, it is possible for there to be a good deal of fudging of issues and compromises between different points of view and forms of community life based on such differences. Accommodations between religious beliefs and their interaction with secular practices and behaviour can be made in these contexts that do not become explicitly a matter of principle and rule. For example, a gay couple seeking a room in a hotel or guest-house whose proprietors are disinclined to provide them with what they want might be told of alternatives. These accommodations may have caused upset and hurt feelings but the issues involved were not made fully explicit and turned into matters of public policy and law. However, there has been a gradual change here which in some respects has culminated in the Human Rights Act 1998 and the Equality Act 2010. This change has made many of the assumptions implicit in the ethos of liberal democracy explicit in terms of rules, laws and regulations which in turn are capable of being made justiciable. Of course, there are differences between these two pieces of legislation, with the Human Rights Act being applicable to public authorities and the Equality Act having wholly general application in the commercial and voluntary sectors as well as in the public sector. Many of the influential proponents and critics of the Human Rights Act have been perfectly clear about seeing it as definitive of basic liberal values and principles (Feldman, 2002; Griffiths, 2003). Similar arguments have been made in relation to the more recently enacted Equality Act, particularly in its stance against discrimination in terms of what are called in the Act 'protected characteristics' which include gender, sexual orientation, ethnicity and, up to a point, religion. This has been thought by many to embody a clear statement of liberalism alive to the need to respect and recognize certain forms of difference and identity within the law. Indeed, it could be argued that from a

Rawlsian perspective the Human Rights Act and now the Equality Act can be seen as part of the 'public reason' of British society – political claims based on whatever set of beliefs have to be advanced and defended in terms embodied in legislation of this sort (Plant, 2006).

However, in making liberal principles more explicit in law and regulation, the scope for easy fudging and compromise has been radically reduced. This is particularly true in relation to Article 9 of the European Convention on Human Rights incorporated into UK law through the Human Rights Act. This article guarantees an absolute right to freedom of religious belief but is also coupled with a degree of conditionality in relation to the expression or manifestation of religious belief, given that religious manifestation affects or may impact on others. The manifestation of religion is subject in the words of the Convention to limitations as are 'prescribed by law and are necessary in a democratic society in the interests of public safety, for the protection of public order, health or morals or for the protection of the rights and freedoms of others'. Many of the issues surrounding these conditions at a previous period may have been settled by convention and habit – for example the possibility for a guest-house owner to refuse to let a room to a gay couple when this room is part of private accommodation. However, this is now turned into a matter of law. This relationship between an absolute freedom of religious belief and a more qualified right to manifest religion is of crucial importance in current debates. If a form of manifestation of that belief – for example the requirement on a Muslim that he or she should pray five times a day – can be regarded as intrinsic to the belief then, a constraint on the manifestation of religion in terms of a practice which is regarded as intrinsic to the belief is tantamount to infringing the absolute right to religious belief. This has led the courts into questions of whether a particular manifestation of religious belief is intrinsic to the religion and, if so, whether a constraint on that manifestation could be regarded as infringing the absolute nature of the right to freedom of religious belief.

Liberalism, equality and identity

It seems fairly clear that the growing explicitness of the basic values and rules of a liberal order comes into question when such explicit rules seem to conflict with forms of identity and practice which many people regard as essential to their lives. The Human Rights Act and the Equality Act provide a basic set of rights for all citizens and yet the impact of these rights may be to limit freedom of religious belief if the manifestation of belief is regarded as intrinsic to the belief but at the same time is held to infringe the rights and liberties of others. If people are prevented from acting on their basic beliefs or 'ground projects', as Bernard Williams calls them in *Moral Luck* (Williams, 1981:13–15), in the public realm – whether political, commercial or voluntary – then this clearly raises the question of how the values, principles and rules of a liberal society which constrain the behaviour of the citizen are to be justified to a citizen who holds what might be regarded as identity-constituting beliefs. What is the basis for the liberal claim to privilege in this context? Why should an individual with such beliefs accept the legitimacy of the principles which constrain his or her behaviour in this way?

It also seems that faith communities have learned something from the growth of the politics of identity/recognition/difference within liberal societies. This has further coincided with the growth of strands within liberal thought which have argued for a greater degree of accommodation to identity, rather than liberalism being seen as identity- or difference-blind. Crucial to this development within liberalism itself have been the arguments of thinkers such as Michael Sandel in *Liberalism and the Limits of Justice* (Sandel, 1982), Will Kymlicka in *Liberalism, Community and Culture* (Kymlicka, 1989) and Anne Phillips in *The Politics of Presence* (Phillips, 1995). These authors point out the need for liberal theories of legitimacy to take account of forms of specific identity found within liberal societies. In addition, the rise of multiculturalism in both theory and practice has posed questions about difference-blind forms of liberalism which liberals have been forced to recognize.

In terms of political and legal theory many of these forms of identity politics and claims have been focused on gender, ethnicity and sexual orientation, demanding from the liberal state some specific form of recognition. Religion has been rather left out of this picture hitherto since it is frequently seen as a form of *self-chosen* identity, or a lifestyle choice. It has been argued that gender, sexual identity and ethnicity are *given* and not *chosen*, they are matters of destiny rather than faith and the conclusion is drawn that, for example, in terms of religious-based discrimination against gays, citizens should not be able to discriminate against an identity which is *not* a matter of choice from the standpoint of one that *is*. The claim here is that religion is, so to speak, a matter of lifestyle choice; being gay is not but is rather a form of given identity. However, the success of identity politics, exemplified in the Equality Act in the legal protection of protected characteristics, has certainly led religious groups to argue that religion is as much a form of fundamental identity, even if based on faith, as are some of the given or naturalized forms of identity mentioned. I shall return to these points later.

Such forms of identity, it is argued, have an internal or necessary relationship to particular forms of public expression. They might be regarded in the words of Anthony Appiah as 'the normative requirements of identity' (Appiah, 2005). As we shall see later these may prove contestable from within and outwith a particular form of identity and faith community but for the moment let us assume that the normative requirements of religious identity involve dress, methods of slaughter of animals, the public wearing of symbols – the crucifix, the burka, the turban and dagger – and other individual and collective behavioural manifestations of belief. Equally they can be broader and more pervasive if a religion is thought to have as part of its own identity demands about the nature of the public realm, the nature of social morality and so forth. This can be seen as quite a fundamental challenge to a liberal understanding of the role of religion, which on the whole liberals have wanted to see as a set of private beliefs and rituals rather than as having an intrinsic public dimension coupled with a demand for recognition of this public dimension. As Catherine Audard has argued in *Qu'est-ce que le liberalisme?* (Audard, 2009: 622ff.), liberals thought that they had accommodated religion through protecting freedom of choice in religion within a private sphere, but in doing so they have failed to understand the internal relationship between religion and what it sees as intrinsic aspects of its claims in the public realm, or, to put the point another way, between belief and intrinsic forms of its manifestation. If this is so then again the issue of what it is that privileges the liberal view of the public realm comes into direct focus and indeed question.

Liberalism and justification

So, we are faced with the following issue. If religious beliefs are thought of, at least by those who hold them, as identity-conferring or identity-constituting then such beliefs fall into what Bernard Williams calls 'ground projects' which are central to the meaning that an individual gives to his or her life. In these circumstances the question has to be asked as to what authority liberal principles can claim over a religious believer when he or she sees the application of principles such as equal negative liberty, equal rights, a discussion-based view about the nature of truth in matters of politics and morality and state neutrality in respect of conceptions of the good and the comprehensive doctrines on which they rest. How should he or she respond to positions, policies, legislation and regulations of the sort identified earlier which may well be deeply inconsistent with these religious ground projects? Why should ground projects be limited, compromised, undermined or constrained by the neutralist principles of a liberal society – one which puts the right before the good and the framework of values of a liberal society before conceptions of the good? Bernard Williams has posed this dilemma very well: 'There can come a point at which it is quite unreasonable for a man to give up, in the name of the impartial ordering of the world of moral agents, something which is a condition of having any interest in being around in the world at all' (Williams, 1981:14).

These questions lead directly to issues of the authority and legitimacy of the liberal order. This issue is fundamental to liberalism because of the centrality of the idea of consent and of rational or reasonable justification within the liberal tradition. In its own self-conception liberalism does not seek to impose itself by force or power but by *consent* – an idea which goes back to section 172 of John Locke's *Second Treatise on Civil Government*, one of the foundational texts of philosophical and political liberalism. It can also be seen as a central theme in the work of modern liberal thinkers such as Rawls, Nagel and Waldron. It has also been seen as central by critics of liberalism such as Carl Schmitt. In his *The Crisis of Parliamentary Democracy* (Schmitt, 1985), Schmitt argues for the view that consent, justification and deliberation are foundational to the liberal position and the source of what he sees as its chronic weakness, namely that it cannot act decisively on the basis of its power because it is constrained by the demand for agreement and consensus. In Schmitt's view this shows something deep about the nature of liberalism, namely that in so far as issues of truth arise at all in politics and ethics what is seen as truth emerges out of debate and discussion. This is why J. S. Mill's essay *On Liberty* is so important to the liberal position. This discussion-based view of truth is one not typ-ically shared by the religious believer in respect of the beliefs held.

So, if liberalism has to base itself on consent and thus on justification how might such justification proceed? Thomas Nagel, for example, argues that in fact there have to be two aspects of the justificatory pro-cess of liberalism (Nagel, 1991):

1 the elaboration of general reasons for liberalism which are applic-able to all and are neutral and impartial in respect of conceptions of the good such as religious conceptions;
2 a justification based on reasons which are salient to the personal beliefs of citizens and to the possibly comprehensive doctrines underwriting such projects.

As Nagel says:

The problem is that since any system must be justified twice, it may be impossible to devise a system which is acceptable from the point of view of what would be impersonally desirable, and from the point of view of what can be reasonably demanded of individuals ... the problem for polit-ical theory is to increase the degree to which both personal and impersonal values can be harmoniously satisfied.

A fully realised social ideal has to engage the impersonal allegiance of individuals while at the same time permitting their personal nature some free play in the consent required by the system. (Nagel, 1991: 31)

Appiah commenting on the same issue argues that what we need there-fore is some idea of a mixed theory of value – one that has space for project-dependent and also objective or more impartial claims; for obligations that are moral and universal and for obligations that are ethical and relative to our thick relations to our projects and our iden-tities (Appiah, 2005: 234). This is a particularly clear statement of the problem which I have tried to identify, but it does not move us any way towards a solution when clearly, as we have seen, impersonal values applied equally, say about non-discrimination, completely cut across values embodied in ground projects.

Liberalism has to see the general framework of rights, equality, nega-tive freedom, state neutrality, impartiality and putting the right before the good as basic but nevertheless there is the hope and perhaps the expectation that such foundational principles at least in general and thin terms may engage with the values implicit in the comprehensive religious doctrines underpinning ground projects. Unless liberals are happy with essentially schizophrenic citizens in a way that increases the psychological burden on religious believers in being members of a liberal society – as Habermas has suggested (Habermas *et al.*, 2010) – there has to be a link between the impersonal rules of a liberal order and such ground projects and agent-relative views. Indeed, some have argued in a positive way that, for example, the Christian position can support the liberal position on issues about rights, freedom, dignity and equality and indeed that the Christian tradition has played a crucial role in forming these ideas. There are others with a more negative view of the legal structure of a liberal order who have equally pointed out the debt that liberalism owes to the Christian religion historically, even though liberalism is engaged in a wholesale distortion of that heritage (Burleigh, 2006). This is a difficult argument since it seems to commit the genetic fallacy of assuming that the origins of a way of thinking have a logical bearing on the current validity of the system of thought which those historical circumstances have engendered. More important, though, would be a philosophical point, namely that some of the ideas central to the impersonal aspects of liberalism and in particular the principle of universalizability and impartiality have a lot in common with the golden rule of Christianity.

This assumption that there might be a pathway between a liberal order linked to central features of Christian belief may be far too optimistic, particularly in the light of what I said before. Firstly, it is of course obvious that Christianity has a strong doctrine of human dignity and it might be argued that this idea underlies the liberal commitment to an impartial order and non-discrimination. However, it might well be argued that unlike liberalism, Christianity's conception of human dignity is intrinsically linked to a specific conception of the good and indeed equally with a conception of sinfulness, the pursuit of which from the point of view of at least some Christians may well detract from the God-given dignity which we all have. If our dignity derives from being created in his image then a failure to live up to that image in our own lives may well detract from that dignity. This is certainly one strand in the thinking of conservative Christians about homosexuality. On the other hand, liberalism cannot link its account of human dignity to any specific moral view about the good, on account of its commitment to respecting moral pluralism and diversity through ideas like neutrality. Secondly, and as a consequence of this first point, while it may be true to say that liberals and Christians share the same *concept* of human dignity, for example, they may well have different *conceptions* of it. Or to put the point another way: there may be agreement over 'thin' concepts but disagreements over 'thick' versions of these concepts, just because the grounds on which these conceptions rest are different in each case. Finally, it might be argued that the only comprehensive doctrines which could underwrite, from their own point of view, liberal principles would be ones which themselves had been liberalized. That is to say, the beliefs of a faith community might well support some or all of the central values and principles of liberal society but would be likely to do this only if that faith community held its beliefs in a liberal manner. This would raise in turn at least two questions: what is a liberal way of holding such beliefs; and how far would it be legitimate for a liberal state to seek to influence how beliefs are held, since historically liberals have believed in a free civil society and the autonomy of the private sphere? This is the issue raised by Eric Besson, in the report in *Le Monde* cited earlier.

The answer to the first question is complex and has led to much controversy. In the literature, holding religious beliefs in a liberal way is the same as holding them in a reasonable way. So what does 'reasonable' mean in this context? Apart from John Rawls, the philosopher who has written most about this is Thomas Nagel, who has argued that 'reasonable' in this context means that the religious believer recognizes that it is reasonable for others to disagree with him or her. Nagel elaborates this to mean that one can hold an internal attitude of complete faith in one's position, believing it to be true while at the same time taking an impartial perspective, looking at one's beliefs from a standpoint outside one's own circle of belief and in so doing recognizing that others disagree and that in this attitude they have reasonable grounds (Nagel, 1987). Part of engaging in what Kymlicka calls the liberalization of faith communities would be to encourage or even require the development of such attitudes, since the legitimacy of liberalism is staked on this: that its values and principles will be supported by those who hold to *reasonable* comprehensive doctrines. However, Nagel's position has been attacked here on two grounds. Raz argues that it is in fact incoherent: my holding X to be true does not follow from my belief in it but from my evidence for it. Given this link between belief and evidence I cannot claim both that X is true and that it is reasonable for others to hold that it isn't (Raz, 1995:

88ff.). Brian Barry insists that a reasonable standpoint on religion as understood by Nagel is in fact exactly the same as a sceptical attitude towards belief (Barry, 1995: 179). It would be odd for a liberal order predicated on the idea of individual freedom to require that people should hold their beliefs in one way rather than another.

Liberalism and pluralism

We now need to explore further the role of the recognition of pluralism in liberal democracy and how faith groups might react to different claims about the nature of pluralism. This is a complex issue as there are different views about the nature of pluralism in modern societies, but consider first what seems to be the problem posed for liberalism by pluralism and why it will just not do to assume that pluralism entails liberalism. The problem is this: if pluralism involves the idea that values are incommensurable – that is to say, that we either do not have some perspective which will reconcile all values into one coherent whole or, more radically, that we cannot have such a perspective – then this applies to liberalism itself. Liberalism involves a constitutional structure which gives weight to values such as liberty (usually of a negative sort), civil and political equality, civil and political rights and so forth. Its weight and ordering of these values is quite different from those embodied in other political positions. So if divergent values are incommensurable how can one set of such values – say those of liberalism – be given a privileged position? Indeed, if incommensurability is so pervasive how can such values be rationally chosen? If, as sometimes is assumed to be the case, pluralism shades into relativism, then on this view the liberal commitment to freedom is only one choice within a world of pluralism. No particular choice is more or less valuable than another. To justify liberalism in such a context looks like trying to pull liberalism up by its own bootstraps. So let us look into the nature of pluralism a bit further.

First of all, pluralism might be noted as a *fact* about modern societies, as it is, for example, by John Rawls (1996: Introduction), on the basis of sociological observations and generalizations. Such claims are not based on controversial philosophical claims about the nature of value. Equally, though, it might be difficult on the basis of purely factual observation alone to arrive at more general philosophical generalizations about pluralism, such as the claim that values are incommensurable or that no monistic account of value can be philosophically feasible. So, for example, to claim that values are incommensurable and that no monistic perspective is possible would require a rejection of utilitarianism, which assumes the opposite. This rejection cannot be based on merely noting the fact of pluralism.

This contrasts with much more philosophically sophisticated accounts of pluralism as, for example, the one elaborated by Isaiah Berlin. This arises out of a critique of the nature of monism and its assumptions. In his essay introducing Berlin's *Concepts and Categories*, Berlin's position is rather oddly described by Bernard Williams as an 'absolute and fundamental truth' about the human situation as revealed by human history (Williams, 1999: xix). This is odd in two respects: firstly, the fact that if such an absolute truth is revealed by history then one needs some rather strong account of history to justify such a claim; secondly, the standpoint of philosophical pluralism itself makes the claim that its own truth is in some sense *absolute* intensely problematic. Williams's own position on pluralism and liberalism is, firstly, that if there is a range of competing values which monists repress and which liberals tolerate, then in some sense more (values) must to some extent mean better and thus liberalism is to be preferred. Secondly, Williams claims that a liberal position is justified in the sense of truthfulness. It is an attempt to live truthfully in the light of the nature of pluralism as revealed in history (Williams, 1999).

A philosophical account of pluralism may also seem to be difficult for the religious believer just because it seems to be inconsistent with a central strand in theism, namely the view that there is 'one God, one morality', as Stuart Hampshire puts it (Hampshire, 1999). If part of the justification of liberalism lies in the fact that it is responsive to the context of pluralism, then at least as a philosophical theory, this may be rejected from the start by the theist just because theism seems to deny the possibility of an authentic pluralism about values. Thus the idea that there is some kind of shared moral ground between liberals and religious believers arising from a mutual recognition of pluralism may not be available, since the nature and indeed possibility of that pluralism may in fact be contested.

However, for the moment I want to concentrate on the problem which pluralism poses for liberalism. Why should liberalism be ceded the fundamental political authority when there is a clash of basic values? There seem to be various answers to this question:

1 Liberalism is a way of coping with the stresses and strains embodied in a society marked by pluralism (Madison, 1961). This cannot be enough of a justification on its own because there are other ways of coping with pluralism – for example, getting rid of it, as fascists believed was important and necessary for the homogeneity of society. The philosophical basis for this was developed by Carl Schmitt in *The Crisis of Parliamentary Democracy* (Schmitt, 1985) and also Adolf Hitler in *Mein Kampf* (Stern, 1975: 49).

2 Liberalism is a basic existential choice as it is treated, for example, by Raymond Aron and in some moods Isaiah Berlin (Aron, 1938: 106, 109, 385, 396, 410; Berlin, 1969: 172; Berlin, 2009: 467–8). The difficulty with this is that many liberals want to privatize religion because it is based on faith and commitment and does not meet the canons of liberal public reason. It is, in Rorty's words, a 'conversation stopper' (Rorty, 1999: ch. 11). It would therefore be utterly inconsistent to privilege liberalism on the basis of existential choice, because this would embody similar faith and commitment. If liberalism is based on a choice of this sort then such an idea seems to consort rather badly with the claim which as we saw earlier is essential to liberalism, namely consent and rational persuasion.

3 Liberalism is justified in the context of deep and irreconcilable value differences in terms of looking at the undesirability of the alternatives. If a state sought to impose an overall conception of the good in the context of diversity of views about the good this would have to lead to high levels of coercion and violence. Rejection of cruelty and violence seems to be a universal value and in so far as liberalism seeks to avoid this it is supported by such universal human values (Shklar, 1998).

4 It can of course be argued, following Rawls and Nagel, that liberalism can be supported by an overlapping consensus drawn from a range of comprehensive doctrines and that this is essential to preserve liberalism's salience for those with strong comprehensive beliefs. But does this apply only if such comprehensive doctrines are held in a liberal way and indeed may have been liberalized by such a liberal state? If this is so then this will not help the legitimacy of liberalism. Liberalism will have to answer the question about the legitimacy of its own position before it can reasonably seek to liberalize, for example, the beliefs of faith communities.

5 Liberalism has a thick moral position of its own which elaborates
   and defends a substantial moral position underpinning liberal principles – what has come to be called, wrongly I think, 'perfectionist'
   liberalism. The work of Joseph Raz is of central importance to such
   a position (Raz, 1986). However, the problem with this, as seen by
   its many critics, is that it makes a conception of liberalism with
   its own thick conception of the good – for example autonomy – a
   further part of the problem of pluralism over the good which liberal political principles were designed to solve. If liberalism has its
   own substantial good, if all goods are part of a social context in
   which goods are controversial and subject to disagreement, what is
   to make the liberal conception of the good authoritative amidst all
   of this diversity?

6 It might be argued that instead of looking for philosophical under-
   pinnings of liberalism in a context of pluralism we should rather
   see it in historical terms. It is a doctrine which has emerged in
   Western history through circumstances such as religious wars
   which have made its appeal intelligible even if it lacks some ultimate philosophical sanction. It is an achievement, not a philosophically grounded theory. However, this will hardly do as it stands as
   a thesis about legitimacy, unless despite fine words about consent
   and rational justification the liberal is just prepared to impose liberal values and their consequences on, for example, faith groups
   who may regard these as illegitimate. This is just how we do things
   around here – to echo Richard Rorty's view. Of course this might
   be a different matter if the position of liberalism in the West could
   be seen as underwritten by a philosophy of history of the sort
   provided by Francis Fukuyama in *The End of History* (Fukuyama,
   1992). However, those like Richard Rorty and Raymond Aron,
   who have taken the view that liberalism should be seen as a historical achievement rather than a philosophical system, have also
   been in the forefront of regarding history as a series of contingencies (Aron, 1938; Berlin, 1969, 2009; Rorty, 1989). Such a view
   of history can hardly provide a firm justification of the priority
   of liberalism in the face of dissenting comprehensive doctrines,
   particularly when some of those doctrines – Christianity would
   be a prime example – may well have their own philosophies of
   history and theodicies underpinned by their own comprehensive
   doctrines.

7 Finally in this list we might draw attention to natural-law ideas of liberalism. It is, of course, worth pointing out that John Locke, a founding father of liberalism, rooted his arguments in a theistic/natural-law view of politics and society. The issue of natural law relates to pluralism in the following way. One of the major natural-law thinkers, St Thomas Aquinas, argued in *Summa contra gentiles* that natural law which could be known by reason and by revelation provided a kind of bridge between the pagan and the Christian and that this bridge was important for communication across cultures and ways of life such as the Christian and the non-Christian. The core idea here is that the nature of human nature and what we are to understand by intelligible forms of human flourishing in the light of that nature provide an important horizon and indeed limiting point for pluralism and diversity. This point is also made at least implicitly by Isaiah Berlin when he argues in *The Crooked Timber of Humanity* that there is a big difference between pluralism and relativism. The pluralist recognizes the fact that the nature of human life provides a horizon based on what is recognizably human as a limitation on the diversity of values, which would otherwise be so great as to lead to relativism (Berlin, 1990: 80).

So there are a large number of different and incompatible answers to the question of what it is that privileges the liberal legal and political order over first-order identity-creating and -sustaining beliefs and this diversity of justificatory strategies weakens the claim to privilege liberalism over other forms of belief.

The neutrality of the public realm

It has been argued that neutrality is essential to modern liberalism in the context of diversity. In a situation of first-order disagreement over conceptions of the good, liberalism has to legitimize itself and does so as a doctrine which is neutral between these first-order controversies. This is why in the view of such thinkers perfectionist liberalism, based on its own substantial moral standpoint, will not work as it will become a further part of the problem of pluralism rather than its solution. Neutrality in public doctrine seems to be quite a powerful tool because its position is that public reason within a neutrally determined public space can deploy only principles and arguments which are not

drawn directly from and do not directly embody contentious comprehensive beliefs and doctrines. The consequence of this is that there can
be no directly religious input into debate in the public realm. It may be
that people of faith will be able to find and utilize neutral arguments
or secular arguments which are widely accepted and may be regarded
as part of public reason as means of backing up their religious position. For example, the ubiquitous health and safety concerns which
are part of public reason might be used in certain circumstances to
back up religious arguments about sexuality, and in this context the
religious person may well be able to make his or her argument about
some aspect of sexuality in a secular way to achieve what is a religious
aim but which would violate the canons of public reason and neutrality if argued on a religious basis alone. However, all of this, which
follows from the idea of the neutrality of the public realm in a liberal
society, may be doubted if it can be shown that some of the central
principles of the public realm as envisaged by liberals are themselves
intensely moralized. It would be good to have space to show that this
is true of freedom, justice and rights, but I will concentrate on freedom, although the case here will indirectly bear on rights, too, whether
these are understood to be protections of negative liberty or for that
matter ways of protecting basic human interests.

A liberal society is a free society and central to it is the ideal of
equal freedom. For most liberals freedom is essentially negative and is
defined in terms of the absence of coercion. The two paradigm cases
of coercion are:

A prevents B from doing X (or, A makes it impossible for B to do X), which
he or she would otherwise do;
   and
A requires B to do Y (or, A makes it impossible for B not to do Y), which
otherwise he or she would not do.

If freedom is the absence of coercion, then it is essential to have an
account of the nature of coercion which is neutral between different
belief systems, otherwise whether someone was coerced would depend
upon that person's beliefs and values. That would collapse the distinction between being free and feeling free. In subjectivizing freedom
to this extent it would render the idea of equal freedom meaningless.
The 'being free' may be objective if we can have an objective account

of coercion; 'feeling free' is subjective in that it engages the individual's beliefs and desires. If freedom and coercion are moralized relative to disputed, controversial and incommensurable conceptions of the good, then there can be no meaning to the phrase 'equal freedom' since each judgement about freedom and coercion would in fact be subjective. Critics of this view assume that there can be some value-free conception of coercion. It is very doubtful that this can be so. It might be argued that if coercion is defined in terms of prevention and impossibility then this might be so. After all, prevention and impossibility are wholly empirical states of affairs and therefore to invoke one or the other is not to make a morally engaged claim. This can be doubted, but for the moment let me pursue a different line. Even if prevention and impossibility are not moralized, most forms of coercion are not covered by them. The law certainly is not. The law works not by prevention and not by impossibility but by threats: if you do X you will go to prison for five years; if you do Y you will be fined £100 and so on. However, threats engage people's sense and scale of values – what matters to them and what is important to them. A threat is only coercive relative to a person's values, indeed given a different set of values it may seem like an offer. The legal notice 'Parking Prohibited: Penalty £50' may be taken by a rich man to be an offer: 'Fancy! I can park in this really good spot for only £50!' To a poor person it may well be a form of coercion in that relative to his scale of values the threat deters him from parking there, which is what he would otherwise do. The same words to one person can be a threat and to another an offer. Take another case: a thief in a church threatens to desecrate the consecrated host unless the priest gives him the keys to the safe. For the priest the host is the body of Christ, the threat is credible and he thinks that he has to comply yet that is not what he wants to do; exactly the same threat may be made to a secular cleaner in the church and it will not be seen as a threat or not that much of a threat. Threats engage our values, and in order to have a common idea of a threat which we would all regard as a form of coercion we have to be able to invoke common values. This is recognized even by Hayek, that great proponent of negative liberty (Hayek, 1960: 138). We have to have a sense of common human goods, a threat against which would be regarded as a basic harm (Plant, 2009).

If there are such moral considerations entering our understanding of the nature of freedom and coercion, why should beliefs about basic goods and harms held by people from within comprehensive doctrines such as religious beliefs be excluded from an account of these basic goods and harms? The answer is essentially epistemological; that is to say, the claim is that such beliefs should be excluded because they do not meet the demands of public scrutiny, they are based upon faith, commitment and so forth rather than objective and intersubjectively shareable evidence. Before this claim is considered we need to notice that even prevention and impossibility as forms of coercion cannot be regarded as de-moralized concepts, either. Take impossibility. What I regard as impossible for me to do, leaving aside forms of logical impossibility like drawing a round square or physical impossibilities like being in two places at once which have nothing to do with coercion, clearly impacts upon our scale of values. It may, for example, be impossible for me to do X if I am to retain my integrity and my beliefs; it may be impossible for me, given my relatively timid character, to make that political speech when I have been threatened with assassination if I do so; it may be impossible for me not to comply with your order to do X since you have said that you will kill my wife and children if I do not – and my love for them is the most important thing in my life. So even impossibility is linked to the scale of values entertained by individuals. Most people would regard these as being so important that a threat against them is coercive because it makes it practically impossible not to comply with the threat. If all this is so then it is not possible to give a de-moralized account of freedom which is an essential building block of a liberal public sphere.

Parallel arguments apply in the case of rights. On the liberal model rights exist to prevent coercion and to protect negative liberty, but if I am right about the relationship between a common conception of coercion and a common set of goods then rights also have to be linked to an idea of such goods and their place in human life. So, whether we think that rights protect negative freedom or more broadly, as, for example, in Joseph Raz's work, that they exist to protect basic and important interests, rights cannot be detached from the good. There can be no question of putting the right before the good if by that is meant the claim that there can be a morally freestanding account of the nature of rights.

There is an additional way, too, that the argument linking negative freedom and central human goods can be made. It is central to neutralist forms of liberalism (Berlin, 1969: 153 n.1) that there can be no moral assessment made of the ends which people choose when they exercise their freedom. The only thing that justifies the restriction of freedom is not a moral and therefore contested critique of the ends for which freedom is used, but rather if A in pursuing Y infringes the rights or negative freedom of B. This has to be so because a moral critique of goals would destroy the neutrality of the liberal order. It follows, at least for Hayek, that the number and significance of the range of choices open to a person have nothing to do with freedom. Freedom is the absence of coercion and that is all. It is not and cannot be linked to disputed accounts of the range and significance of the choices made. However, as Charles Taylor has argued, such views lead to very paradoxical results (Taylor, 1985). If a neutralist liberal is asked what makes society A freer than society B, the answer has to be in terms of the number of coercive rules and regulations in one society compared with another. It cannot be answered by citing the greater moral importance of the choices available in society A compared with B. However, this quantitative rather than qualitative approach to the issue will lead us to the view that the simpler a society is the freer it is likely to be. A society with little or no traffic, with little or no financial and property-transfer system, with little industry and trade requiring laws to do with contract and the like is likely to have far fewer laws than a complex Western society. So however oppressive the first sort of society may be, it is freer in quantitative terms than the other. Taylor cites Western societies versus Hoxha's Albania as an example. Surely Taylor is right to argue that what makes Western societies freer than Albania is what people are able to do and how these thing relate to accounts of the human good: they are allowed to be mobile, to leave the country, to participate in politics if they wish to, to criticize the government, have a wide variety of cultural goods available to them, etc. On the quantitative approach none of these things can enter into the judgement since to do so would moralize the concept of negative liberty, which in a context of moral diversity would undermine one of the building blocks of the neutral state.

So both in terms of an understanding of coercion and the understanding of why freedom matters to us we have to invoke a conception of goods which we have in common. This is why, as I said earlier, it seems to me that something like a natural-law approach which presumes some agreement over the central goods of human life in the context of what human beings need to flourish is central to making sense of freedom and coercion.

If a conception of the good or goods lies at the heart of an account of liberal society and any attempt to banish such ideas will lead to illusion, why should not the religious perspective with its view of the good and of human flourishing have a role in deliberating about what the core or essential goods are? In the recent literature on liberalism one can find two positions. One position would effectively privatize religious belief and debar it from having any kind of legitimate voice in the public realm; the other would demand the reshaping of religious belief as a prerequisite of entry into the public realms and would in all probability have the effect of privatizing religion as much as the first position.

The first position is that in so far as participation in the public realm is concerned an exacting epistemological standard has to be met, namely that for public reason to operate claims in the public realm have to be made subject to public scrutiny, testing and contestation. The *sources* of authority for claims made in particular must be capable of being open to such scrutiny. This is not the case, so it is argued, with faith-based claims. They depend on personal faith and commitment; they may be based on revelation and on personal religious experience. On the liberal view we are examining they do not meet the threshold to have a place in the public realm.

The second position is less radical at first sight. It involves the idea that in order to be part of the public realm faith claims need to be reasonable, and the criterion of reasonableness which is held in very broadly the same way by Rawls and Nagel is that I hold to my faith or to my comprehensive doctrine in a reasonable way if I recognize that it is reasonable for others to disagree with me. The reason for this account is that public justification has to have some sort of impersonal or impartial character. So in terms of public reason one has to be able to take both the personal position of faith in my own position while at the same time being able to take on the impersonal position, too; stepping as it were outside of my belief, I recognize that it is reasonable for others to disagree with me. This is very close to arguing that in order to be part of the public realm religious belief itself has to be of a liberal form. Indeed Kymlicka makes this achievement part of his own liberal project (Kymlicka, 1989).

There is a great deal to be said about both of these claims, but here I will just make two points which bear upon the legitimacy of liberalism in the context of debarring the religious voice. As regards the first argument, it would be very odd for a liberalism which at least in the terms of some of its most prominent proponents depends upon a kind of basic commitment or existential choice – the whole point of which is that this has to happen when we run out of shared rational grounds for belief. If liberalism itself depends upon some kind of faith which cannot be given an ultimate foundation, then it is hardly on strong grounds in attempting to block the religious voice in public debate which in turn depends on faith and commitment. Equally many of those arguing for the debarring of the religious voice do so because they take scientific reasoning as their paradigm of right reason and there is a lot to argue about here. However, one small point can be made, which is that it is not at all clear how scientific or factual evidence is going to be able to provide a justification for liberal principles to define the public realm if, as I have argued, those such as freedom, rights, justice and so forth are normative principles. The reason why factual and scientific enquiry cannot do this is the fact–value distinction which is usually taken to be central to empiricism. If all the reasoning that we are allowed is factual reasoning, then that is going to underdetermine in a radical way the normative realm of liberalism and again we are left with a commitment to liberalism as just that – a commitment. So on this basis it seems that liberalism itself has to be open to faith in itself and commitment to itself, and it would then be wholly inconsistent to rule out faith-based claims from the public realm.

The second argument about liberalizing faith groups in a way raises the same question, namely: what is the authority of liberalism to do this? What is the basis of its legitimacy such that it can challenge the way others interpret and understand their own beliefs? As we have seen, this is not an easy question to answer unless liberals are prepared to leave their unsustainable comfort zone of neutrality and argue their case in terms of a basis for liberalism in terms of a substantive good or set of goods which in turn have some salience for the substantive beliefs of those whose faith commitments they wish to liberalize. So the question then is how could this possibly be done?

One possible answer would be to look at some sort of account of natural law. Recall that Aquinas argued that natural law can be a

bridge between the pagan and the believer; could it also be a bridge in
the case of contending comprehensive doctrines and liberalism? One
thing that might be repeated at this juncture is that many who have
embraced moral pluralism have wanted to say that this can be differentiated from relativism (see Berlin, 1990), since the values embodied
in pluralistic moralities are all in some sense universal or objective and
that the nature and circumstances of human nature and human life
constitute a kind of moral horizon within which diversity occurs. So
how might such views be built upon?

There are two complementary ways. The first owes a lot to Alan
Gewirth in *Reason and Morality* and *The Community of Rights*
(Gewirth, 1978, 1996), the second is indebted to John Finnis in *Natural
Law and Natural Rights* (Finnis, 1980).

The argument derived from Gewirth would go like this. Any moral
or religious doctrine is going to have to have a place for the ideas of
agency and responsibility. Even the most authoritarian set of religious
doctrines has to have a place for agency. After all, its proscriptions
on evil or sinful behaviour only have a point and a purpose if the
adherents of that religion have some capacity either for following its
dictates or being condemned because they do not. The idea of agency,
therefore, can be seen as being centrally important to any comprehensive doctrine which seeks to guide action. However, agency has its own
generic goods, which are universal or general aspects of agency rather
than agency exercised within the perspective of one comprehensive
doctrine. Such goods of agency will be both negative and positive.
The negative ones will involve typical negative forms of liberty to be
free from coercion. When I wrote above about coercion I suggested
that the idea itself had to be linked to the idea of some goods, a threat
against which would always be regarded as coercive. The approach I
am now outlining would give some analytical framework within which
to think about that idea. Agency will also involve some account of
positive goods – a case which was developed by Rawls in his account
of primary goods. One cannot exercise agency without some degree
of education, some degree of physical security, some degree of healthy
functioning and some degree of power in order to exercise agency.
These are the basic goods of agency a threat against which will be coercive. Such goods would also provide us with a general account of harm
so that either threatening these goods, which are crucial to agency, or
withholding them would constitute harm. On this view, therefore, we

can develop the idea of the generic goods of agency, which have to be seen as general since, as I have said, any comprehensive action-guiding doctrine has to presuppose a capacity for exercising agency.

The second argument is indebted to Finnis's position in *Natural Law and Natural Rights* and it is an attempt to meet the need in any plausible theory of freedom pointed out by Charles Taylor for freedom to be linked to an idea of the good and human flourishing. Otherwise, freedom is purely a quantitative matter of counting up restrictions rather than considering what one can do with it. One response to such an argument will be to say, that is all very well, but people will differ fundamentally in their conceptions of the good and therefore freedom will be subjective. Finnis provides reasons for doubting that the goods associated with human flourishing and fulfilment are as diverse and subjective as this. To put his point in an absurdly brief form, he argues that there are a variety of human goods reference to which provide a kind of stopping place in justification. If I seek to explain why I am doing something, then, depending on the context, I will stop my justification by invoking some kind of basic good which an interlocutor would normally find an intelligible reason for doing something. Life and beauty are straightforward examples. If my ultimate justification for my course of action is that without pursuing that course I will die, then this will be taken as an ultimate reason giving intelligibility to what I am doing. Equally, beauty, or more generally aesthetic experience, can provide a foundational form of intelligibility in a different context. Similarly, the point is the same in relation to the goods of reason and rationality. These are not to be seen as sociological observations about the point at which people run out of arguments, but can be given a rational basis by forms of a reflexive argument focused on the idea of self-refutation. This is clear enough in the case of rationality. Any argument that I mount against the case for acting in a rational way will itself involve the use of the very forms of rational argument which I am seeking to undermine. So the process of critique confirms what it is seeking to undermine.

An elaborated account of the generic goods of action would also enable us to provide a rationale for rights and justice. Generic goods of both a negative and positive sort would provide the foundation for rights, because as necessary goods for all human agents any threat to such goods would be coercive. This approach tends to favour the interest or benefit theory of rights rather than the will or choice theory, just because of the fact that while negative liberty is part of the core set of generic goods of agency, this approach is broader and emphasizes positive goods, too, which can be turned into positive rights. These generic goods go beyond the importance of will and choice and encompass what must be regarded as basic interests of all human agents.

So there is a case for saying, against the pluralist view that we are faced with incommensurable comprehensive doctrines, that in fact there can be some types of universals in human life and practice rooted in the common idea of agency and common values relating to those forms of human flourishing which when invoked provide for the intelligibility of practical activity. In particular, this will help to provide an account of the moral context of the public realm, rather than one rooted in the idea of neutrality.

Identity- and difference-blind politics

Where does such an approach leave us in terms of the question of whether a liberal political order should recognize specific forms of identity including religious identities and grant them legal privileges and legal immunities? To do this would or could sanction the legal protection for the ways identities would manifest themselves in the public realm in dress, in the utilization of symbols and so forth. I would favour the alternative view that, as far as possible, a legal and political order should be difference-blind if it can draw upon a normative structure – a set of goods – which are universal, as I have suggested that it can.

In order to provide more reasons for this point of view we need to look at some of the negative aspects involved in claims about identity. I can go into these only in a skeletal way but they include the following. At the most abstract level it is arguable that the ascription of identity is always open-ended in two senses. The character Daniel in Sartre's novel *Le sursis* (Sartre, 1972: 151) says that he wants to be a pederast as an oak tree is an oak tree, so that he can come to be what he is, to realize his nature ('être ce que je suis'), but this is impossible for a human being because one cannot turn oneself into a kind of an object defined by an essential nature. For Sartre, and indeed de Beauvoir in *Le deuxième sexe* (de Beauvoir, 1949: part I), there is neither an essence in general for human beings to fulfil nor an essence in respect of particular roles. There is always a strong element of belief and of construction about social roles, and to believe that one can assume or be defined in terms of an essential identity neglects this fact that what we regard as essences are in fact social constructions.

Further, even if we regarded our identities as essentially fixed whether by biology or inherited culture, Sartre considers it possible for any person in any circumstances to take up an attitude of their own towards whatever they perceive their essential nature to be. To assume that in human life one has to fulfil one's nature as an oak tree is an oak tree is always to extinguish the radical freedom which human beings have, even if it is a freedom limited to taking up an inner mental attitude towards one's identity. To see one's identity as fixed is for Sartre to 'éteindre le regard intérieur'. If this has some salience then identity is always going to have highly contestable features, just because of its constructed and intentionalist nature. For a liberal state to recognize identities as ineluctable and as part of some kind of fate is, in the light of the Sartrean critique, to freeze something about types of human flourishing and development at important moments.

This freezing may well also empower conservative elements within any group claiming a specific identity to determine what the nature of that identity is, what claims to political and legal recognition are implied and what forms of behaviour in the public realm are required by a religious identity, for example. Another way of making the same point would be to claim that this presupposes a high degree of essentialism – that there is an essential core to a religious community which legitimates and indeed requires behaviour and appearance of a particular sort. However, there is quite a literature on the contestability of religious identities and there is also the point that any kind of legal recognition of religion in identity terms requires treating a religion in a rather generic way, whereas there might be quite substantial doctrinal and denominational differences, which in turn may sanction or for that matter constrain public forms of manifestation of those beliefs. The same points apply to other forms of identity, including gender and sexual orientation.

One further point about the philosophy of identity. Some will, of course, argue that identity does have an essence and that it is fixed by biology, say, in relation to gender and sexual orientation, for example. Even if the biology supports the view that some aspects of human life are genetically determined this still leaves two questions unresolved. Given that claims to identity in the law and politics are going to be

normative – that is to say, how people with such an identity ought to
be treated and what kind of self-expression of their identity ought to
be tolerated and/or ought to be protected by rights – because of the
fact–value distinction the factual nature of the biological underpin-
nings of identity will wholly underdetermine the normative aspects of
identity, which is what matters for politics and the law. These claims
also leave untouched Sartre's point about attitudinal and behavioural
freedom (as a consequence) in relation to any such identity claim.

In political debates about issues of identity and discrimination this
is a contrast which looms large. It is often argued that gender, race
and sexual orientation are given or naturalized forms of identity and
religion is not. Naturalized forms of identity are things that you discover about yourself, whereas religious identity is something that you
choose to assume. Therefore there is no case for special protection of
religious identity any more than any other lifestyle choice. In particular
the law should not allow self-assumed identities to be a basis on which
to discriminate against those with given or naturalized identities. As
it stands, however, this contrast is far too stark. In both cases we are
talking about the normative aspects, or more controversially requirements, of identity – how people with a particular identity should be
treated and what sorts of claims they ought to be able to make on the
basis of their identity. We cannot just read off answers to these questions from only an account of the givenness of the identity, any more
than we can read off what should or should not be allowed in terms
of the manifestation of religious identity. In all of these cases there
has to be deliberation about these sorts of questions in a democratic
society. So what might count as important in such deliberation? For
some it will be the identity itself which in their view will embody in
some way the authentic forms of expression appropriate for that identity. On this view, given that a liberal state will protect given forms of
identity it should also protect authentic forms of the manifestation of
that identity. However, this cannot be correct as its stands for two reasons. Firstly, if what makes the givenness of identity or its naturalized
form is some kind of biological basis then that in and of itself cannot
sanction an account of how a person with that identity ought to be
treated or what sorts of claims he or she ought to be able to make
on others. The empirical account of the biological nature of identity
cannot of itself provide an account of why others should be put under
an obligation in respect of this identity. To do this we have to explain

how and why the identity so given should be respected and protected by others. This is a normative argument and not an empirical one. This point in itself parallels the situation in respect to religious identity, where similar moral arguments arise. It is not that we have one type of identity which is given and naturalized with no contestation about what its requirements are in terms of its manifestation, on the one hand, and the contested requirements of religious identity, on the other. Both types of identity involve strong normative claims, and in this sense the contrast between naturalized and self-assumed identity is far too stark, at least in terms of what is claimed to follow from these identities. Secondly, we have to consider what follows from a manifestation of identity, given that both the naturalized and chosen form involve the rights and interests of others. Ways of manifesting an identity of any sort are likely to be constrained by the rights and interests of others and whether others may be harmed by particular ways in which identities of any sort are manifested. The idea of harm and our understanding of that in respect of rights, interests and basic goods are crucial here.

My own view is that politics and the law have taken a wrong turn here and we would be much better turning back towards a difference-blind type of politico-legal system. Threats and potential harms to any of the basic goods of agency are to be regarded as coercive irrespective of questions about identity. In these circumstances something akin to laws against threatening words and behaviour ought to be enough without qualifying them or constraining them with religious or other types of identities. On this view what we need to consider is harm to basic goods. If a form of religious expression can be shown in a court to pose a threat or do potential or actual harm to others who also have the same rights to the same goods, then that is a good basis for constraining the forms of expression in question. If such forms do not pose threats or forms of harm to basic goods they should be tolerated without having to get into metaphysical disputes about whether they are essential to the form of religious identity being claimed. Emphasis on harms and the threat of harm would allow us to conduct a debate about the toleration of various ways in which religion is manifested in a public and accessible discourse which is in fact denied when the focus is on identity, the normative requirements of identity and the authoritative articulation of these requirements by religious authorities. It might be argued that my proposal will not work because the idea of harm differs in a pluralistic society between the various groups making up such a society. However, two responses can be made to this. The first is to reiterate the point already made that in trying to determine the harmfulness or otherwise of tolerating a particular manifestation of religious belief we can conduct the debate about that in an accessible public discourse. Secondly, there is a benchmark of harm that can be shared across all groups within a pluralistic society, because of the link between harm and the basic goods of agency already noted. We need a citizen-focused approach to these issues, not one based upon a hermetic appeal to religious authority and claims about the internal requirements of religious identity.

References

Appiah, K. A. 2005. *The Ethics of Identity*. Princeton University Press.
Aron, R. 1938. *Introduction à la philosophie de l'histoire*. Paris: Gallimard.
Audard, C. 2009. *Qu'est-ce que le liberalisme?* Paris: Gallimard.
Barry, B. 1995. *Justice and Impartiality*. Oxford: Clarendon Press.
Berlin, I. 1969. *Four Essays on Liberty*. Oxford University Press.
    1990. *The Crooked Timber of Humanity*, ed. Henry Hardy and J. Murray. London: Fontana.
    2009. *Enlightening*, ed. Henry Hardy and Jennifer Holmes. London: Chatto and Windus.
Burleigh, M. 2006. *Sacred Causes*. London: HarperCollins.
de Beauvoir, S. 1949. *Le deuxième sexe*. Paris: Gallimard.
Feldman, D. 2002. *Civil Liberties and Human Rights in England and Wales*. Oxford University Press.
Finnis, J. 1980. *Natural Law and Natural Rights*. Oxford University Press.
Fukuyama, F. 1992. *The End of History and the Last Man*. London: Hamish Hamilton.
Gewirth, A. 1978. *Reason and Morality*. University of Chicago Press.
    1996. *The Community of Rights*. University of Chicago Press.
Griffiths, J. A. G. 2003. 'The Brave New World of Sir John Laws', *Modern Law Review*, 63, 159–76.
Habermas, J., Brieskorn, N., Reder, M., Ricken, F. and Schmidt, J. 2010. *An Awareness of What is Missing: Faith and Reason in a Post-Secular Age*, trans. C. Cronin. Cambridge: Polity Press.
Hampshire, S. 1999. *Justice is Conflict*. London: Duckworth.
Hayek, F. A. 1960. *The Constitution of Liberty*. London: Routledge and Kegan Paul.

Kymlicka, W. 1989. *Liberalism, Community and Culture*. Oxford: Clarendon Press.

Madison, J. 1961. 'The Federalist X', in A. Hamilton, J. Madison and J. Jay, *The Federalist*. London: Dent.

Nagel, T. 1987. 'Moral Conflict and Political Legitimacy', *Philosophy and Public Affairs*, 16, 215–40.

1991. *Equality and Partiality*. New York: Oxford University Press.

Phillips, A. 1995. *The Politics of Presence*. Oxford University Press.

Plant, R. 2006. 'Liberalism, Religion and the Public Sphere', in J. Garnett, M. Grimley, A. Harris, W. Whyte and S. Williams, eds., *Redefining Christian Britain: Post 1945 Perspectives*. London: SCM Press, 254–66.

2009. *The Neo-liberal State*. Oxford University Press.

Rawls, J. 1996. *Political Liberalism*. New York: Columbia University Press.

Raz, J. 1986. *The Morality of Freedom*. Oxford University Press.

1995. *Ethics in the Public Domain*. Oxford: Clarendon Press.

Rorty, R. 1989. 'The Contingency of a Liberal Community', in *Contingency, Irony and Solidarity*. Cambridge University Press, 44–72.

1999. *Philosophy and Social Hope*. London: Penguin.

Sandel, M. 1982. *Liberalism and the Limits of Justice*. Cambridge University Press.

Sartre, J. P. 1972. *Le sursis*. Paris: Gallimard.

Schmitt, C. 1985. *The Crisis of Parliamentary Democracy*, trans. E. Kennedy. Cambridge, MA: MIT Press.

Shklar, J. 1998. *Political Thought and Political Thinkers*, ed. S. Hoffmann. University of Chicago Press.

Stern, J. P. 1975. *Hitler: The Führer and the People*. London: Fontana.

Taylor, C. 1985. 'What's Wrong with Negative Liberty?', in *Philosophical Papers*, vol. II. Cambridge University Press, 211–29.

Williams, B. 1981. *Moral Luck*. Cambridge University Press.

1999. 'Introduction', in I. Berlin, *Concepts and Categories*. London: Pimlico, xiii–xx.

2 | The European Court of Human Rights and religious neutrality

IAN LEIGH

Introduction: the meanings of religious neutrality

It is often said that the state should be neutral in matters of religion, but neutrality is a problematic concept, capable of several different meanings. Despite that, the term is on the whole less problematic than 'secular'. Several authors have noticed the differing senses of 'secular' when used in relation to the state (Taylor, 2009): from its original meaning denoting a division in jurisdiction between political and religious authorities (Benson, 2000) to official indifference (Rivers, 2010) or antipathy towards religion.[1] Even in states such as France with constitutional provisions on secularity there can be considerable debate as to meaning (Laborde, 2008). Debates using the term 'secular state' are now so prone to terminological confusion that for the present purpose, in discussing the jurisprudence of the European Court of Human Rights (ECtHR), it is more helpful to focus on different aspects of neutrality.[2]

Of these the least controversial perhaps is the duty of state officials to behave *impartially*, that is without judging between the merits of different religions and in a non-discriminatory way. Even this does not prevent controversy over whether there is scope for recognizing the religious beliefs of officials over matters of conscience in the workplace or whether to do so compromises the state's position, as in *Ladele* v. *London Borough of Islington* (Malik, present volume). Beyond impartiality, however, conceptual controversy begins and at

I am grateful to the participants in the 2010 Zutshi–Smith seminar, and especially to Malcolm Evans and Julian Rivers, for helpful comments on earlier drafts.
[1] Julian Rivers contrasts this with separationism and notes the tendency to slip from one to the other (Rivers, 2010: 331).
[2] For an alternative discussion of the ECtHR jurisprudence identifying no fewer than twelve different senses of secularism, see Bader, 2010.

least four further variants can be identified, with different implications for both individuals and religious organizations. One strand stresses neutrality as the *equi-distance* of the state from all religions so they are treated even-handedly and none is favoured. This is often taken to entail separation of religion and state, although strictly it does not entail that. A second strand focuses on strict *equality of treatment* of religions by the state. A third strand – equal respect – permits differences in treatment by the state in situations either where fundamental rights are not engaged or where differences in treatment can be justified (described below as *equal respect*). A fourth sense of neutrality – as *objectivity* – can also be identified: its characteristics are to treat religions equally as subjective belief systems so that, at best, the state is indifferent towards them or, at worst, they are seen as equally irrelevant or misguided.

No reference to neutrality appears in the European Convention on Human Rights articles most clearly touching religion – Article 9 (freedom of thought, conscience and religion) and Article 2 of the First Protocol (respect for parents' religious and philosophical convictions).[3] Although neutrality might be considered to be implicit in Article 14 (preventing discrimination inter alia on grounds of religion) this is tempered by the subordinate status of that provision, since another Convention right must also be engaged, and by the possibility of justifying differences in treatment on reasonable and objective grounds (*Belgian Linguistics Case*).

Despite such textual silence this chapter argues that neutrality is becoming increasingly prominent in the Convention jurisprudence on religious freedom. For some time the ECtHR has gravitated towards neutrality as equi-distance and strict equality of treatment. This trend is especially evident in the Court's decisions on religious education and religious dress in schools. This, it will be argued, is inconsistent with

---

[3] The text of Article 9 of the ECHR states:

1. Everyone has the right to freedom of thought, conscience and religion; this right includes freedom to change his religion or belief and freedom, either alone or in community with others and in public or private, to manifest his religion or belief, in worship, teaching, practice and observance.
2. Freedom to manifest one's religion or beliefs shall be subject only to such limitations as are prescribed by law and are necessary in a democratic society in the interests of public safety … or for the protection of the rights and freedoms of others.

its own earlier jurisprudence that was more in line with neutrality as equal respect. This development, it will be contended, is undesirable for two reasons. Firstly, it fails to respect historic and cultural differences among European states and, secondly, the secular state model which is in effect promoted as a result suffers from profound difficulties concerning its own claims to neutrality. There are indications in the 2011 Grand Chamber judgment in *Lautsi* v. *Italy* that some members of the Court now appreciate this difficulty, although it is too early to say if, as a result, there will be a sustained change of direction in the jurisprudence.

Pluralism in European religion–state relations (neutrality as equal respect)

The European Convention on Human Rights was adopted by European states with a variety of models of state–religion relations and notably omits an establishment clause, unlike the US First Amendment. Historically the variety of different state–religion models within Europe has not been regarded as inconsistent with religious freedom.

Overall, the conventional European approach is not to assume a particular pattern of religion–state relations. As the Court explained in *Otto-Preminger Institute* v. *Austria*, 'it is not possible to discern throughout Europe a uniform conception of the significance of religion in society; even within a single country such conceptions may vary' (paras. 57–8).

The Convention jurisprudence and the variety of European models is an inconvenient truth for those who claim that separatism is the European norm for religion–state relations. For example, the Parliamentary Assembly of the Council of Europe chose to largely disregard it when it 'reaffirmed' in 2007 that 'one of Europe's shared values, transcending national differences, is the separation of church and state' (Council of Europe, 2007). This is partially correct, of course: there *is* a European tradition of separation, but it is much stronger in some countries than others and it exists alongside other traditions of establishment and, indeed, cooperation in church–state relations (Evans and Thomas, 2006: 699; Temperman, 2010b).

Nor should separatism here be conflated with state secularity: a recent survey by Madgeley notes that within contemporary Europe

'what distinguishes the European model is not so much state secularity as state religiosity, particularly when contrasted with the separationist model in the USA' (Madgeley, 2009: 185). For example, he
notes, none of the former Communist states which joined the EU in
2004 opted either for a formal state–religion model or strict separation, preferring instead what can be termed 'benevolent separation'
or 'cooperation'. To emphasize the separatist tradition while downplaying the establishment and cooperation strands is both misleading
and historically inaccurate. The European Parliament's assertion that
separatism *transcends* other church–state models is therefore highly
questionable.

This plurality of approaches to religion–state relations has been
accommodated within the European Convention in three ways, which
can be distinguished from one another. Taken together I shall argue
that they represent an approach which can be characterized as neutrality by equal respect. The three means of accommodation are: by
limiting the scope of the individual Convention right to freedom of
thought, conscience and religion; the use of the margin of appreciation
where qualified Convention rights *are* taken to be engaged; and the
availability of justification to the state for limited formal differences in
its approach towards religions.

The limited scope of individual rights is a symptom of the European
practice of treating the questions of free exercise of religion and
non-establishment as discrete matters (Ahdar and Leigh, 2004). The
European Convention on Human Rights is different in major respects
from the US First Amendment ('Congress shall make no law respecting
an establishment of religion, or prohibiting the free exercise thereof').
Under the Convention there is no non-establishment clause, and the
European Court of Human Rights has declined to find that links
between religion and the state necessarily violate individual freedom
of religion. This has important implications for the approach taken
towards state neutrality on religious matters.

The jurisprudence of the ECtHR affirms that the existence of a state
church does *not* necessarily violate Article 9. In *Darby* v. *Sweden* the
European Court of Human Rights found that:

A State Church system cannot in itself be considered to violate Article 9 of
the Convention. In fact, such a system exists in several Contracting States and
existed there when the Convention was drafted and when they became parties

to it. However, a State Church system must, in order to satisfy Article 9, include specific safeguards for the individual's freedom of religion. (para. 45)

The question at stake was the liability of a non-national to pay a tax which went in part to the Swedish Lutheran Church to support its religious activities. The former Commission had found a violation of Article 9, since the only way that the applicant could avoid paying the tax was to change nationality. The Court of Human Rights approached the issue differently. It found no violation of Article 9 but that the tax constituted discrimination as regards the enjoyment of property since Swedish nationals could opt out of supporting the Lutheran Church if they chose but foreigners were denied this choice.

The decision in *Darby* v. *Sweden* is nearly two decades old but the Court has reaffirmed the point with reference to the second means of accommodation relevant to state–religion relations – the use of the margin of appreciation. In the recent decision of *Spampinato* v. *Italy* the ECtHR declared inadmissible a challenge to the Italian income-tax provision requiring a taxpayer to stipulate which religion a portion (eight-thousandths) of his income tax should be apportioned to, failing which the amount would be shared in defined proportions between recognized religions. The Court reiterated that such arrangements were within the state's margin of appreciation in taxation matters under Article 1 of the First Protocol (the right to peaceful enjoyment of possessions). There is 'no common European standard governing the financing of churches or religions such questions being closely related to the history and traditions of each country'. A complaint under Article 9 was also found to be manifestly ill-founded: the Court found that because the taxpayer could choose not to make an election he was not required to indicate his religious affiliation contrary to the article.

Using the margin of appreciation under Article 9, some states have been permitted to justify prohibitions on the wearing of Islamic veil for students or teachers by appealing to *constitutional provisions* on secularity – for example Turkey, Switzerland and France (see respectively, *Leyla Şahin* v. *Turkey*, *Dahlab* v. *Switzerland* and *Dogru* v. *France*). The logic of this position, however, is that states with different constitutional religion–state arrangements, establishing a state church[4]

---

[4] For example, Constitution of Greece, 1975: Article 3; Constitution of Norway, 1814: Article 2.2; Constitution of Malta, 1964: Article 2.

or recognizing a plurality of religions,[5] should in principle equally be able to appeal to those arrangements under the margin of appreciation. This was the basis on which the former common-law offence of blasphemy was found not to violate the Convention despite its unequal coverage in preventing certain attacks on Christianity (especially Anglicanism) but not Islam (*Choudhury* v. *UK*). In *Wingrove* v. *UK* the Court also invoked the margin of appreciation and stated that 'there is no uniform European conception of the requirements of "the protection of the rights of others" in relation to attacks on their religious convictions' (para. 58).

The third technique for accommodating local religious diversity is one of proportional difference. Support for this can be derived from decisions under Article 14 (which prohibits discrimination in the enjoyment of Convention rights, inter alia on grounds of religion). Here the jurisprudence does *not* require complete equality of treatment by the state of all religions, rather it permits some difference in treatment on religious grounds. Discrimination is treated as suspect only if there is 'no reasonable and objective justification'. This does not mean that the Court is required to defer uncritically to all existing differences; rather, it promotes a measured approach to testing the legitimacy of different treatment. Consequently two decisions under Article 14 of the ECHR hold that the preferential tax treatment of the Catholic Church in Spain over that of Protestant Churches is justified, referring to the former's responsibilities to provide public access to its monuments and artefacts under a concordat with the state (*Iglesia Bautista 'El Salvador' and Ortega Moratilla* v. *Spain*; *Alujer Fernandez and Caballero Garcia* v. *Spain*). The Court reiterated this stance concerning Article 14 in *Spampinato* v. *Italy*.

There are, however, some limits to the use of these three techniques. The *Darby* v. *Sweden* approach is not a *carte blanche*: some forms of state preference for one religion do fall foul of Article 9 if they go too far. Consequently the protection of the Greek Orthodox Church as the historical or dominant religion from competition by newer religions through criminalizing proselytism was found to violate Article 9 in *Kokkinakis* v. *Greece*. Likewise, the Court has found that a political

---

[5] For example, Constitution of Belgium, 1970: Article 181; Constitution of Finland, 1999: Section 76 (establishing the Evangelical Lutheran Church) alongside separate legislation recognizing the position of the Orthodox Church.

party's programme to implement state endorsement of sharia law (even in *millet*-type arrangements) in Turkey would violate the Convention (*Refah Partisi* v. *Turkey*). The Court found that there was no violation of Article 9 in the prohibition for unconstitutional activities of Refah Partisi, a political party which supported the introduction of plural legal systems according to which Muslims would be bound in private law matters by sharia. The Grand Chamber characterized Refah Partisi's policy as applying some of the precepts of sharia law to the majority of the population (Muslims) within the framework of a plurality of legal systems. This went beyond freedom to follow religion as a matter of individual conscience since it assigned private-law obligations according to membership of a religious group (paras. 127 and 128).

As regards non-discrimination in several cases from Greece, the ECtHR has also taken a sceptical approach to preferential treatment of the Orthodox Church (which is established under the Greek constitution) as compared to other religious groups. When the Greek authorities denied the Catholic Church the right to take legal proceedings on the ground that it had not accomplished certain formalities whereas the Orthodox Church of Greece had access to courts without any formality or particular procedure, the Court found this situation to be discriminatory (*The Canea Catholic Church* v. *Greece*). The Court rejected the Greek government's argument that the special legal status of the Orthodox Church of Greece stemmed from the close and ancient relations between it and the state, the overwhelming majority of Greek citizens being of the Orthodox faith. However, it did not object in principle to the possibility of the government conferring to the Orthodox and Catholic Churches, respectively, different types of legal personality, that is personality in public law and personality in private law, in view of their different positions in the Greek society and legal order.

Moreover, the Court's decision in *Alexandridis* v. *Greece* shows how the approach to accommodating religious differences among states can be vulnerable to changes in the level of protection given to the individual under Article 9. The ECtHR held in that case that the procedure by which an advocate taking a professional oath to be admitted to practise law could opt to make a 'solemn declaration' rather than swearing an oath on the Gospels violated Article 9. The affirmation process was an exceptional one instituted in effect against a societal assumption that every Greek lawyer was a

Christian Orthodox and would wish to take an oath on the Gospels (*Alexandridis* v. *Greece*, para. 36). The Court found that the process for making an alternative 'solemn declaration' violated freedom of religion, by in effect requiring an advocate to reveal his or her religious affiliation. The Convention text gives no explicit protection against an individual being compelled to reveal their religious identity. This is a recent trend within the jurisprudence that brings within the range of review a number of state practices reflecting majority religion beliefs that in previous decades would not have been considered incompatible with the Convention (see also *Grzelak* v. *Poland*).

In summary, then, under the conventional position based on equal respect the European jurisprudence focuses on the *effect* of state preference for one religion over another or none on the exercise of the religious freedom of minorities. Where the law embodies appropriate safeguards of minority rights (as in *Darby* v. *Sweden*), or where differences in treatment have a reasonable and objective justification, neither full separation of church and state nor complete equality of treatment has been seen as necessary.

While this orthodox position has not been formally abandoned, nevertheless in some recent pronouncements the ECtHR has significantly moved its position increasingly to emphasize other interpretations of state neutrality. Before turning to the more controversial application of this concept (especially as regards state education) it is worth rehearsing its use in the less contentious religious-liberty question of how the state should deal with inter- and intra-religious disputes.

Neutrality as impartiality in religious disputes

Where there is conflict between religious groups the ECtHR has found that the state's role is to be a 'neutral and impartial organiser of the exercise of various religions, faiths and beliefs' and 'this role is conducive to public order, religious harmony and tolerance in a democratic society' (*Refah Partisi* v. *Turkey*, para. 33). Moreover, '[t]he State's duty of neutrality and impartiality, as defined in the Court's case-law, is incompatible with any power on the State's part to assess the legitimacy of religious beliefs' (*Refah Partisi*, para. 91).

The close similarity to classic liberal statements of neutrality under which the state must not endorse any 'comprehensive view' is immediately obvious (Dworkin, 1978: 127; Rawls, 1999: 80–1; Raz, 1986: 110).

Neutrality as impartiality does not mean, however, that the state can remain passive in the face of religious conflict. In its decision in *Otto-Preminger Institute* v. *Austria* the Court laid the groundwork for an argument that Article 9 encompasses a *positive* obligation upon the state to protect religious freedom, as well as the more familiar negative duty to refrain from interfering with religious liberty:

> [T]he manner in which religious doctrines are opposed or denied is a matter which may engage the responsibility of the State, notably its responsibility to ensure the peaceful enjoyment of the right guaranteed under Article 9 to the holders of those beliefs and doctrines. (*Otto-Preminger Institute* v. *Austria*, para. 47)

This implies that the role of the authorities where there is conflict between religious groups is not to remove the cause of tension by eliminating pluralism, but to ensure that the competing groups tolerate one another (*Serif* v. *Greece*, para. 53). A significant 2007 decision of the Court in a case from Georgia illustrates and applies this obligation (*97 members of the Gldani Congregation of Jehovah's Witnesses and 4 others* v. *Georgia*). An application was brought by members of the Gldani Congregation of Jehovah's Witnesses following the failure by the state authorities in Georgia to take action following numerous physical attacks and intimidation of the congregation by a group of Orthodox extremists. Although in total 784 complaints had been lodged with the relevant authorities, no careful and serious investigation had been carried out into any of those complaints. Against this background the ECtHR concluded that the Georgian authorities had violated Article 9 because of their failure to take the necessary measures to ensure that the group of Orthodox extremists tolerated the existence of the applicants' religious community so as to enable them to exercise freely their rights to freedom of religion (para. 134).

Moreover, it is clear from another decision of the Court that the state's duty to stand impartially between religious groups devolves to the actions of individual officials and the courts also. Thus in *Kuznetsov and others* v. *Russia*, where the chairwoman of the regional Human Rights Commission, accompanied by police officers in uniform, acted illegally in breaking up a Sunday meeting of the applicant Jehovah's

Witnesses and the authorities refused to prosecute, there was a violation of the applicants' rights under Article 9. The ECtHR also found a violation of Article 6 (the right to a fair hearing) since the domestic courts had failed to state the reasons for their decisions or to demonstrate that the parties had been heard in a fair and equitable manner (*Kuznetsov and others* v. *Russia*, para. 85).

Together these judgments take a significant step forward in converting Article 9 into a positive obligation upon the state, building on *Otto-Preminger Institute* v. *Austria*. There is, however, something of a tension between this emerging strand of Convention jurisprudence and other decisions in which the ECtHR has allowed member states to significantly curtail the exercise of rights by religious groups in order to avoid the stirring up of religious controversy. Rather than emphasizing the state's duty to positively ensure mutual tolerance, on some occasions at least the Strasbourg court has taken the path of least resistance in permitting, under the margin of appreciation doctrine, national authorities to curtail religious expression simply because there is a risk of courting controversy with other, opposed, religious groups.

In *Murphy* v. *Ireland* the ECtHR permitted Ireland to ban *all* religious advertising on radio under this justification. The Court noted that there was no European consensus on the approach to religious advertising (*Murphy* v. *Ireland*, para. 81). The Irish government argued that a total prohibition was necessary because of the place of religious conflict in Irish history, the need for a 'level playing field' and the position of broadcasters in maintaining a position of religious neutrality and the difficulty of distinguishing between different categories of religious advertisement. The ECtHR accepted these as relevant and sufficient reasons for the restriction, despite a concession by the Irish government that religious conflict was not a live current concern.

Somewhat inconsistently, the margin featured to the opposite effect in a recent decision from Germany in which a state publicity campaign aimed at warning young people of the dangers of (named) religious sects was found by the majority of the Court *not* to breach the state's duty of impartiality towards those groups (*Leela Förderkreis EV and others* v. *Germany*). Although the majority of the Court proceeded on the basis that Article 9 was engaged, it nevertheless concluded that the campaign had the legitimate aim of protecting the safety of others and did not amount to a disproportionate interference. This doubly unsatisfactory judgment fails to specify either the precise interference with the sect's freedom of religion or the alleged public-safety threat, preferring instead to revert to the margin of appreciation doctrine.

So far as *intra*-religious disputes are concerned it is clear that the state must avoid taking sides. As it was put in *Manoussakis* v. *Greece*, freedom of religion 'excludes any discretion on the part of the State to determine whether religious beliefs or the means used to express such beliefs are legitimate' (para. 47).

In a series of decisions from Eastern Europe the Court has found that Article 9 is violated when state authorities overstep the mark by intervening in religious disputes. For example, a 2009 decision from Bulgaria concerned a dispute arising from attempts to replace the patriarch of the Bulgarian Orthodox Church imposed during the Communist era (Patriarch Maxim) and the subsequent government's decision to reinstate him in order to end the ensuing confusion within the church (*Holy Synod of the Bulgarian Orthodox Church (Metropolitan Inokentiy) and others* v. *Bulgaria*). The Bulgarian government argued before the European Court that 'the unity of the Bulgarian Orthodox Church was an important national goal of historical significance, with ramifications affecting the very fabric of the Bulgarian nation and its cultural identity', and therefore their reinstatement of Patriarch Maxim was a necessary and proportionate interference with Article 9. Despite referring to a wide margin of appreciation in the 'particularly delicate' area of relations between states and religious communities, the ECtHR disagreed:

The State's duty of neutrality and impartiality, as defined in the Court's case-law, is incompatible with any power on the State's part to assess the legitimacy of religious beliefs. Furthermore, in democratic societies the State does not need to take measures to ensure that religious communities remain or are brought under a unified leadership ... State measures favouring a particular leader of a divided religious community or seeking to compel the community, or part of it, to place itself under a single leadership against its will would constitute an infringement of the freedom of religion. (*Holy Synod of the Bulgarian Orthodox Church (Metropolitan Inokentiy) and others* v. *Bulgaria*, paras. 199–200)

In this and similar decisions something approaching a doctrine of separation of state and religion is identifiable, grounded upon the effect of state interference with collective religious liberty – the autonomy of a religious group to govern itself being central (*Hasan and Chaush* v. *Bulgaria*; *Metropolitan Church of Bessarabia and others* v. *Moldova*; *Mirolubovs* v. *Latvia*). That is different, however, from the more controversial use of neutrality to which we now turn – in state education. Here the issue is one of impact on individual conscience, which in turn raises two questions. Does neutrality require state, firstly, objectivity and, secondly, equi-distance from all religions? The first question can be considered with regard to decisions on religious education in Norway, Turkey, Poland and Germany and the second by reference to the recent decisions on religious symbols in French and Italian schools.

Neutrality, objectivity and religious education

Perhaps nowhere are the difficulties and contradictions over the idea of state neutrality or impartiality clearer than in relation to education. Few if any states can be said to be neutral in the sense of wholly disinterested in the values that are communicated by schools to pupils. In the field of religious and ethical education in particular there are sharply diverging, conflicting philosophies and individual, parental and communal interests (Leigh, 2012; Temperman, 2010a).

Arguably, some minimum of religious education is necessary to fulfil one commonly stated liberal goal for education – training for citizenship – because of the undeniable historical importance of religion in shaping present-day culture and its contemporary social significance. On the same basis, learning about the religious beliefs of others may be a foundation for promoting the liberal virtue of toleration. It can, for example, combat ignorance among pupils of the beliefs of those from other religious backgrounds. In societies divided on ethnic and religious lines religious education may play a part in helping to reduce mutual intolerance and in validating and integrating as citizens pupils from minority groups. Aspirations like these represent the modern European orthodoxy, reflected, for example, in pronouncements from the Council of Europe Parliamentary Assembly and the Organisation for Security and Cooperation in Europe (Council of Europe, 2005; OSCE, 2007).

Alongside these aspirations is another commonly held objective, albeit negatively stated – that the state should not take on the confessional responsibility for inducting pupils *into* religious belief. In other words state religious education should be *about* religion but should not have a religious objective. While this may seem uncontroversial, many who hold religious beliefs question a closely connected assumption: that a detached viewpoint of this kind (a so-called 'view from nowhere') is attainable by state educators.

There is considerable potential for tension between the various perspectives on religious education, especially viewed from the vantage point of families with clearly fixed religious or atheist beliefs. It is unsurprising that these tensions have both given rise to a growing number of Convention challenges and are reflected in cross-currents within this jurisprudence. The most relevant Convention provision in adjudicating between these claims is not Article 9 but rather the specific right given by Article 2 of the First Protocol to parents that their children should be educated in accordance with their religious and philosophical convictions. For the most part, even where Article 9 has also been pleaded in religious education challenges, the Court has used Article 2 of the First Protocol as the primary vehicle to determine the issues. However, there are exceptions, notably *Grzelak* v. *Poland*.

The chosen yardstick of the ECtHR in determining the legitimacy of state action in these disputes is that of objectivity:

The State ... must take care that information or knowledge included in the curriculum is conveyed in an objective, critical and pluralistic manner. The State is forbidden to pursue an aim of indoctrination that might not be considered as respecting parents' religious and philosophical convictions. (*Kjeldsen Busk Madsen and Pedersen* v. *Denmark*, para. 53)

Bearing in mind the well-rehearsed objections to comprehensive or perfectionist liberalism as a neutral umpire between differing conceptions of the good, a claim that states must behave objectively in matters of religious education might appear naïve (Ahdar and Leigh, 2003: ch2). Although the Court has not elucidated the problematic concept of objectivity in detail, the ways in which it has been employed give some indications of its thinking, although it must be said these are not always fully consistent with one another. On closer examination, it can be argued that used in this context objectivity is primarily a proxy for neutrality as impartiality, equi-distance, equal treatment and equal respect, rather than a strong claim to intellectual superiority in its own right.

In *Folgerø and others* v. *Norway* a challenge was brought by a group of humanist parents to the arrangements for religious education in Norwegian state schools. Norway had introduced a compulsory course on 'Christian Knowledge and Religious and Ethical Education' in 1997 which was designed to provide a general introduction to Christianity (which occupied around 55 per cent of the teaching) and to other major world religions and outlooks, including non-religious life stances. The parents objected to the failure to allow a total exemption from the course. The state contended, however, that a total exemption would defeat the objectives of promoting dialogue among pupils from various faiths, and of providing all pupils with a basic knowledge of the religions covered in the course. Successive challenges brought by the parents before the Norwegian Courts failed. Both the ECtHR and the UN Human Rights Committee, to which a similar complaint was brought, concluded, however, that the course was insufficiently objective not to require the possibility of an exemption and that the partial opt-out scheme established by Norway did not prevent violations of the claimants' right to have their children educated in accordance with their religious and philosophical convictions (*Leirvåg* v. *Norway*). The judgment of the Grand Chamber of the ECtHR is noteworthy for the serious division that it produced over fundamental questions: the Court ruled by a majority of 9:8 that there had been a violation of Protocol 1 Article 2 of the Convention (the right of parents to have their children educated in accordance with their religious and philosophical convictions).

The majority applied the standard of whether the syllabus was critical, objective and pluralistic in its treatment of religions (*Folgerø and others* v. *Norway*, para. 102). Pluralism and objectivity did not require that equal treatment be given to all religions and philosophies. The Grand Chamber found that it was within the margin of appreciation of the Norwegian government to adopt a syllabus that devoted greater attention to Christianity than to other religions (para. 89). This did not *in itself* constitute a departure from the necessary principles of pluralism and objectivity amounting to indoctrination. However, on closer analysis the curriculum was unbalanced to the extent that it raised concerns: there was a clear difference in the depth of knowledge required concerning Christianity as compared to other religions, which in the majority's view undermined the objective of 'understanding, respect and the ability to maintain dialogue between people with different perceptions of beliefs and convictions' (para. 95).

The minority opinion, by contrast, recognized greater discretion for a state to give preference to the historical majority religion:

The notion of pluralism embodied in these provisions should not prevent a democratically elected political majority from giving official recognition to a particular religious denomination and subjecting it to public funding, regulation and control. Conferring a particular public status on one denomination does not in itself prejudge the State's respect for parents' religious and philosophical convictions in the education of their children, nor does it affect their exercise of freedom of thought, conscience and religion. (*Folgerø and others* v. *Norway*, Joint Dissenting Opinion, p. 51)

Whereas the majority had emphasized the predominance of Christianity in the syllabus, the minority stressed that the duty on teachers to present all religions and philosophies from the standpoint of their particular characteristics applied equally. Differences in the treatment of religions were quantitative rather than qualitative and these differences were within the margin of appreciation, having regard to the place of Christianity as the state religion in Norway and to Norwegian history (*Folgerø and others* v. *Norway*, Joint Dissenting Opinion, p. 52). In any event the dissenting judges noted that other religions made up roughly half the subject matter of the curriculum. The minority disagreed also concerning the partial exemption provisions, finding them not to be excessively burdensome or intrusive, and that to allow exemption by observation fell within the national margin of appreciation. This was in line with an earlier case (*CJ, JJ and EJ* v. *Poland*) holding that there was no violation of Articles 8 or 9 despite the applicants' claim that their daughter had been stigmatized by reason of claiming exemption from religious-education classes.

Folgerø and others v. *Norway* was followed by a further decision in which the ECtHR ruled unanimously that Turkey's system of religious education violated the rights of a parent from the Alevi stream of Islam (*Zengin* v. *Turkey*). The key issue in this instance was not the legal favouritism given to one religion. Rather, it was the way in which the religious-education syllabus was implemented, which the court found was insufficiently critical, objective and pluralistic. Although the Court found that the 'intentions' behind the syllabus for the 'religious culture and ethics' course (which referred to secularism, freedom of thought and religion and fostering toleration) were compatible with the principles of pluralism and objectivity enshrined in Protocol 1 Article 2, the execution of the course nonetheless violated these (para. 59). The portrayal of Islam was limited to the Sunni understanding and gave no recognition to the Alevi faith until the ninth grade; in addition only fifteen pages of the course-book used were devoted to religions other than Islam (para. 67). Moreover, exemption from the course appeared to be available only to parents of children who identified themselves as Christian or Jewish.

The majority opinion in *Folgerø and others* v. *Norway* and the judgment in *Zengin* v. *Turkey* show the Court engaging in close scrutiny of religious education arrangements, including the proportions of time devoted in the classroom to each religion and the specific exercises undertaken. It is clear that the ECtHR does not take assertions by a state that the objective of religious education is to instil cultural knowledge or foster toleration at face value.

In two later judgments the Court seems, however, to have reverted to a somewhat less interventionist approach, emphasizing instead the breadth of the state's margin of appreciation.

In *Grzelak* v. *Poland* two agnostic parents challenged the failure of their son's primary school to offer a course on ethics as an alternative to religious education. The number of pupils was too small to make delivery of such a course viable. As a result of this failure their son had no school record for religious education/ethics. The parents claimed that this gap in his school profile would in future result indirectly in the disclosure of his lack of religious belief and to consequent prejudice against him. The ECtHR confirmed that the state retains discretion under Article 2 of the First Protocol over how religious education is organized 'to decide whether to provide religious instruction in public schools and, if so, what particular system of instruction should be adopted. The only limit which must not be exceeded in this area is the prohibition of indoctrination' (para. 104). Thus the decision to provide optional ethics classes subject to demand was within the state's margin of appreciation and there was no violation of Article 2 of the First Protocol.

The ECtHR found, however, that there had been a violation of Article 14 in conjunction with Article 9 because of the implications of the lack of a recorded mark for religion/ethics in the context of the prevailing educational arrangements and the social realities in Poland (para. 95). In an otherwise predominantly Roman Catholic society the absence of a mark for 'religion/ethics' on the applicant's school certificates therefore amounted to a form of 'unwarranted stigmatisation' by, in effect, clearly signalling the applicant's religious affiliation (para. 99). The Court was 'not satisfied that the difference in treatment between non-believers who wished to follow ethics classes and pupils who followed religion classes was objectively and reasonably justified and that there existed a reasonable relationship of proportionality between the means used and the aim pursued' (para. 100). This was particularly the case since more recent curriculum reforms had been introduced under which the mark for religion/ethics would contribute to a pupil's average mark and, thus, the non-availability of the ethics alternative would in future adversely affect the pupil's school record as a whole.

What this ruling gives with one hand it takes away with the other. Although the Court pays lip-service to the state's autonomy under Article 2 of the First Protocol, the practical effect of the discrimination ruling is to detract from the margin of appreciation. In order to avoid the prejudice identified by the Court while also avoiding the necessity to mount ethics courses for very small numbers of pupils, Poland would be required in effect to marginalize the teaching of religion or ethics within its school system by making it non-assessed. Bearing in mind that the parents and the child in the case were able to opt out of religious education in any event, the effect is rather similar to *Folgerø and others* v. *Norway* in that the Court prioritizes the marginal prejudice to a minority group over the cost of accommodation to the majority religious group, notwithstanding the lack of coercion of the minority. The key point is the Court's finding that the difference in treatment was not reasonably and objectively justified and was disproportionate. It is striking, however, that there is no indication that in reaching this conclusion the Court evaluated the effect of the change on the majority or the cost to the state of the alternatives.

In *Appel-Irrgang and others* v. *Germany* Protestant parents challenged the requirement applicable in schools in Berlin that pupils attend a compulsory course in ethics, to which they objected on the grounds that it gave insufficient attention to Germany's Christian heritage. The ECtHR noted the legal requirement that the purpose of the course was 'to examine fundamental questions of ethics independently of pupils' cultural, ethnic and religious origins' and that teachers were not allowed to unduly influence pupils. These requirements conformed, the Court found, with the principles of pluralism and objectiveness established by Article 2 of Protocol 1. Nor did the requirement to attend violate Article 9 in the Court's view since

it fell within a State's margin of discretion to decide whether or not a school curriculum was, in view of the country's tradition, to dedicate more attention to a particular religion and whether ethics should be taught in separate classes, split on the basis of pupils' religious beliefs, or in one common class. As regards the applicants' claims that the ethics course was contrary to their religious belief, the Court observed that neither the School Act nor the curriculum gave priority to one particular belief. It was not possible to deduce from the Convention a right not to be exposed to convictions other than one's own.

This may partly miss the point – presumably the parents' objection was in part that by ignoring the undoubted historical position of Christianity the course had forfeited its claim to objectivity and neutrality.

On the other hand, the proposition that there is no right not to be exposed to other beliefs is plainly correct – indeed it is often argued that exposure of this kind is part of the rationale of religious or ethics education in the first place. The logic can conversely be extended, however: in the case of religious education it suggests that parents should not be permitted to opt out merely in order to be able to cocoon their child within the family's agnostic or atheist beliefs. Somewhat inconsistently, the Court seems to reiterate earlier jurisprudence that opt-outs are a way of offsetting prejudice where a course does not meet the standard of objectivity.

A confused and inconsistent picture emerges from these four decisions. Although the Court has consistently stressed the state's margin of appreciation under Article 2 of the First Protocol, in practice the margin is more evident in the breadth recognized in *Appel-Irrgang and others* v. *Germany* (and to a lesser extent in *Grzelak* v. *Poland*) than in *Folgerø and others* v. *Norway* or *Zengin* v. *Turkey*. The latter two judgments show close scrutiny of the operation in practice of the state's decisions concerning religious-education syllabuses that contradict the general pronouncements about the discretion available. In both *Grzelak v. Poland* and in *Zengin v. Turkey* the effect of the Court's jurisprudence on religious discrimination and non-disclosure of religious beliefs further undermines the margin of appreciation. Moreover, in referring to these concepts the Court has increasingly sidelined its own earlier jurisprudence suggesting that opt-out provisions will act as a safeguard against religious education perceived to lack sufficient objectivity. Although the jurisprudence contains clear statements that strict geometric equality of attention to different religions is not required, comparing *Folgerø and others v. Norway* and *Appel-Irrgang and others v. Germany* one could easily conclude that the state which takes this route will face less strict scrutiny.

Religious dress and symbols in schools: neutrality as equi-distance

Further ambiguities about the nature of state neutrality are obvious in recent decisions in which the ECtHR has rejected challenges to the French law banning the display of ostensible religious symbols by pupils in schools (Article L. 141-5-1 of the Education Code, inserted by Loi no. 2004–228, 15 March 2004), whilst finding that the official display of crucifixes in Italian state schools violates the Convention.

In *Dogru v. France* the expulsion of a secondary school pupil who refused to remove her Islamic headscarf during physical education classes was found not to violate Article 9 of the ECHR. The Court found that the decision of the school authorities that wearing a headscarf was incompatible with sports classes for reasons of health or safety was not unreasonable and exclusion was a justified and proportionate response. Although the facts occurred in 1999 the ECtHR nevertheless also had before it the government's submission of the 2004 law banning conspicuous religious symbols. Applying its earlier jurisprudence the Court found that 'the State may limit the freedom to manifest a religion, for example by wearing an Islamic headscarf, if the exercise of that freedom clashes with the aim of protecting the rights and freedoms of others, public order and public safety' (para. 64, citing especially *Leyla Şahin v. Turkey*). The ECtHR paid particular attention (as had the French authorities and courts) to the constitutional principle of secularism applicable in France. Protection of this principle, and to a lesser extent protection of health and safety, was a legitimate aim for restricting the right to manifest one's religion through the wearing of a religious symbol or clothing:

The Court also notes that in France, as in Turkey or Switzerland, secularism is a constitutional principle, and a founding principle of the Republic, to which the entire population adheres and the protection of which appears to be of prime importance, in particular in schools. The Court reiterates that an attitude which fails to respect that principle will not necessarily be accepted as being covered by the freedom to manifest one's religion and will not enjoy the protection of Article 9 of the Convention (*see Refah Partisi (Prosperity Party) and Others*, para. 93). Having regard to the margin of appreciation which must be left to the member States with regard to the establishment of the delicate relations between the Churches and the State, religious freedom thus recognised and restricted by the requirements of secularism appears legitimate in the light of the values underpinning the Convention. (*Dogru v. France*, para. 72)

Just before this, the Court had stated that

it was for the national authorities, in the exercise of their margin of appreciation, to take great care to ensure that, in keeping with the principle of respect for pluralism and the freedom of others, the manifestation by pupils of their religious beliefs on school premises did not take on the nature of an ostentatious act that would constitute a source of pressure and exclusion … In the Court's view, that concern does indeed appear to have been answered by the French secular model. (para. 71)

Even by the frequently opaque and terse standards of Strasbourg judgments this is an extraordinarily confused passage. Under the vague rubric of 'failing to respect' secularity the constitutional duties of public bodies were projected (apparently unconsciously) by the ECtHR onto individuals, so as to limit their rights. In so doing the Court failed to deal with the central question to be decided: that of how private dress choices by pupils can be said to threaten that principle. The Court failed to explain also why, even accepting that the defence of secularity was a legitimate aim under Article 9.2, the restriction on the wearing of symbols was *necessary*. The question of proportionality of the restriction was not really analysed – it was simply presented as a conclusion.

Little clarity was added by the Second Chamber decision in *Lautsi* v. *Italy* in which the ECtHR dealt with an equally controversial challenge to the display of crucifixes in state schools from Italy – a country that does *not* have a constitutional provision requiring secularism in the same way as Turkey, France or Switzerland. Nevertheless, the Court found that the display of crucifixes in state schools was incompatible with the state's duty of neutrality in the exercise of public services, particularly in the field of education, and therefore violated Article 2 of Protocol 1 taken in conjunction with Article 9.

The applicant alleged that the display of the crucifix clashed with her convictions and violated the right of her children not to profess the Catholic faith (para. 53). The Italian government had argued success-fully before the domestic courts that the crucifix acquired a neutral and secular meaning as well as its religious significance also by reference to Italian history and traditions, representing tolerance (*Administrative Court of Veneto*). The Strasbourg Court found, however, that the cru-cifix had 'a plurality of meanings among which the religious meaning is predominant' (para. 51), and that 'the presence of crucifixes in the classrooms goes beyond the use of symbols in specific historical con-texts' (para. 52). The ECtHR accepted that the applicant's concern that the display of the crucifix was 'a signal that the state is on the side of the Catholic religion' was a tenable one, not least because the Catholic Church officially ascribed this meaning to it (para. 53).

The display of the crucifix in the classroom was 'necessarily per-ceived as an integral part of school' and could therefore be regarded as a 'powerful external symbol' (para. 54, citing *Dahlab* v. *Switzerland*). Controversially in *Dahlab* v. *Switzerland* the Court had earlier con-cluded that the wearing of the veil by a solitary teacher in a school was a display of religious symbols with a coercive power over those observing it that engaged Article 2 of Protocol 1. In the case of the crucifix, students could easily feel that they were being educated in a school characterized by a religious environment and this could be 'emotionally disturbing' to students from minority religions and those professing no religion. The fact that students were *compelled* to attend classes in rooms where crucifixes were prominent weighed heavily with the Court:

The presence of the crucifix can be easily interpreted by students of all ages as a religious symbol and they will feel they are being educated in a school environment characterized by a particular religion. What may be encouraging for some religious students can be emotionally disturbing for students from other religions or those who profess no religion. This risk particularly affects students belonging to religious minorities. The negative freedom is not limited to the absence of religious services or religious instruction. It covers the practices and symbols expressing, in particular or in general, a belief, a religion or atheism. This negative right deserves special protection if the State expresses a belief and if a person is placed in a situation from which he cannot escape or only by an effort and cost that are disproportionate. (*Lautsi v. Italy*, para. 55)

It is clear then that in the Second Chamber's view by requiring the display of crucifixes in its schools the Italian state was both coercing pupils and aligning itself with the Catholic Church in a way that compromised its duty of neutrality:

The state is obliged to religious neutrality in public education where attendance is required irrespective of religion and must seek to instill [*sic*] in students critical thinking. The Court does not see how display in classrooms of public schools of a symbol that it is reasonable to associate with Catholicism (the majority religion in Italy) could serve the educational pluralism that is essential to the preservation of a 'democratic society' as conceived by the Convention. (para. 56)

In reasoning thus the Court imported into the Convention text a strong duty of state neutrality as equi-distance from all religions. The ideal pattern of state–religion relations that the Court appeared to have in mind is one of separation:

The Court believes that the required display of a symbol of a given religious confession in the exercise of public functions relating to specific situations under government control, particularly in classrooms, restricts the right of parents to educate their children according to their beliefs and the right of schoolchildren to believe or not believe. The Court considers that this constitutes a violation of these rights because the restrictions are inconsistent with the duty of the State to respect neutrality in the exercise of its public functions, particularly in the field of education. (para. 57)

This, however, ignored the specific context in which previous dicta about neutrality were given – namely in decisions applying the margin of appreciation to states, such as Turkey and France, that (unlike Italy) do have a constitutional guarantee of secularity. The Second Chamber failed to explain why states that could demonstrate equal respect for different religions should nevertheless be required to conform to a pattern of equi-distance. Court-enforced removal of crucifixes certainly distances the state from religion but whether it is otherwise a neutral act is much more debatable. It risks being interpreted instead as promoting a distinctive secular vision, which religious adherents may themselves feel threatened or alienated by. This perception partially underlay the vociferous reaction in Italy to the decision, where it was condemned by the Catholic Church and leading politicians alike in strong terms.

The Grand Chamber's decision in the case, given in March 2011, overturned the Second Chamber ruling and was considerably more attuned to these criticisms (Leigh and Ahdar, 2012; McGoldrick, 2011; Mancini and Rosenfeld, 2012). A majority of the Grand Chamber (15 to 2) found that there was no violation of Article 9 or Article 2 of the First Protocol and the Court held unanimously that there was also no violation of Article 14.

The majority found that the state's duty of neutrality had not been breached since the crucifix was 'an essentially passive symbol' albeit one of religious significance for the majority of the population (*Lautsi* v. *Italy*, Grand Chamber, para. 72). The applicants had not established 'indoctrination' contrary to Article 2 of Protocol 1: display of the crucifix was not accompanied by any teaching so that it could be deemed proselytizing, and minority religions were accommodated (para. 71). Moreover the display of the crucifix in the school did not interfere with Mrs Lautsi's right to bring up her children according to her secularist beliefs (para. 75). In response to charges of 'cultural vandalism' that had been levelled at the Second Chamber decision, the majority reverted to Italy's margin of appreciation in organizing the school environment (paras. 69–70).

There are a number of interesting and controversial aspects of this ruling that cannot be explored at length here (Leigh and Ahdar, 2012). What should be noted, however, are comments made by two of the judges concerning neutrality in their concurring opinions. Judge Bonello distinguished sharply between freedom of religion protected under the Convention and 'values cognate to, but different from, freedom of religion, like secularism, pluralism, the separation of Church and State, religious neutrality, religious tolerance' (*Lautsi* v. *Italy*, Grand Chamber, Concurring Judgment of Judge Bonello, para. 2.2).

He emphasized that to require the removal of the crucifix 'would have been a positive and aggressive espousal of agnosticism or of secularism – and consequently anything but neutral' (para. 2.10). Judge Bonello's reasoning is perhaps ambivalent towards neutrality, on the one hand downplaying its significance, while on the other hand reinterpreting it. In the latter vein Judge Power argued that:

Neutrality requires a pluralist approach on the part of the State, not a secularist one. It encourages respect for all world views rather than a preference for one. To my mind, the [Second] Chamber Judgment was striking in its failure to recognise that *secularism* (which was the applicant's preferred belief or world view) *was, in itself, one ideology among others.* A *preference for secularism* over alternative world views – whether religious, philosophical or otherwise – *is not a neutral option.* (para. 3, emphasis added)

She continued:

[T]he display of a religious symbol does not compel or coerce an individual to do or to refrain from doing anything. It does not require engagement in any activity though it may, conceivably, invite or stimulate discussion and an open exchange of views. It does not prevent an individual from following his or her own conscience nor does it make it unfeasible for such a person to manifest his or her own religious beliefs and ideas. (para. 5)

There is a clear contrast here not only with the Second Chamber ruling but also with *Folgerø and others* v. *Norway* and *Grzelak* v. *Poland*. In those decisions the Court appeared unaware of the extent to which its own judgments could be seen as promoting a distinctive secular vision under the guise of neutrality. This at least has now changed, although it is nonetheless improbable that at this point the Court will forswear future use of neutrality. What remains to be seen, however, is whether the Grand Chamber's ruling will presage a more sophisticated and nuanced approach, one that favours pluralism over equi-distance.

Conclusion

In this chapter it has been argued that recent decisions of the ECtHR show that the court's position with regard to religious neutrality is inconsistent with its earlier doctrine and confused in appealing to different senses of neutrality. Some of the inconsistency may be explained if the jurisprudence is regarded as being in a transitional phase. The conventional approach, based on equal respect, which emphasized the margin of appreciation, the absence of a single European model and toleration of differences provided religious freedom was not de facto impeded, seemed for a time to be out of fashion. In its place there emerged an increased emphasis on neutrality entailing geometrical equi-distance of the state from all religions – a preference for a particular secular-state model in other words. Peripheral aspects of religious establishment such as oath-taking and religious preference in state education have already fallen to this new approach and, if followed through, it may not be long before constitutional aspects also are treated by the Court as violating the Convention. In part these developments rest upon an expanding notion of what constitutes interference with an individual's freedom of religion, for example by recognition of a right to non-disclosure of belief under enlarged notions of coercion and on increasing attention to non-discrimination. Without the textual underpinning of a US-style establishment clause the ECtHR seems sometimes to have behaved as though the Convention required strict separation of religion and the state. Followed to its conclusion this pattern could well lead to the demise of the hitherto distinctively European approach to religious liberty based on equal respect and its replacement with a separatist model of religious neutrality. In its *Lautsi* v. *Italy* decision, however, the Grand Chamber appears to have recognized the force of the criticism of religionists that this would be tantamount to the Convention-sponsored imposition across the continent of secularism in the name of neutrality. The majority in that decision revert to a more modest understanding of freedom of religion, drawing on a narrower concept of coercion. This approach also reverts to toleration of plural state–religion models, based on the margin of appreciation. The tension between these competing approaches is so far unresolved.

Political philosophers have long been attuned to the paradoxical claims of liberalism as a neutral arbiter when it comes to matters of religion. Michael W. McConnell, an American academic, now judge, has remarked insightfully of the First Amendment jurisprudence:

The beginning of wisdom in this contentious area of law is to recognize that neutrality and secularism are not the same thing. In the marketplace of ideas, secular viewpoints and ideologies are in competition with religious viewpoints and ideologies. It is no more neutral to favour the secular over the religious than it is to favour the religious over the secular. It is time for a reorientation of constitutional law: away from the false neutrality of the secular state, *toward* a genuine equality of rights. (McConnell, 1998: 33)

The judges of the European Court of Human Rights have on occasion seemed to be a long way from the same self-knowledge when it comes to interpreting the Convention. If the Court is to retain legitimacy and respect in the eyes of all Europe's citizens, of diverse religious *and* secular faiths, its pronouncements on religious matters need to be considerably more literate in handling delicate religious and philosophical controversies, not to mention more consistent, transparent and better reasoned, than some of those in the past. In *Lautsi* v. *Italy* the Grand Chamber has taken a promising first step which may turn out to be a watershed in the jurisprudence.

References

Ahdar, R. and Leigh, I. 2004. 'Is Establishment Consistent with Religious Freedom?', *McGill Law Journal*, 49, 3, 635–81.

2013. *Religious Freedom in the Liberal State*, 2nd edn, Oxford University Press.

Bader, V. 2010. 'Constitutionalizing Secularism, Alternative Secularisms or Liberal-Democratic Constitutionalism? A Critical Reading of Some Turkish, ECtHR and Indian Supreme Court Cases on "Secularism"', *Utrecht Law Review*, 6, 3, 8–35.

Benson, I. 2000. 'Notes Towards a (re)Definition of the "Secular"', *UBC Law Review*, 33, 519–49.

2004. 'Considering Secularism', in D. Farrow, ed., *Recognizing Religion in a Secular Society*. Montreal: McGill-Queen's University Press, 83–98.

Council of Europe. 2005. Recommendation 1720 (2005) on Religion and Education, text adopted by the Parliamentary Assembly of the Council of Europe on 4 October 2005.

2007. Recommendation 1804 (2007), text adopted by the Parliamentary Assembly of the Council of Europe on 29 June 2007.

Dworkin, R. 1978. 'Liberalism', in S. Hampshire, ed., *Public and Private Morality*. Cambridge University Press, 113–43.

Evans, C. and Thomas, A. 2006. 'Church–State Relations in the European Court of Human Rights', *Brigham Young University Law Review*, 3, 699–726.

Laborde, C. 2008. *Critical Republicanism: The Hijab Controversy and Political Philosophy*. Oxford University Press.

Leigh, I. 2012. 'Objective, Critical and Pluralistic? Religious Education and Human Rights in the European Public Sphere', in C. Ungureanu and L. Zucca, eds., *Law, State and Religion in the New Europe: Debates and Dilemmas*. Cambridge University Press, 192–214.

Leigh, I. and Ahdar, R. 2012. 'Post-Secularism and the European Court of Human Rights (or How God Never Really Went Away)', *Modern Law Review*, 75, 6, 1064–98.

McConnell, M. W. 1998. 'Equal Treatment and Religious Discrimination', in S. Monsma and J. Soper, eds., *Equal Treatment of Religion in Pluralist Society*. Grand Rapids, MI: Eerdmans, 30–54.

McGoldrick, D. 2011. 'Religion in the European Public Square and in European Public Life – Crucifixes in the Classroom?', *Human Rights Law Review*, 11, 451–502.

Madgeley, J. 2009. 'Religion and State', in J. Haynes, ed., *The Routledge Handbook of Religion and Politics*. Abingdon: Routledge, 174–91.

Mancini, S. and Rosenfeld, M. 2012. 'Unveiling the Limits of Tolerance: Comparing the Treatment of Majority and Minority Religious Symbols in the Public Sphere', in C. Ungureanu and L. Zucca, eds., *Law, State and Religion in the New Europe: Debates and Dilemmas*. Cambridge University Press, 160–91.

OSCE. 2007. Office of Democratic Institutions and Human Rights, Toledo Guiding Principles on Teaching about Religion and Beliefs in Public Schools: Warsaw, 2007, www.osce.org/odihr/item_11_28314.html (accessed 18 July 2012).

Rawls, J. 1999. *A Theory of Justice*. Oxford University Press.

Raz, J. 1986. *The Morality of Freedom*. Oxford University Press.

Rivers, J. 2010. *The Law of Organized Religions: Between Establishment and Secularism*. Oxford University Press.

Taylor, C. 2009. 'Foreword: What is Secularism?', in G. B. Levey and T. Modood, eds., *Secularism, Religion and Multicultural Citizenship*. Cambridge University Press, xi–xxii.

Temperman, J. 2010a. 'State Neutrality in Public School Education: An Analysis of the Interplay between the Neutrality Principle, the Right to Adequate Education, Children's Right to Freedom of Religion or Belief, Parental Liberties, and the Position of Teachers', *Human Rights Quarterly*, 32, 865–97.

2010b. *State–Religion Relationships and Human Rights Law: Towards a Right to Religiously Neutral Governance*. Leiden: Martinus Nijhoff.

Cases

97 members of the Gldani Congregation of Jehovah's Witnesses and 4 others v. Georgia, Appl. No. 71156/01 (3 May 2007).

Administrative Court of Veneto, Appl. No. 1110 (17 March 2005).

Alexandridis v. *Greece*, Appl. No. 19516/06 (21 February 2008).

Alujer Fernandez and Caballero Garcia v. *Spain*, Appl. No. 53072/99 (14 June 2001).

Appel-Irrgang and others v. *Germany*, Appl. No. 45216/07 (20 October 2009).

Belgian Linguistics Case, 1 EHRR 252, 284 (1968).

The Canea Catholic Church v. *Greece*, Appl. No. 25528/94 (16 December 1997).

Choudhury v. *UK*, Appl. No. 17439/90 (1991) 12 HRLJ 172.

CJ, JJ and EJ v. *Poland*, Appl. No. 23380/94 (Commission decision of 16 January 1996, DR 84).

Dahlab v. *Switzerland*, Appl. No. 42393/98 (15 February 2001).

Darby v. *Sweden*, 13 EHRR 774 (1991).

Dogru v. *France*, Appl. No. 27058/05 (4 December 2008).

Folgerø and others v. *Norway*, Appl. No. 15472/02 (29 June 2007).

Grzelak v. *Poland*, Appl. No. 7710/02 (15 June 2010).

Hasan and Chaush v. *Bulgaria*, 34 EHRR 55 (2000).

Holy Synod of the Bulgarian Orthodox Church (Metropolitan Inokentiy) and others v. *Bulgaria*, Appl. Nos. 412/03 and 35677/04 (22 January 2009).

Iglesia Bautista 'El Salvador' and Ortega Moratilla v. *Spain*, 72 D&R 256 (1992).

Kjeldsen Busk Madsen and Pedersen v. *Denmark*, 1 EHRR 737 (7 December 1976).

Kokkinakis v. *Greece*, 17 EHRR 397 (1993).

Kuznetsov and others v. *Russia*, Appl. No. 184/02 (11 January 2007).

Ladele v. *London Borough of Islington*, EWCA Civ 1357 (2009).

Lautsi v. *Italy*, Appl. No. 30814/06, Grand Chamber (18 March 2011).

Leela Förderkreis EV and others v. *Germany*, Appl. No. 58911/00 (6 November 2008).

Leirvåg v. *Norway*, UN Human Rights Committee, Communication No. 1155/2003 (23 November 2004), www.unhchr.ch/tbs/doc.nsf/(Symbol)/6187ce3dc0091758c1256f7000526973?Opendocument (accessed 18 July 2012).

Leyla Şahin v. *Turkey*, Appl. No. 44774/98, Grand Chamber (10 November 2005).

Manoussakis v. *Greece*, 23 EHRR 387 (1996).

Metropolitan Church of Bessarabia and others v. *Moldova*, Appl. No. 45701/99 (13 December 2001).

Mirolubovs v. *Latvia*, Appl. No. 798/05 (15 September 2009).

Murphy v. *Ireland*, Appl. No. 44179/98 (10 July 2003).

Otto-Preminger Institute v. *Austria*, 19 EHRR 34 (1994).

Refah Partisi v. *Turkey*, 37 EHRR 1 (2003).
Serif v. *Greece*, 31 EHRR 20 (2001).
Spampinato v. *Italy*, Appl. No. 23123/04 (29 April 2010).
Wingrove v. *UK*, 24 EHRR 1 (1997).
Zengin v. *Turkey*, Appl. No. 1448/04 (9 October 2007).

3 | Religion and sexual orientation: conflict or cohesion?

MALEIHA MALIK

Raymond Plant's chapter is a powerful argument in favour of rebalancing contemporary debates about religion away from identity politics towards a more traditional liberal concern with preventing harm as the criterion which guides when and how law should regulate religion.

One reason for the popularity of identity politics was the failure of political liberalism to recognize the problems which were inherent in its claims to neutrality and universalism. A range of writers have addressed the problem of 'difference' and revealed the way in which the chimera of 'universalism' masked the reality of hegemony (Taylor, 1992; Young, 1990). Liberal elites who had greater social, economic and political power than minorities were given yet more power through their control over concepts, language and the ability to define the conceptual categories through which minorities made their legal and political claims. The claim to liberalism's neutrality and universalism, it was argued, allowed this powerful elite to represent their subjective viewpoints and interests as the truth about all citizens and dominate legal and political discourse irrespective of differences of race, culture and religion or gender and sexuality. The postmodern critique of liberalism, as well as the political 'identity' movements which it has inspired, have made an important contribution to revealing these oppressive aspects of traditional liberalism and by increasing our understanding of 'difference'. This intellectual shift has, in turn, led to refinements within liberal political theory that are more sensitive to 'difference' (Phillips, 2007).

This rebalancing of liberalism to take greater account of 'difference' has come at a considerable price. One cost has been a splintering of political alliances that are able to transcend racial, cultural or religious divides by focusing on common issues such as social justice or gender equality. Another conceptual problem, especially in the context of religion, has been that the focus on identity politics carries within it a risk of the early closure of identity. An essentialist approach has given too much weight to religious identity as a monolithic faith system with only one absolute truth about what constitutes a valid form of religious belief or conduct. This view of religion underestimates the extent to which religious belief is socially constructed and needs to be subject to critique. It also gives too much power to established forms of religion, and organized religious authority, at the expense of those with more heterodox views. In Plant's terms, '[t]his freezing may well also empower conservative elements within any group claiming a specific identity to determine what the nature of that identity is, what claims to political and legal recognition are implied and what forms of behaviour in the public realm are required by that religious identity' (Plant, this volume: 33).

Plant is correct to warn us that 'politics and the law have taken a wrong turn here and we would be much better turning back towards a difference-blind type of politico-legal system' (Plant, this volume: 35). He proposes the harm principle as one difference-blind liberal principle which could guide legal regulation. He concludes that '[e]mphasis on harms and the threat of harm would allow us to conduct a debate about the toleration of various ways in which religion is manifested in a public and accessible discourse which is in fact denied when the focus is on identity, the normative requirements of identity and the authoritative articulation of these requirements by religious authorities' (Plant, this volume: 35). He also develops a more sophisticated understanding of the harm principle by positioning it within deeper foundations about the basic goods that underpin human agency which can be shared by all citizens in a pluralist society. He concludes that 'there is a benchmark of harm that can be shared across all groups within a pluralistic society, because of the link between harm and the basic goods of agency already noted. We need a citizen-focused approach to these issues, not one based upon a hermetic appeal to religious authority' (Plant, this volume: 36).

In this chapter, I address the tensions and conflicts between religion and sexual-orientation equality which are increasingly emerging in political and legal disputes. This issue, in turn, raises one central issue which Plant explores in his analysis: how should a modern liberal state which is committed to human rights and equality regulate religion? My argument is that tensions and conflicts between sexual-orientation equality and religious freedom can be resolved through a focus on harm as the guiding principle for political and legal regulation. I also argue that the principle of equality, as enshrined in legislation such as the European Convention on Human Rights, the Human Rights Act 1998 and the Equality Act 2010, is now one benchmark of harm which is shared across almost all groups within a pluralistic society. There will be individuals and groups who do not agree with these standards, especially religious groups who disagree with equality for women, gays and lesbians. I argue that a liberal society can be 'pluralist' by allowing these individuals and groups an expansive space to live as long as they do not cause harm to others, rather than 'muscular' by imposing liberal values in all spheres of life. First, I set out the ways in which religion and sexual-orientation equality are increasingly coming into conflict in political and legal disputes. Second, I explore some of the available techniques such as the belief–conduct distinction or the use of exemptions to manage these conflicts.

The question of how a liberal state should respond to the tensions and conflicts between religion and sexual-orientation equality is a potentially vast topic. Here, I want to narrow the analysis of these wide-ranging interrelated issues by considering, first, the way in which conflicts between religion and sexual orientation emerge in liberal democracies. I start with a brief discussion of some of the key legal cases in which the religion and sexual orientation conflict has arisen in contexts such as employment or student activities. These cases shed light on the way in which these conflicts are emerging at a grassroots level. I then discuss a series of cases in the UK, USA and Canada in which tensions, or conflicts, between religion and sexual orientation have arisen. These cases point to the problems with using traditional legal techniques such as the belief–conduct distinction or exemptions to balance competing interests in this context. Although there is no resolution, finally, I offer a way forward which minimizes the possibility of conflicts between religious freedom and sexual-orientation equality.

Religion and sexual-orientation equality

The emergence of equality and non-discrimination as important constitutional values, as well as the expansion of the protected grounds of non-discrimination to sexual orientation, has raised the prospect of a conflict, or at the very least significant tension, between religion and sexual orientation.

There is also a widespread public perception that an increase in the protection of equality through human rights and discrimination law has led to an increase in 'conflicts' between different social groups. A Christian registrar of marriages has argued that a requirement for her to carry out a civil partnership between a same-sex couple constituted discrimination on the ground of religion or belief. The 'Catholic adoption agencies' debate led to public discussion about whether organized religion can provide public goods and services without fully complying with the requirements of equality law for gays and lesbians.

The clash between religion and sexual orientation is not just a theoretical prospect. A survey of even a very short time frame of two years between 2008 and 2010 confirms that many of the recent political struggles and legal cases in the USA and UK have involved a conflict between religion and sexual orientation. In the USA, political struggles over the recognition of same-sex partnerships continue in a number of state jurisdictions. California provides a good illustration of the way in which this conflict involves both political and legal activism. Following a decision by the US Supreme Court that a state law banning same-sex marriage was unlawful discrimination in May 2008, opponents launched the Proposition 8 initiative to ban same-sex marriage. In November 2008, they won the vote by 52 per cent and ensured that same-sex marriages were banned in California.

Opponents of Proposition 8 launched their own political and legal campaign.[1] This, in turn, led to the decision of the California Ninth Circuit Court of Appeal in *Perry* v. *Brown* that Proposition 8 was unconstitutional. In *Perry* v. *Brown*, Judge Stephen Reinhardt established a narrow principle which is limited in its application to the specific facts of Proposition 8 because California sought to withdraw the right to same-sex marriage after it had been granted. That is, Proposition 8 stripped same-sex couples of the right to have their marriage relationships recognized by the state with the designation of 'marriage' which had previously been granted to them. Moreover, Proposition 8 singled out same-sex couples for unequal treatment compared with others because, without a legitimate reason, it took away their established right to marry that had already been granted to them as a right. This narrow principle prevents *Perry* v. *Brown* from

---

[1] 'Same-Sex Marriage, Civil Unions, and Domestic Partnerships', *New York Times*, 28 June 2010.

establishing a wider principle concerning the constitutional nature of same-sex partnerships throughout the USA.

There is also considerable emerging case-law. In *Christian Legal Society* v. *Martinez* decided in June 2010, the US Supreme Court held that a public higher education institution's 'all-comers' policy that required the Christian Legal Society to open up its membership to individuals who did not agree with its views on homosexuality did not breach First Amendment free speech and expressive-association claims.

In the UK, same-sex partnerships have been officially recognized since the enactment of the Civil Partnership Act 2004. This has not, however, resolved the conflicts between religion and sexual orientation. In a case that was decided by the Court of Appeal in December 2009, *Ladele* v. *London Borough of Islington*, a registrar of births, deaths and marriages claimed that her employer had subjected her to direct discrimination, indirect discrimination and harassment on the grounds of her religion by requiring her to participate in civil partnership services against her orthodox Christian beliefs. In April 2010, in *McFarlane* v. *Relate Avon Ltd*, a Christian counsellor argued that his employer's insistence that he provide relationship and sexual therapy to same-sex couples subjected him to unlawful religious discrimination.

These political and legal struggles confirm the difficulty faced by liberal democracies simultaneously seeking to safeguard religious freedom and equality for gays and lesbians. Of course, religion raises general problems for liberals and the religious. For liberals, many of the beliefs and practices of the main religions either conflict – or at the very least are difficult to reconcile with – key human rights and equality norms. For the religious, although liberal societies guarantee freedom of religion and belief, they seem to do so from a position of superiority where the framework and terms of the debate are unilaterally dictated by secular liberalism. One classic way in which liberals address this tension is through the distinction between belief and manifestation. It is an often-repeated mantra that liberals are comfortable with religious belief and seek to regulate only religious practice.

The legal framework within which the conflict between religious freedom and sexual orientation emerges is complex. It is well established that freedom of religion is protected in a range of international, European and domestic human rights instruments, such as Article 9 of the ECHR. Freedom of religion, understood in this way, is a recognized individual and associational right. What is less established is the emerging equality norm of religious equality that can be found in constitutional provisions (e.g. Article 15 of the Canadian Charter and Article 14 of the ECHR), as well as European Union and domestic discrimination law (e.g. the EU Employment Equality Directive and the UK Equality Act 2010). Article 14 of the ECHR, for example, introduces a norm of non-discrimination on the grounds of discrimination in the enjoyment of any of the ECHR rights: 'The enjoyment of the rights and freedoms set forth in this Convention shall be secured without discrimination on any ground such as sex, race, colour, language, religion, political or other opinion, national or social origin, association with a national minority, property, birth or other status.'

The right to freedom of religion has been incorporated via the Human Rights Act, which gives it special status via section 13(1). This approach builds on a core assumption that it is possible to distinguish between belief and conduct in relation to freedom of religion. Article 9(1) contains a provision that protects 'the right to freedom of thought, conscience and religion'. Crucially, the first part of the text of Article 9(1) does not contain a reference to 'belief'. It gives special status to the internal aspect of this right that is associated with 'thought and conscience'. The second part of Article 9(1) deals with the freedom to act upon these inner beliefs. This is more limited than the translation of the inner freedom of belief into all the external manifestations that follow from that belief.

Although the first part of Article 9 does not contain a reference to belief it seems probable that belief would be included within the term 'right to freedom of thought and conscience' (C. Evans, 2001: 52–3; Bamforth *et al.*, 2008). This internal aspect, sometimes known as the *forum internum*, of the right to religious freedom in Article 9(1) is unqualified under Article 9(2). The vision of religion in Article 9, therefore, relies on a dichotomy between belief and conduct (or action). Belief is given unconditional protection. This is in comparison to the right to manifest religion and belief, limitations of which can be justified under Article 9(2). A number of commentators have noted the way in which this dichotomy underestimates the relationship between belief and conduct and, in particular, the way in which restrictions on action can have an important impact on the inner dimension of religion and belief (M. D. Evans, 2008). The belief–conduct dichotomy is also part of the legacy of the Reformation, which ensures that our concept of freedom of religion focuses on preventing the coercion of belief, especially the punishment of heresy and forced conversion (MacCulloch, 2004).

More recently, Lord Nicholls has also acknowledged the distinction between belief and conduct but at the same time stated that there is an important relationship between these aspects:

It is against this background that Art.9 of the European Convention on Human Rights safeguards freedom of religion. This freedom is not confined to freedom to hold a religious belief. It includes the right to express and practise one's beliefs. Without this, freedom of religion would be emasculated. Invariably religious faiths call for more than belief. To a greater or lesser extent adherents are required or encouraged to act in certain ways, most obviously and directly in forms of communal or personal worship, supplication and meditation. But under Art.9 there is a difference between freedom to hold a belief and freedom to express or 'manifest' a belief. The former right, freedom of belief, is absolute. The latter right, freedom to manifest belief, is qualified. (*R (Williamson)* v. *Secretary of State for Education and Employment*, para. 16)

Yet, despite this confident confirmation of the central place of the belief–conduct distinction, what precisely constitutes an illegitimate interference with the inner aspects of religious belief is not a clear issue. As Moens has noted, the distinction between a wide range of latitude for belief and a more restrictive approach to action depends on some consensus about the social values which underlie religion (Moens, 1989). In increasingly plural societies it will be difficult to apply the doctrine because it provides no substantive guide to what types of manifestation of belief fall within the permissible range (Bader, 2007). In the context of the religion versus sexual-orientation debate, in particular, there is very little social consensus which allows us to determine how we should develop and police the boundaries of what constitutes a legitimate sphere of inner religious belief or lawful manifestation of that belief.

The established individual right to freedom of religion now coexists with an increasingly sophisticated regime of discrimination law that operates at the European Union, Council of Europe and domestic level (Bamforth *et al.*, 2008). In the UK, the political and legal goals of 'equality' and 'non-discrimination' have become a project of cultural transformation of key areas such as education and employment, as

well as the public sphere more generally. Although the new Equality
Act 2010 treats all the grounds of discrimination – race, sex, religion
and belief, sexual orientation, disability and age – in the same way,
it is far from clear that they all enjoy the same degree of legitimacy
in the wider society. Established equality norms – for example racial
or gender equality – may enjoy a greater degree of social consensus
as compared with emerging social norms around sexual-orientation
equality. In 1960s London, refusing a bed-and-breakfast room to
an Indian family was a common occurrence. In 2010, most people
accept that this would be unlawful race discrimination. Yet there is
not the same degree of consensus about excluding a gay couple from a
bed-and-breakfast hotel.[2]

This lack of social consensus about sexual orientation raises
particular problems for regulating religious conscience and belief
because regulatory concepts – such as the belief–conduct distinction – depend on a degree of consensus about what types of manifestation of religious belief fall within the permissible range (Moens,
1989). Although the legal norm that sexual orientation discrimination should be prohibited is now well established, there is still a
wide diversity of views about the topic. Significantly, there is a large
degree of diversity within religious organizations and communities
about the correct ethical approach to the issue (Leigh, 2006). This
raises a dilemma for liberal democracies about how they should
respond to this diversity of viewpoints in a secular society (Audi,
2000) and within religious communities (Cane *et al.*, 2008). Is the
right approach that debate about sexual orientation is encouraged?
Should state and legal regulation be used unapologetically to pursue the goal of sexual-orientation equality even if there is a considerable cost to the individual right to freedom of religion? If, as
Malcolm Evans has demonstrated, the European Court of Human
Rights has evolved its interpretation of freedom of religion from one
that focuses on the right of the individual towards a more 'state cen-
tric' approach (Evans, 2008), this suggests that the state interest in
promoting the goal of non-discrimination on the ground of sexual
orientation is more likely to 'trump' religious freedom. As the discussion in the next section suggests, although there are a number of legal

[2] See the report of the incident in 'Gay Couple Turned Away from B & B by
Christian Owners', *Guardian Observer*, 21 March 2010.

techniques, such as the use of exemptions or the belief–conduct distinction, that seek to achieve an optimal balance between two competing rights or interests, in practice this balance is tilting very firmly in the direction of sexual-orientation equality.

Regulating religion and sexuality conflicts

The belief–conduct distinction

The belief–conduct distinction provides one analytical technique for regulating conflicts and tensions between religion and sexual-orientation equality. On this analysis, harm caused by conduct is treated as a more significant factor that justifies legal regulation of religion. Belief, on the other hand, is given a wider range of latitude as part of the liberal commitment to safeguard freedom of speech and religious conscience. *Ladele* v. *London Borough of Islington* illustrates how this approach may be applied. In *Ladele* v. *London Borough of Islington*, a registrar of births, deaths and marriages successfully claimed that her employer had subjected her to direct discrimination, indirect discrimination and harassment on the grounds of her religion by requiring her to participate in civil partnership services against her orthodox Christian beliefs. The employment tribunal found in favour of the applicant on all three grounds: direct and indirect discrimination on the ground of religion or belief, as well as harassment on the ground of religion or belief. The Employment Appeal Tribunal allowed an appeal from this decision in favour of the London Borough of Islington. The Court of Appeal refused the appeal of Ms Ladele and confirmed the decision in favour of the London Borough of Islington.

In *Ladele* v. *London Borough of Islington*, the applicant's post as a registrar of marriages would not fall within any exceptions to allow her a defence to an act of sexual-orientation discrimination for failure to perform (same-sex) civil partnerships as compared with other forms of marriages. Moreover, given ECtHR case-law which endorses the 'contracting out' approach, she could not easily argue that there had been an interference with her Article 9 ECHR right, because she has the option either not to take up that form of employment or to leave her employment altogether (C. Evans, 2001: 127). Restrictions on acting on religious conviction in employment are not, in themselves, a restriction of freedom of religion or belief.

The employment tribunal decision in favour of Ms Ladele considered the importance of the Article 9 ECHR right to freedom of religion, although it failed to apply the 'contracting out' limits placed on Article 9 in employment contexts. The Employment Appeal Tribunal (EAT) decision in favour of Islington Borough Council reaffirmed the 'contracting out' doctrine, as well as the belief–conduct distinction. This narrower approach confirms that Article 9 ECHR does not require that one has the right to manifest the right to all religious belief at all times and in all contexts. Moreover, Elias J in the Employment Appeal Tribunal also confirmed that rights to religious freedom are limited by the rights and interests of others. More specifically, in the context of a conflict between the grounds of religion and belief and sexual orientation, Elias J stated 'the right to manifest religious belief must give way to rights of same-sex partners to have their partnership recognised by law' (EAT, para. 126).

The Court of Appeal (CA) also dismissed Ms Ladele's appeal from the decision of the EAT in December 2009, as well as refusing leave to appeal to the Supreme Court. Ms Ladele's claim of direct and indirect religious discrimination was rejected. The Master of the Rolls (with whom Dyson and Smith LJJ agreed) stated:

[It] appears to me that the fact that Ms Ladele's refusal to perform civil partnerships was based on her religious view of marriage could not justify the conclusion that Islington should not be allowed to implement its aim to the full, namely that all registrars should perform civil partnerships as part of its Dignity for All policy. Ms Ladele was employed in a public job and was working for a public authority; she was being required to perform a purely secular task, which was being treated as part of her job; Ms Ladele's refusal to perform that task involved discriminating against gay people in the course of that job; she was being asked to perform the task because of Islington's Dignity for All policy, whose laudable aim was to avoid, or at least minimize, discrimination both among Islington's employees, and as between Islington (and its employees) and those in the community they served. (CA, para. 52)

Ladele v. *London Borough of Islington* is clear on the issue that a religious believer cannot expect to be granted an exemption from the requirement of non-discrimination on the ground of sexual orientation beyond that which has been agreed in equalities legislation. There is some scope for an exemption from human rights and equalities legislation as well as the requirements of sexual-orientation equality, as contained in the Equalities Act 2010. Nevertheless, where there is a clear conflict between religion and sexual-orientation equality which falls outside these exemptions there will be almost no scope to argue that religious conscience should be accommodated. The fact that Ms Ladele was already working as a marriage registrar in Islington before the introduction of the Civil Partnership Act 2004 made this a difficult case to adjudicate. There is also an overwhelming argument that there should have been transitional arrangements in place that took into account employees such as Ms Ladele who were in their posts as marriage registrars before the Civil Partnership Act 2004. In the Court of Appeal, Lord Neuberger, the Master of the Rolls, noted that Ms Ladele and her employers were faced with a dilemma. Nevertheless, from the wider perspective of examining the relationship between religion and sexual-orientation equality there are good arguments to justify the decision in *Ladele* v. *London Borough of Islington*. In those situations where the accommodation of religion raises issues about symbols (headscarves or crosses) there can be accommodation without a significant cost or harm to others. In some situations the manifestation of religion may require a balancing with other interests and costs to employers and public institutions: for example, permitting beards in a factory that produces food may raise questions about health and safety. However, *Ladele* v. *London Borough of Islington* raised a different type of issue because it was a claim for an exemption from sexual-orientation equality that is part of the human rights and equality legislation. Sexual-orientation equality has become part of the normative structure of human rights and equality legislation that, in Raymond Plant's terms, has become 'a benchmark of harm that can be shared across all groups within a pluralistic society'. On this analysis, the fundamental nature of sexual-orientation equality provides a key building block of the normative values that bind liberal political order and guide the harm principle. It follows, therefore, that there is an important difference between the accommodation of religion that does not conflict with these normative values (such as the accommodation of symbols) and those accommodations that conflict with human rights and equality values such as sexual-orientation equality. Once liberal political order is defined in these terms, *Ladele* v. *London Borough of Islington* is correct law and politics. There should be no accommodation for the religious where the exemption is from a key constitutional or human right such as the right to equality. Individuals cannot expect to directly influence public services that are provided to the general public, so that they conform to their personal religious beliefs, where that accommodation constitutes a breach of the constitutional or human right of another citizen.

Yet there are aspects of the case which illustrate the way in which these incidents raise unresolved practical as well as legal conflicts. At first instance, the employment tribunal (ET) had relied on the fact that Islington Council gave insufficient weight to the religion or belief of the applicant in making decisions about how to manage this conflict in the workplace, and they failed to consider whether there were ways of ensuring that the applicant's religion or belief could be accommodated. Most significantly in the context of free speech, there was evidence that the management at Islington Borough Council failed to consider alternative ways of resolving the conflict because they had already reached the view that the failure to perform a civil partnership was in itself a form of homophobia which breached their 'Dignity for All' equal opportunities policy (ET, paras. 27–8). The EAT decision also recognized that there had been poor 'human resources' management of this particular case. Elias J noted: 'There were clearly some unsatisfactory features about the way the Council handled this matter. The claimant's beliefs were strong and genuine and not all of management treated them with the sensitivity that they may have done' (EAT, para. 130).

In situations that involve a religion and sexual-orientation conflict there is the risk of a reactive vicious cycle: a religious person voices their reservations about homosexuality or same-sex partnerships; this is interpreted as inherently homophobic and triggers equal opportunities policies and sanctions. This general atmosphere in the workplace, in turn, creates an indirect risk for religious belief. *Ladele* v. *London Borough of Islington* also suggests that the reason conflicts emerge may be because of the failure of management to take proper steps to resolve the dispute. It is, therefore, preferable that areas such as the workplace or public-service delivery are designed to prevent individuals being put into a position where their religious conscience is tested. The use of greater non-legal measures, as discussed in the concluding comments, can play a crucial role in ensuring that conflicts between religious freedom and sexual-orientation equality are prevented, and appropriately managed, before they give rise to a legal problem.

The Canadian Supreme Court has also endorsed a version of the belief–conduct distinction in *Trinity Western University* v. *British Columbia College of Teachers*. This case concerned a conflict between freedom of religion and the constitutional right to equality. The case also shows that religious freedom and sexuality conflicts become most clear in situations where religious institutions (particularly those linked to the public sector) seek to impose codes of conduct or belief in relation to homosexuality. Trinity Western University (TWU) was a private institution in British Columbia (BC) associated with the Evangelical Free Church of Canada. TWU had a teacher-training course and applied to the BC College of Teachers (BCCT) for permission to assume full responsibility for teacher training, in part to give a Christian view of the world. BCCT refused, citing as its reasons that it was contrary to public policy to approve a teacher-training programme offered by a private institution which appears to follow discriminatory practices. BCCT's concern was that TWU Community Standards applicable to all staff embodied discrimination against homosexuals. At first instance, the BC Supreme Court found that there was no reasonable foundation to support the BCCT's decision with regard to discrimination and granted mandamus allowing approval of the TWU proposed teacher-training programme subject to a few conditions. The BC Court of Appeal found that the BCCT had acted within its jurisdiction, but affirmed the trial judge's decision on the basis that there was no reasonable foundation for the BCCT's finding of discrimination. The Canadian Supreme Court dismissed the appeal and found that the BCCT had jurisdiction to consider discriminatory practices in dealing with the TWU application.

In *Trinity Western University* v. *British Columbia College of Teachers*, much of the discussion in the Canadian Supreme Court turned on the issue of the standard of review used by the BCCT and in Canadian administrative law. There is also, however, some discussion of the conflict between a right to freedom of religion or belief and the right to equality on the ground of sexual orientation. One significant aspect of the decision of the Canadian Supreme Court is the weight which the court gave to the constitutional right to freedom of religion. The majority stated that: 'A hierarchical approach to rights, which places some over others, must be avoided, both when interpreting the Charter and when developing the common law. When the protected rights of two individuals come into conflict ... Charter principles require a balance to be achieved that fully respects the importance of both sets of rights' (paras. 29–33). Therefore, not only should the BCCT have considered the importance of sexual-orientation equality, they should have also given weight to freedom of religion. The Canadian Supreme Court went on to state that there was a particular need to understand the importance of freedom of religion in the context of Canada as a diverse society, and of maintaining a private sphere of freedom of association for religious groups and individual believers (para. 25). Finally, the majority of the Canadian Supreme Court stated that one key concept devised for resolving a conflict between rights such as freedom of religion or belief and sexual-orientation equality is to use the distinction between belief and conduct (para. 36).

It is possible to extract a number of principles from the decision of the majority in *Trinity Western University* v. *British Columbia College of Teachers*. First, in cases where there is a potential conflict between two constitutional rights, a hierarchical analysis which tries to decide which right is more important should be avoided in favour of an analysis that seeks to balance and give importance to both sets of rights. Second, the Canadian Supreme Court confirmed the importance of the public–private distinction in an analysis of constitutional and human rights law by confirming that freedom of religion is an important constitutional right which entails respecting a private sphere that is not subject to the requirements of non-discrimination on grounds such as sex and sexual orientation. Third, and related to the private–public distinction, there is a wider margin of appreciation for freedom of belief as compared with the freedom to act upon beliefs. Therefore, an individual or group has a wider sphere of freedom to hold or express beliefs that are discriminatory (e.g. believing that LGBT people should be subject to discrimination) as compared with acting on those beliefs (e.g. discriminatory acts against LGBT people).

It is also worth pointing out that there was a strong dissent by L'Heureux-Dubé J against the majority decision and reasoning in *Trinity Western University* v. *British Columbia College of Teachers*.

Specifically, L'Heureux-Dubé J challenged the separation of the private and public sphere by arguing that beliefs and actions in the private sphere can have a considerable impact on the public sphere and stated:

[F]reedom of religion like any other freedom is not absolute. It is inherently limited by the rights and freedoms of others. Whereas parents are free to choose and practice the religion of their choice, such activities can and must be restricted when they are against the child's best interests, without thereby infringing the parents' freedom of religion ... there is a similar intersection between the asserted private religious beliefs and the public interest in the present appeal. Actions in the private sphere can have effects in the public realm. Everyone must assume the legal consequences of his or her private beliefs, so long as these consequences do not violate fundamental rights. (para. 62)

L'Heureux-Dubé J also stated that 'there can no longer be any doubt that sexual-orientation discrimination in education violates deeply and widely accepted views of elementary justice' (para. 70). Finally, she was sceptical about the use of the belief–conduct distinction as a basis to allow discriminatory beliefs a much wider margin of appreciation, and also questioned why the code of conduct in this case was construed as a matter of belief rather than conduct: 'with respect, I do not see why my colleagues classify this signature as part of the freedom of belief as opposed to the narrower freedom to act on those beliefs' (para. 72). A different line of analysis is, therefore, represented by the L'Heureux-Dubé minority dissent which is sceptical about the belief–conduct distinction, and suggests a greater willingness to intervene in the affairs of religious organizations, even those in the private sphere, which breach the right to sexual-orientation equality.

Scepticism about the use of the belief–conduct distinction as a solution is also expressed in a recent decision of the Saskatchewan Court of Appeal *In the Matter of Marriage Commissioners Appointed under the Marriage Act 1995*. The court had to consider a situation similar to that which arose in *Ladele* v. *London Borough of Islington*. The Saskatchewan Court of Appeal was asked to rule on the constitutionality of proposed amendments to Saskatchewan's Marriage Act, which would have allowed marriage commissioners to decline to perform marriage ceremonies that were contrary to their religious beliefs.

The Court found that the proposed amendments violated the equality rights of gays and lesbians under section 15 of the Canadian Charter of Rights and Freedoms, and that this violation could not be justified under section 1 of the Charter. Significantly, in reaching their decision the majority reasoned that requiring the marriage commissioners to perform the solemnization of a same-sex partnership would have breached their individual right to freedom of religion. They accepted that there was a conflict between two rights – the right to religious freedom of the marriage commissioners and the equality rights of gays and lesbians. They went on to focus on the issue of accommodation and balancing under section 1 of the Canadian Charter and emphasized the 'public' nature of the work of the marriage commissioners as 'public officials' who were delivering a 'public service'. 'In relation to the third leg of the proportionality test, the balancing of the salutary and deleterious effects of the legislation, I fully agree that the fact that these proposals would permit discrimination by a public official in the delivery of a public service is so contrary to fundamental principles of equality in a democratic society that these amendments cannot pass this test' (para. 161).

The focus on the 'publicness' and 'official' nature of the work or the delivery of service was also important to the reasoning of the Court of Appeal in *Ladele* v. *London Borough of Islington*, where Neuberger LJ stated: 'Ms Ladele was employed in a public job and was working for a public authority; she was being required to perform a purely secular task, which was being treated as part of her job' (para. 52). This shift towards considering the private–public distinction, rather than analysing whether the claim relates to belief or conduct, may provide a more productive way of resolving the religious freedom and sexual-orientation equality conflict. As the US Supreme Court decisions discussed in the next section suggest, a focus on whether the interference with sexual-orientation equality is in the private or public sphere provides one conceptual mechanism for delineating the precise latitude that will be given to religious individuals and associations to be permitted to discriminate on the ground of sexual orientation.

Regulating religion in the public sphere

The US Supreme Court jurisprudence on the extent to which religious individuals and associations can exclude gays and lesbians provides some useful guidance on the limits to religious freedom in the public sphere. In *Boy Scouts of America* v. *Dale* the applicant James Dale was a former Boy Scout who had remained a volunteer in the organization after entering college. He had been a member of the Boy Scout movement for over twelve years, during which time he had earned twenty-five badges of honour and other commendations. In 1990, after the Boy Scout movement became aware that Dale was the head of his college's gay student group, the local Scout leader wrote to tell him that his membership was revoked because the Boy Scout movement prohibits membership by gays. Dale sued the Boy Scout movement under New Jersey state discrimination law, which prohibits discrimination on the grounds of sexual orientation in accessing public accommodation and states: 'all persons shall have the opportunity ... to obtain all the accommodations, advantages, facilities, and privileges of any place of public accommodation ... without discrimination because of ... sexual orientation'. The New Jersey (state) Supreme Court found that the Boy Scouts did fall within the public accommodation sphere of the discrimination law statute. Therefore, prima facie, the Boy Scouts had discriminated against Dale on the grounds of sexual orientation. However, the Boy Scouts had a claim that the statute breached their First Amendment Rights to freedom of association. On this point, the New Jersey Supreme Court found that the 'ethos' of the Boy Scout movement was diverse: some within the movement opposed homosexuality, whilst others were opposed to discrimination on the grounds of freedom of association. The New Jersey Court also found that the belief that homosexuality was immoral was not a core aspect of the associational beliefs, or 'ethos', of the Boy Scout movement: therefore, they granted a judgment in favour of Dale and concluded that this decisions, and the New Jersey discrimination provision, did not violate the Boy Scout movement's First Amendment right to freedom of association.

On appeal, the US Supreme Court overturned the decision of the New Jersey Supreme Court and found in favour of the Boy Scout movement. A bare majority (expressed in the opinion of Reinquist CJ) found that the New Jersey discrimination provision had violated the movement's First Amendment rights to freedom of association. They used the test of whether the discrimination provision (the public accommodation statute) would be a 'serious burden' to the ideas of the organization and the ability of the association to express its message.

The majority found that the Boy Scout movement does have an 'official position' that is anti-gay and they deferred to this official position for the purposes of constructing the First Amendment rights to freedom of association. The majority also accepted the Boy Scouts' conclusion that the presence of Dale would interfere with their ability to maintain this aspect of their beliefs and expressive message. In contrast to the views of the majority, there was a powerful dissent (expressed in the opinion of Stevens J and Souter J) that used a different test for examining the conflict between the discrimination law (public accommodation) provision that prohibited sexual-orientation discrimination and the First Amendment rights to freedom of association of the Boy Scouts. This dissenting view argued that for the conflict to be resolved in favour of the rights to free association of the group there should be a test applied that 'at a minimum, a group seeking to prevail over a discrimination law must adhere to a clear and unequivocal view' (676; 686). If, for example, there were a substantial body of 'internal critics' or a minority within the movement who did not agree that it was an anti-gay organizations, then this would suggest that there was not a clear conflict that needed to be resolved in favour of the First Amendment rights of the group.

Most recently, in June 2010, in *Christian Legal Society* v. *Martinez*, the US Supreme Court has again considered the problem of the religion and sexuality conflict in the context of the First Amendment. The case raised the issue of whether a public law school could place a condition on its official recognition of a student group – and the attendant use of school funds and facilities – on the organization's agreement to open eligibility for membership and leadership to all students in a way that was non-discriminatory. The Christian Legal Society (CLS), argued that an 'accept-all-comers' policy that was instituted by Hastings Law School as part of its policy on non-discrimination on a number of grounds including, inter alia, sexual orientation, infringed its First Amendment rights to free speech, expressive association, and free exercise of religion by requiring it to accept members who do not share the organization's core beliefs about religion and sexual orientation. Non-compliance would lead to giving up the advantages of official recognition. CLS sought a special dispensation from the 'accept-all-comers' policy.

The US Supreme Court was split 4:3 in reaching a decision that the school's 'accept-all-comers' policy did not infringe CLS's First

Amendment rights. Ginsberg J delivered the opinion for the majority. A critical part of her analysis turned on the fact that the case fell within what US First Amendment jurisprudence categorizes as a limited public forum, that is, a forum the boundaries of which can legitimately be limited by an owner who has proprietary-type interests. It therefore followed that Hastings' insistence that CLS follow an 'accept-all-comers' policy was an indirect rather than direct measure to encourage CLS to modify its membership. This distinguished the *Christian Legal Society* v. *Martinez* case from *Boy Scouts* v. *Dale*. Unlike the Boy Scouts, CLS were an organization which was effectively seeking a state subsidy for their activities on the campus of a public higher education institution. CLS could exclude any person they choose for any reason but – crucially – the consequence of this would be that they give up public recognition and public funding. This was quite different from a situation in which a group was being coerced into accepting unwanted members with no choice, as exemplified by the situation in *Boy Scouts* v. *Dale*.

It was also essential to the majority's argument in *Christian Legal Society* v. *Martinez* that the non-discriminatory 'accept-all-comers' policy was treated as being viewpoint-neutral. Stephens J, concurring, argued that the policy did not discriminate against those with religious beliefs (e.g. that homosexuality is a sin) but it only targeted those who acted on these beliefs to exclude some individuals from membership of the CLS. Moreover, the fact that in practice the 'accept-all-comers' policy would have a disparate impact on religious groups who may be more likely to want to exclude individuals from their groups and association was not an infringement of the First Amendment. Alito J, dissenting, strongly disagreed with this characterization of the 'accept-all-comers' policy as viewpoint-neutral. His statement that 'Hastings' accept-all-comers policy is not reasonable in light of the stipulated purpose of the RSO [registered student organizations] forum: to promote diversity of viewpoints "among" – not within – registered student organizations' suggests a very different vision of what is required by the First Amendment. Whereas for Stevens J, First Amendment free-speech values are guaranteed by ensuring that each student has access to membership of each of the organizations, for Alito J these values are safeguarded through a strategy of pluralism which ensures that a range of distinct voices are all represented within the forum. Once again, Stevens J's response to these arguments focused on the fact that the First Amendment protects CLS's right to discriminate in the private sphere; it need not provide them with public funds and a public forum. Free speech, he argued, requires us to tolerate organizations such as the CLS rather than granting them equal access to public forums and public funds.

The disagreement between Stevens J and Alito J on this point has significance for the scope of religious freedom in the public sphere beyond the issue of freedom of speech and association. If, as Stevens J argued, even the most minimal connection with the public sphere and public funding means that the issue is 'public' then this will significantly favour sexual-orientation equality over religious freedom. This has particular relevance not only for the application of sexual-orientation equality as the preferred norm in the public sphere, but also for current debates about the reach of discrimination law into the private sphere. For example, will the increasing delegating of public functions to civic society, and the 'Big Society' agenda, be subject to the requirements of non-discrimination? If religious organizations step forward to provide important public services (e.g. care and counselling) using public funds, is it reasonable that they should comply with sexual-orientation equality norms? The principle underlying the decision in *Christian Legal Society* v. *Martinez* suggests that the requirement that religious organizations comply with non-discrimination standards, even where these conflict with a central doctrine of their religion, will not be a breach of their right to free speech or association. It also confirms the willingness of courts to prefer sexual-orientation equality as a state aim even if this interferes with religious freedom. If a religious individual or association cannot, in good conscience, provide the public service without sexual-orientation discrimination then the solution is that they should withdraw from the public activity.

Concluding comments: managing conflicts between religious freedom and sexual orientation

Religious freedom and sexual-orientation equality conflicts are, as the previous discussion confirms, proliferating, as well as being a focus of considerable political and legal activism. There are, as the previous discussion has suggested, ways of developing our existing legal concepts and principles to minimize or avoid a conflict. One important guiding principle is that where there is a religion and sexuality conflict it is important to take an approach that does not create a hierarchy between rights or equality grounds. As Judge Tulkens has stated in a different context of the ECtHR headscarf cases, in which there was an alleged conflict between equality and constitutional rights: 'In a democratic society, I believe it is necessary to seek to harmonize the principles of secularism, equality and liberty, not to weigh one against the other' (*Leyla Şahin* v. *Turkey*, Judge Tulkens, para. 4).

The belief–conduct distinction provides one way of balancing the need to respect freedom of religion with the need to regulate the manifestations of religion that constitute conduct that is causing harm to others. As Raymond Plant notes in his chapter, our understanding of harm will depend on a benchmark that can be shared across all groups in a pluralist society, which in turn provides the link between harm and the basic good of agency. In contemporary liberal democracies, human rights and equality standards will provide the normative benchmark that guides our understanding of harmful conduct as well as providing the common public discourse for debating the limits of tolerating religion. It is, therefore, not surprising that manifestations of religion that require discrimination against gays and lesbians will be the subject of legal regulation.

Requiring religion to comply with the standards of human rights and equality can lead to tensions and conflicts for some adherents whose religious beliefs are not compatible with equality for women, gays and lesbians. Legal techniques such as the belief–conduct distinction or the grant of an exemption are a crucial means of securing religious freedom for these individuals.

It is also important to recall Raymond Plant's observation that our present approach to religion runs the risk of assuming that all individuals adhere to the most conservative interpretation of a religious practice. Plant's analysis suggests that there will be difficult questions about how to determine which sorts of manifestations of religion are to be regarded as essential or intrinsic to religion.

This approach would slow down the analysis to investigate more closely whether a conflict between religion and sexual-orientation equality is inevitable. It may be possible to develop solutions which treat a religious individual who is gay or lesbian as a member of his or her preferred religious community, rather than assuming the incompatibility of his or her sexual orientation with religious doctrine. Significantly, in many of these situations the applicant often wants to stay within the religious group rather than exercising a right to exit.

This suggests that techniques such as mediation or alternative dispute resolution should be explored in preference to the all-or-nothing structure of litigation, which forces an individual to choose between his or her religion and sexual orientation.

Where a conflict between religion and sexual-orientation equality cannot be avoided, recent decisions such as *Ladele* v. *London Borough of Islington* (UK Court of Appeal) or *Christian Legal Society* v. *Martinez* (US Supreme Court) confirm the willingness of the judicial branch to impose a legal solution despite the lack of social consensus about sexual-orientation equality. Religious groups often point to these decisions to argue that they are uniquely disadvantaged when faced with secular political institutions, and some have argued in favour of separate religious courts (Meikle, 2010). In the UK, cases such as *Ladele* have led to claims that Christians are being marginalized and in some situations 'persecuted' (Donald, 2012: section 7). In recent comments, Archbishop Rowan Williams criticizes 'those on the Church's evangelical wing, such as his predecessor Lord Carey, who have said that Christians in Britain suffer from persecution'. Dr Williams concludes: 'But ... our problem is not simply loud voices attacking faith (and certainly not 'persecution' as some of the more highly coloured apologetics claim).'[3]

Legal devices such as the belief–conduct distinction and the public–private distinction are useful to safeguard the rights of individuals (such as gays and lesbians) in key areas such as employment or on campuses. Yet, in these contexts, falling back on the belief–conduct distinction is not without costs. It is difficult to argue that there has been no compromise to religious conscience in cases such as *Ladele v. London Borough of Islington* which require compliance with sexual-orientation equality norms by religious individuals. In these situations, human rights and equality legislation provides us with an imperfect solution. In situations such as *Ladele* v. *London Borough of Islington*, the religious individual is being presented with a difficult choice between following the requirements of their religion and private conscience or participating in a key public institution such as employment or in the public sphere.

---

[3] Quoted in 'Archbishop Launches Parting Attack on Critics', *Sunday Telegraph*, 9 September 2012.

Ideally it should be possible to allow an individual to participate in public life without having to compromise their religion. Yet, in situations where there is a tension or conflict between religion and sexual-orientation equality, this may not be possible. The final decision against Ms Ladele may be correct law and politics in a liberal political order. Nevertheless, it is possible to acknowledge that Ms Ladele was faced with a choice between her religion and her preferred employment which required an unreasonable compromise. These situations should be avoided because, as Sheldon Leader has noted, 'to erect barriers between one's conscience and action manifesting that conscience – as happens when one is blocked from school or employment because of an intense religious conviction – is an invitation to withdraw into angry or cynical indifference towards one's society' (Leader, 2007: 730).

Moreover, one consequence of these techniques is that they will tend to silence and marginalize religious voices within liberal democracies in ways which could be damaging and counterproductive, as well as detrimental to free-speech values. As Carl Stychin has argued, a willingness to enter into, and encourage, debate between those on different ends of the spectrum in the religion and sexuality conflict is an important part of developing stable solutions (Stychin, 2009).

Given these issues, it is especially important to focus on developing non-legal responses which can avoid or minimize tensions and conflicts between religion and sexual-orientation equality. In its recent analysis of religion and belief in the UK, those interviewed by the Equality and Human Rights Commission emphasized the importance of public debate and non-legal solutions. They also identified some key principles (such as proportionality) that can underpin dispute resolution and public debates in situations that involve religion (Donald, 2012: sections 7 and 8).

Some conflicts could be resolved in a forum other than courts through processes of arbitration or mediation within religious communities (Malik, 2008). In some situations, it may be appropriate to have a more wide-ranging discussion that allows greater public participation in debates about the appropriate balance between conflicting equality groups or between equality and other human rights. In the context of the exemptions that have been granted to religious organizations to discriminate on the ground of sexual orientation, the Joint Committee on Human Rights could hear evidence from a wide range

of individuals and groups in civil society, including organizations such
as Stonewall, about their experience of the exemptions granted to
religious organizations (Stonewall, 2007). The Committee could then
evaluate and report on the impact of these exemptions in an annual
review that would be an open and transparent procedure.

Local authorities implementing an equality duty (under the Equality
Act 2010) which covers religion or belief, and sexual orientation or
gender could be encouraged to devise processes of consultation with
local communities and civil society which bring together a wide range of
groups and individuals before significant conflicts arise. An early process
of consultation may help to resolve conflicts within and also between different groups. It could also inform the design and implementation of an
equality action plan. Better training and management in the workplace
should be supported to prevent disputes (for example, between religious
conscience and sexual-orientation equality) becoming acrimonious. In
some cases, the reallocation of work duties and rosters can address the
issue without the need for disciplinary proceedings or litigation. ACAS
should consider whether there is a need to issue guidance or a code of
practice about how employers can reconcile their responsibilities under
the Employment Equality (Religion or Belief) Regulations 2003 and the
Employment Equality (Sexual Orientation) Regulations 2003 (ACAS,
2005, 2007). As the comments in the Employment Appeal Tribunal
decision in *Ladele* v. *London Borough of Islington* confirm, there is considerable scope for addressing these conflicts through the intelligent use
of human-resources policy rather than through litigation.

Religion and sexuality conflicts require a range of responses. Legal
devices, such as the use of the belief–conduct distinction, or drawing
distinctions between the public and private sphere, can only provide
a partial solution. There is a considerable role for non-legal strategies
in this context. Although law has a role to play, it cannot provide a
substitute for tolerance as a political and ethical virtue (Jones, 2012)
or the transformation of social attitudes on the part of both religious
believers and advocates of sexual-orientation equality. This may be
one area in which – as one commentator argues – 'you can't hurry
love' (Koppelman, 2006).

References

ACAS. 2005. *Management of Sexual Orientation, Religion and Belief in the
    Workplace*. Research Paper. London: ACAS.

2007. *Sexual Orientation and Religion or Belief Discrimination in the Workplace*. Prepared by Ben Savage. London: ACAS.

Audi, R. 2000. *Religious Commitment and Secular Reason*. Cambridge University Press.

Bader, V. 2007. *Secularism or Democracy? Associational Governance of Religious Diversity*. Amsterdam: IMISCOE/Amsterdam University Press.

Bamforth, N., Malik, M. and O'Cenneide, C. 2008. *Discrimination Law: Theory and Context*. London: Sweet and Maxwell.

Cane, P., Evans, C. and Robinson, Z., eds. 2008. *Law and Religion in Theoretical and Historical Context*. Cambridge University Press.

Donald, A. (with the assistance of Karen Bennett and Phillip Leach). 2012. *Religion or Belief, Equality and Human Rights in England and Wales*. Equality and Human Rights Commission Research Report, 84. London: EHRC.

Evans, C. 2001. *Freedom of Religion under the European Convention on Human Rights*. Oxford University Press.

Evans, M. D. 2008. 'Freedom of Religion and the European Convention on Human Rights', in P. Cane, C. Evans and Z. Robinson, eds., *Law and Religion in Theoretical and Historical Context*. Cambridge University Press, 291–316.

Jones, P. 2012. 'Toleration, Religion and Accommodation', *European Journal of Philosophy*, 20, 5.

Koppelman, A. 2006. 'You Can't Hurry Love: Why Antidiscrimination Protections for Gay People Should Have Religious Exemptions', *Brooklyn Law Review*, 72, 125–46.

Leader, S. 2007. 'Freedom and Futures: Personal Priorities, Institutional Demands and Freedom of Religion', *Modern Law Review*, 70, 5, 713–30.

Leigh, I. 2006. 'Homophobic Speech, Equality Denial and Religious Expression', in I. Hare and J. Weinstein, eds., *Extreme Speech and Democracy*. Oxford University Press, 375–99.

MacCulloch, D. 2004. *Reformation: Europe's House Divided 1490–1700*. London: Penguin.

Malik, M. 2008. *From Conflict to Cohesion: Competing Interests in Equality Law and Policy*. London: Equality and Diversity Forum.

Meikle, J. 2010. 'Ex-archbishop Attacks Judges over Gay Counselling Ruling', *Guardian*, 29 April.

Moens, G. 1989. 'The Action–Belief Dichotomy and Freedom of Religion', *Sydney Law Review*, 12, 195–217.

Phillips, A. 2007. *Multiculturalism without Culture*. Princeton University Press.

Stonewall. 2007. *Consultation Response, Discrimination Law Review.* London: Stonewall.

Stychin, C. 2009. 'Faith in the Future: Sexuality, Religion and the Public Sphere', *Oxford Journal of Legal Studies*, 29, 4, 729–55.

Taylor, C. 1992. *Multiculturalism and the Politics of Recognition.* Princeton University Press.

Young, I. M. 1990. *Justice and the Politics of Difference.* Princeton University Press.

Cases

Boy Scouts of America v. Dale, 530 US 640(2000).

Christian Legal Society v. Martinez, 561 US (2010).

In the Matter of Marriage Commissioners Appointed under the Marriage Act 1995, SKCA 3 [2011].

Ladele v. London Borough of Islington, ET 2203694/2007, unreported (3 July 2008); ICR 387 (Employment Appeal Tribunal (EAT)) [2009]; 1 WLR 955 (Court of Appeal (CA)) [2010].

Leyla Şahin v. Turkey, 44 EHRR 5 [2007].

McFarlane v. Relate Avon Ltd, ICR 507 (Employment Appeal Tribunal) [2010]; IRLR 872 (Court of Appeal) [2010].

Perry v. Brown, 671 F.3d 1052 (2012).

R (Williamson) v. Secretary of State for Education and Employment, 2 AC 246 [2005].

Trinity Western University v. British Columbia College of Teachers, 1 SCR 772 [2001].

X v. United Kingdom, App. No. 8160/78 22 DR 27 (1981).

4 | Liberal religion and illiberal secularism

LINDA WOODHEAD

You are at liberty to seek your salvation as you understand it, provided you do nothing to change the social order.

Attributed to Josef Goebbels

The way in which recent conferences about religion and politics have been framed reveals hidden assumptions: 'Religion Confronts the Secular State', 'Is Religion Compatible with Liberal Democracy?', 'Post-Secular Conditions: Challenges to Citizenship, Law, and Democracy'. Such titles lend support to a widespread view that secular states are the norm, and that they are being challenged by a recent 'resurgence' of (illiberal) religion, a development which threatens to shift religion from the private to the public sphere, and in doing so raises urgent new questions about whether liberal-democratic states and societies can or should accommodate the unexpected intruder. This chapter questions every one of these assumptions: that religion was ever separate from the modern state, politics and public life; that religion and liberalism are inevitably at odds with each other; and that secularism has a more constitutive relation with liberalism than religion. For the sake of brevity, examples are taken from the British situation, but the argument applies more widely.

Let me begin by sketching what I mean by liberalism. First, I mean something wider than 'liberalism' as it appears in those political theory textbooks where it is presented as a political ideology alongside conservatism, socialism, Marxism and so on. This is a bloodless abstraction of liberalism: detached from history, institutional embodiment, compelling symbolic forms and social life.

Second, I mean not a single ideology but a family of affirmations and commitments, which in practice take their place in much wider constellations of commitment and structure. Few liberals affirm all of the following commitments, but most affirm some, in a variety of combinations:

1 Individual freedom. For liberals, individuals are sovereign 'choosers'. As such, each one is the ultimate authority on how he or she should conduct his or her own life. Such choice should be abrogated only in extraordinary circumstances. This implies some belief in human dignity and unique individuality, and often entails a suspicion of authority, including that of the state. In relation to religion, it means that each person has the right, and should have the freedom, to choose his or her own 'religion or belief' (as many human rights instruments phrase it). Matters of conscience are sacrosanct.

2 Universalism. Liberalism has a universalist tendency in the sense that its generalizations about human dignity and freedom are taken to hold for all times and places. It considers universal certain characteristics which it considers to be common to all human beings (such as a sovereign will). The contingencies of socialization are not considered sufficiently constitutive of the individual to override will and responsibility. Nor are the differing conditions of societies and their members considered sufficient to justify the conclusion that the freedom of some is more important than that of others.

3 Liberalism and democracy have a close affinity; indeed, in contemporary politics they are so closely associated that the common phrase 'liberal society' is generally used as inclusive of both. As John Dunn (1979: 80) puts it, 'democratic theory is the unthinking normative political theory of the modern West ... and liberalism is its painfully precarious reflective normative theory'. Some commitment to equality is also implied, at least to equality with regard to possession of a sovereign will and the freedom of opportunity to exercise it.

4 Liberalism tends to be progressivist and teleological. It is bound up with meliorist metanarratives which look with hopeful expectation, if not towards the perfection of human nature and society, at least to a situation in which optimized wants of individuals are successfully coordinated. This often forms the horizon of its practical and theoretical reflections, especially in its contemporary versions. However, there is a more pessimistic version of liberalism which rests its commitment to human freedom not on belief in human perfectibility, but human sinfulness: because no individual or group can be trusted to make uncorrupted decisions on behalf of others, it is vital to maximize choice in order to minimize corruption.

This constellation of views is what is meant by liberalism in what follows, though full account is taken of the fact that in practice individuals and schools may hold some of these tenets but not others, and that in practice the different elements take their place in wider constellations of meaning and commitment and institutional realization. I do not assume that liberalism is incompatible with other value-commitments, nor that it does not need to be checked by them. It is perfectly possible to be a liberal *and* a moral pluralist, believing that freedom needs to be constantly checked and balanced by the demands of justice, equality and solidarity.

As a corollary, I reject a normative fug which too often surrounds the notion of liberalism, and which implicitly defines it as 'the doctrine to which all decent and tolerant people subscribe' – or, as John Maynard Keynes (Eccleshall *et al.*, 1984: 39) expresses the same sentiment – 'a Liberal is anyone who is perfectly sensible'. Along with this, I am suspicious of what is so often a mirror 'yah boo' term to liberalism: 'fundamentalism'. The latter term applies to the form of Christianity which arose in the early twentieth century in the USA and which coined it in order to describe its programme of returning to the 'fundamentals' of the Christian faith (Marsden, 1982, 1987, 1991). To stretch it beyond that use is at best analogical, and at worst an ill-informed way of dismissing forms of religion which, on superficial acquaintance, seem 'illiberal' or 'not the sort of thing to which decent and tolerant people like us subscribe'.[1]

Finally – and this is the main point of this chapter – I reject the idea that 'secular liberalism' is identical with liberalism, 'true liberalism' or 'liberal liberalism'. By 'secular liberalism' and 'secularism' I mean not only the view that religion should be kept out of politics and that there should be a strict separation between the state and religion (an idealized prescription for keeping politics and religion, and the state and

---

[1] The 'Fundamentalism Project' (1987–95), directed by Martin E. Marty and R. Scott Appleby and resulting in five edited volumes (Marty and Appleby, 1991–5), was a serious attempt by distinguished scholars to analyse different forms of fundamentalism and, in some of the volumes, to arrive at a characterization of the phenomenon. Some scholars, like David Martin in the UK, disassociated themselves from the enterprise from the outset because of their hostility to the central concept, and others remain sceptical about its success in establishing the usefulness of the term for scholarly analysis beyond Christianity, whilst acknowledging that the project gathered together many valuable studies of various forms of modern religion which share a few common characteristics.

religion, autonomous of one another – something which no society has managed without forcible suppression of religion), I also mean the linked and more radical view that religion has no place in politics *or* 'the public sphere', and that it should be a wholly private matter. Even when it does not admit it, secularism in this far-reaching sense drives at the complete elimination of religion, because the proscription of 'private religion' would consign religion to a position of insignificance and powerlessness, and cut out its very heart (not unlike a prescription for 'private politics'). What would a private religion be? One can perhaps imagine an entirely self-created domestic religion, but even that would be influenced by existing cultural resources, linked to wider traditions and practices, and would no doubt play a role in publicly significant activities like the socialization of children. A religion which is never expressed does not exist; once it is expressed it is communicative and public. Moreover, at the level of the individual, religion is such an important aspect of identity (of *habitus*, of moral direction, of conviction, of belonging), that the demand to 'keep it private' is an impossible one. Nevertheless, such secularism devotes great energy to showing that modern societies, like the UK, actually *are* secular, and that religion *has* been privatized. In doing so it shows how easily an 'ought' (religion should be private) shades into an 'is' (it is privatized). The slippage – or linkage – is bound up with secular narratives of progress and modernization which assume that enlightened rationality has vanquished superstition, and that secular liberalism has vanquished religious tyranny (Woodhead, 2009). As such, religion not only ought not be, it cannot be, and is not, of continuing public significance. This routine conflation of normative with descriptive claims makes it necessary to deal with both in order to reveal the empirical errors as well as the prescriptive flaws at the heart of such secularism.

Thus the focus of this chapter is not 'moderate secularism' which allows religion some role in politics (and is therefore in my view a rather confusing term), but more radical forms of secular liberalism which seek the complete elimination of religion from state and society, from politics and public life. I argue that such secular liberalism is conflicted because of its manifest failure to respect the freedom, rights and normal conditions of existence of decent religious people and institutions. (By decent, I mean lawful and, in that sense, minimally moral; it is not my intention to defend the 'freedom' of any form of religion to cause criminal harm either to wider society or to its own members, nor to deny that religion is perfectly capable of such things. Though if one is not to treat the law of the day as infallible, there will be exceptional cases where religious conflict with the law is justified, and may lead to a necessary development of legal reasoning.) I also suggest that such secular liberalism is historically forgetful of the role of religion in the establishment of liberal-democratic societies, and, in so far as it claims to describe the current situation in the UK, that it misrepresents the actual socio-political situation. Thus I agree with Veit Bader (2007) that, to quote the title of his book, Europe currently faces an urgent choice between 'Secularism *or* [Liberal] Democracy'. In making this argument I will focus mainly on the UK, and make the case by way of four propositions:

1 That secularism is illiberal.
2 That religion is an important ingredient in liberalism, intellectually and historically, and that in Britain today illiberal religion is the exception not the norm.
3 That Britain – like other Western European countries – is only secular in theory, not in practice.
4 That secularism benefits from religious critique and opposition, and vice versa.

None of this implies that all forms of religion are liberal. It is quite clear that many forms can be, and have been, on the side of reaction against liberal reform, and that some forms of religion continue to be deeply illiberal. These observations are so commonly made in radical secular literature that it is not necessary to expatiate upon them here (for recent examples of a critique which stems from Enlightenment times see, for example, Harris, 2004 and Hitchens, 2007; for a counter to the view that religion tends naturally towards violence and tyranny see Cavanaugh, 2009 and Martin, 1992).

Finally by way of ground-clearing, a note on the meaning of 'religion'. There is a tendency in political discussion to identify religion with historically contingent forms of post-Reformation (and currently declining) church Christianity. These are typified by hierarchical male leadership, local congregational forms, national or supra-national bureaucratic institutions, sacred texts and rituals, authorized and 'policed' moral and theological doctrines, communal worship and dedicated buildings. Those other religions commonly classified as 'world religions' tend to be assimilated to this model, or some aspects of it. The problem, as many have pointed out, is that this is an unduly narrow, imperialist, 'confessional' model of religion (see, for example, critiques by Asad, 1993; Balangangadhara, 1994; Cantwell Smith, 1962; Smith, 1988). It ignores the most commonly practised non-elite forms of everyday, lived religion and 'misfortune management' which are the dominant forms of religious practice in Europe and elsewhere – today as in the past (Stringer, 2008). It overlooks the fact that a 'spiritual revolution' has occurred in Western countries since the 1980s whereby 'spirituality' has become a more popular category of identification than 'religion' (Heelas and Woodhead, 2005). And it assimilates all the world's hugely varied forms of religion – and their even more diverse forms of internal and external organization – to a very particular, modern, Christian manifestation of religion whose origins and form – and, arguably, demise – are bound up with those of the modern nation state.[2] Of course, because modern states and politicians *themselves* work with a very narrow understanding of religion, thereby reinforcing the approach I am criticizing, it does make some sense for political science to narrow its focus accordingly – to 'see like a state'. But the moment the lens draws back to take in civil society as well, the flaws in this approach become apparent. In what follows, 'religion' is therefore used in a broad rather than a narrow sense – as a concept which draws our attention to complex and varied constellations of symbols, institutions and practices by means of which individuals and groups believe that they come into contact with mysterious powers which exceed the reach of everyday human abilities and perceptions, but which are nevertheless integral to the 'deep structure' of life (Riis and Woodhead, 2010). This opens the debate to institutionalized and non-institutionalized forms of religion, regulated and non-regulated, national and transnational, local and global, elite and popular, Western and non-Western.

I do not think there is anything in the argument which follows which directly conflicts with Raymond Plant's in his opening chapter, but

---

[2] Even Catholicism and Orthodoxy have accommodated themselves to national frameworks, despite their transnational forms, and the history of Protestantism is, of course, inseparable from that of modern nationalism. However, it is actually more accurate to say that modern nation states and their bureaucratic apparatuses mirrored and often borrowed from the forms of late medieval and early modern religion – including, above all, the centralized institutions of the Roman Catholic Church (see, e.g., Mann, 1993; Woodhead, 2004).

our different disciplinary approaches will be apparent. As a political philosopher, he approaches the question of the compatibility of religion and liberalism by considering possible conflicts of principle, and constitutional dimensions. I am a historical sociologist, also trained in theology, a specialist in the empirical study of religion. That means that I focus more on the empirical nature of, and past and present relations between, religion, liberalism and secularism. Like me, however, Lord Plant is aware of the internal diversity of the religious arena (or at least of Christianity, which is his main reference point), and like me he is well aware of the liberal tradition *in* religion and theology. Where our chapters are most complementary, perhaps, is in their coordinating awareness that current debates about the compatibility of religion and liberalism deal only with the most conservative, illiberal forms of religion (and secularism), which constitute only a fraction of religion in the UK. Lord Plant makes the interesting point that the disputes over religious freedom which are generated in the context of the new equalities law have the effect of pushing to the fore the most conservative and illiberal forms of religion. I make the related point that such religion is the exception within the contemporary religious arena, and that the tendency of the debate to 'fundamentalize' all forms of religion is a distortion. I think we agree on the important, but neglected, point that by speaking as if *all* religion is necessarily a problem for, and an intruder upon, liberal societies, a great deal of debate on this topic continues to propagate this divisive myth.

Secularism is illiberal

I start by affirming the basic liberal principle that individuals should be free to make their own choices, except where those choices cause harm to others. Like most liberals I would also argue that causing offence does not count as a harm (and so is not regulated by law), except where (a) there is incitement to hatred which creates a clear danger for the targeted individual or group and (b) the offence is persistent and personalized and, as such, constitutes harassment or abuse. (I would add that both (a) and (b) are usually much more serious where the individual or group is a minority, whether by religion, class, race, gender or some other ascription.)

If we take this fundamental liberal principle seriously, it is hard to deny that many recent legal and regulatory measures taken towards religion and religious people by 'secular' states, sometimes with the endorsement of the European Court of Human Rights (ECtHR), are straightforwardly illiberal. The regulation of Muslim dress for women is a prominent example. A series of ECtHR decisions have upheld the rights of some European countries and accession candidates to ban headscarves in certain public places (most notably *Dahlab* v. *Switzerland* (2001), *Şahin* v. *Turkey* (2004) – for an overview see McGoldrick, 2009). I take public to mean at least some of the following: open, not secret, widely accessible or publicly accountable in some ways. In some, but not all, cases, it also implies a link to the state. On this account, schools, universities, law courts and workplaces – which have frequently been sites of controversy over the wearing of religious dress – count as public. On liberal principles, to prevent a person from choosing to dress as they wish is only justified if their choice causes harm to others. How can wearing a headscarf cause harm? Even if you could make a plausible argument that it harms the wearer (and I do not think you can), that is not material if it is a free choice. There are, of course, those who argue that it is *not* a free choice – including some academics. Some, like Okin (1999, 2005), go even further, and consider multiculturalism itself potentially 'bad' for women, a position which assumes that minority cultures are more patriarchal than majority culture. I have not yet found empirical evidence to support the smaller claim (that *hijab*- or *niqab*-wearing women are coerced), or the larger (that minority cultures, perhaps by virtue of being religious, are more patriarchal than majority culture). The latter may be true, but would require detailed and systematic auditing for each subculture (if it could be isolated), but the former actually runs against everything which empirical research in Europe, including my own, has found to date. Muslim women in Britain assert forcefully that their dress is their own choice, and sometimes their parents endorse this (Woodhead, 2009). In the face of such plausible claims, it is the antithesis of liberalism to say that 'I have fuller access to the springs of volition than you do.'

Nor can legal regulation be justified by arguing that covering causes offence. It is clear that face-veiling (*niqab*, not merely *hijab*) does offend some non-Muslims and indeed some Muslims. But that is beside the point, since a liberal society should not legislate against offence. So defenders of this intolerance toward religious people have to make extremely strained appeals to security issues (which makes no sense for *hijab* and is easily dealt with for *niqab*, e.g. by disallowing it in the context of a riot or a bank) or – and this is what the ECtHR has done – affirm that states are free – subject to European scrutiny – to decide for themselves according to the 'margin of appreciation' if religious symbols threaten the 'public order' (an appeal to Article 9(2) of the European Convention on Human Rights and Fundamental Freedoms). But how does Muslim covering threaten public order? To make this case it is necessary to identify order with constitutional principles of secularism, as was done in *Şahin* v. *Turkey*. This leads to a circular argument: public order depends on upholding secularism, secularism requires the repression of religion, the repression of religion is required to uphold public order. In other words, the widespread banning of religious dress in public spaces in many European countries, sometimes with the support of the ECtHR, brings into sharp relief an illiberalism which seems to sit much too easily with many European forms of secularism.[3]

So far the UK has taken a fairly liberal stance towards religious dress and the display of religious symbols. But in other areas it has not been so liberal. A British example of secular illiberalism concerns government policy, under New Labour and the Preventing Violent Extremism (PVE) initiative, towards so-called religious 'radicalization' and 'deradicalization'. Of course liberalism does not condone the use of violence, except by the individual in very constrained situations of self-defence and by the state under specified conditions. For citizens to use violence against one another is illiberal in the extreme, since it denies their freedom, dignity and equality. So liberals can agree that it is right to strive to detect and prevent and punish terrorism, religious or otherwise. But the UK has gone further, by claiming that 'radicalization' should also be subject to surveillance and control, where radicalization is defined not only as planning and using violence, but as holding and/or expressing certain (in parentheses: religious) beliefs. These may include beliefs about the legitimacy of the use of violence in overthrowing perceived injustices, beliefs about the illegitimacy of liberal democracy and even the theological affirmation – common

---

[3] It has not always been so. In a series of earlier judgments, particularly regarding the purported violation of the religious freedom of individuals (often belonging to minority religions like Jehovah's Witnesses) by former communist countries, the ECtHR upheld the rights of claimants against the secular illiberalism of these nation states. For details see Beckford and Richardson, 2007.

to most religions – that the state does not command one's ultimate loyalty. In other words, the mere holding and expressing of certain beliefs – and even the mere reading of certain forms of literature – is under official suspicion in the UK. This is illiberal. It is even more illiberal to believe that rational, choosing human beings can have their brains 'programmed', ' washed', radicalized or deradicalized: for these are all ways of saying that some individuals have no reason and volition, or that reason and volition are so shallow and unreliable they can be overturned by quick and simple techniques. What is objectionable here is not only the wilful refusal to attend to the overwhelming scientific evidence which discredits the notion of brainwashing and 'decontamination' (a literature stemming from the earlier panic about 'cults' and 'new religious movements' in the 1970s; see Dawson, 2006: 95–119), but the willingness to assume that only a narrow set of contemporary secular affirmations could possibly be freely held (hence also the assertion that a veiled Muslim must be forced to cover), and the deeper assumption that human dignity and liberal treatment is somehow conditional on the beliefs a person holds. A truly liberal society is one which tolerates the holding and expression of even the most offensive and illiberal views – anti-semitism and other forms of racism, vile forms of sexism, fascism and other forms of totalitarianism – so long as others are not harmed or harassed. To try to ban opinion and its expression is illiberal, and to focus almost exclusively on *religious* opinion, is a sign of the distinctively secular strain of illiberalism.

A final example of illiberalism is provided by the outcome of several recent cases in which new equalities legislation has been applied to issues of religious conscience. One of the most revealing and controversial cases is that of Lillian Ladele, a Christian registrar who refused to officiate at civil partnerships. Ladele was employed before civil partnerships were instituted. She is a black Christian belonging to a conservative congregation who believes that sex outside marriage is contrary to the word of God. She denies being homophobic. In good conscience she believed that she could not officiate at civil partnerships, though she did agree to fill in the preliminary paperwork. Her colleagues, who did not share her objections, were happy to swap duties with her so that no partnership ceremonies would be affected, and she would continue to officiate at weddings. But complaints were brought against Ladele by two of her colleagues, themselves gay, and she was harassed, disciplined and threatened with dismissal. In the face of this treatment, Ladele took her case to an employment tribunal in 2008, which found that she had indeed suffered harassment and discrimination due to her religion, and upheld her complaint. Islington Council then successfully appealed the decision at the Employment Appeals Tribunal. In 2009 Ladele's appeal against this decision at the Court of Appeal failed. Lord Neuberger expressed some sympathy for her position but said that in a 'modern liberal democracy', only 'very limited exceptions' could be made. This ruling has set an important precedent. The decision in the Court of Appeal on the Gary McFarlane case (*McFarlane* v. *Relate Avon* (2010)) was based very largely on the earlier Court of Appeal decision in *Ladele* v. *London Borough of Islington*: McFarlane, a black Christian from Bristol, was sacked by Relate after refusing to give directive sexual counselling to gay and lesbian couples.

On purely liberal principles, the ruling against Ladele is surely wrong. Certainly Ladele caused offence to her gay colleagues. But no one was harmed – except for her, and the principle of conscientious objection. Ladele was abiding by a principle which conscientious objectors have often tried to maintain: that in the face of what you consider to be wrong but which you are powerless to prevent, and/or which the majority in a democratic society approve, you sit on your hands and do nothing. What we are now seeing is a situation in which legislation is making this impossible. I am not suggesting that in such cases religion is necessarily in the right; it may lead people to believe objectionable things which are offensive to many, myself included. But people have a fundamental freedom to believe such things and to express such belief, so long as no harm is done. (I am also aware that the fact that Ladele is a state official is germane to the case. However, first, she took the position before civil partnerships were instituted, and, second, it is open to argument whether state employment makes someone somehow 'the face of the state', or a mere functionary – or a citizen with the right to conscientious objection.)

One worry here is that we are witnessing the rise of a form of secular illiberalism expressed in an inconsistent application of equalities legislation which means that other 'protected grounds' are given more protection than religion. Thus the rights of women or same-sex couples, for example, are in effect being allowed to trump those of religious people when there is a clash between them. One more liberal course would be to strive for a 'reasonable accommodation' of religious conscience, and to give much greater priority to protection of freedom of belief – religious and secular – and its manifestation. Another, which Raymond Plant hints at in his chapter, would be to rely on more universal requirements to treat people with equal concern and respect and as civic equals, whatever their identity might happen to be. This might involve a more publicly accessible debate about the goods and harms involved and how, if at all, they can be balanced (Plant, 2011).

The accommodation principle may imply that some people, most often members of religious minorities, should be exempted from generally applicable laws for reasons of conscience (Nussbaum, 2008). To fail to accommodate is to impose a majority opinion – here a secular orthodoxy – upon everyone, even those who do not accept its truth. This may well be inappropriate in a liberal society. To quote Justice Jackson's famous opinion protecting Jehovah's Witnesses from having to recite the Pledge of Allegiance in American schools:

> If there is any fixed star in our constitutional constellation, it is that no official, high or petty, can prescribe what shall be orthodox in politics, nationalism, religion, or other matters of opinion or force citizens to confess by word or act their faith therein. If there are any circumstances which permit an exception, they do not now occur to us. (Quoted in Nussbaum, 2008: 3)

Lord Plant's chapter contains more profound reflections upon this whole area.

Religion is a constitutive part of liberalism

Why *have* such examples of secular illiberalism become so prominent in the last few decades? Part of the reason seems to be that there is a growing fear of religion which is fed by the ideologically loaded distinction between liberalism (good) and religion/fundamentalism (bad), which is reinforced by historical forgetfulness and a progressivist narrative which presents Western liberalism as the fruit of a historical triumph of secularity over religion – and of reason over superstition and freedom over tyranny. This narrative both implies and reinforces the idea that all religion is essentially fundamentalist, which is to say illiberal and affirming of dogmatic principles which are considered infallibly true, not amenable to rational debate, historical criticism or change. This secular narrative is invidious because it survives by fostering a historical ignorance which is the condition of its own survival (if the past is benighted, why study it?). But it is only wilful blindness to our own cultural and political history – a history which is relevant because it still lives in the present – which leads to the false conclusion that religion is always the opponent of liberalism.

It is impossible in the compass of this short chapter to make the point by rehearsing religion's contribution to the rise of liberal democracy, so instead I will simply point out a few familiar examples already highlighted in major contributions to philosophy and the social sciences. Though these examples confine themselves to the example of Christianity and its influence in Western societies and intellectual traditions, the liberal contribution of other religions in the West and elsewhere should not be ignored.

First, consider Norbert Elias (1978), whose account of the 'civilizing process' in the West rightly draws attention to the central importance of the humanism exemplified by Erasmus. Elias tends to present Erasmus as a secular humanist, but this is inaccurate. Like many sixteenth-century humanists and reformers, Erasmus – part of the new intellectual bourgeoisie, the champions of liberalism – was inspired by the levelling example of Jesus Christ, who opposed both social and religious hierarchies. Erasmus mocks and unmasks both princes and prelates, and contrasts their pretension with the simplicity of true Christian piety. He praises virtue over status, wisdom over learning, self-discipline over display, rationality over passion, service over self-seeking, humility over self-importance and human dignity over conferred status (Rummel, 2006). The call to a recognition of common humanity below the level of social convention is of a piece with Erasmus' dislike of inequality and belief in tolerance, and his brand of Protestant conviction has enormous importance in the history of liberalism.

Second, consider Charles Taylor (C. Taylor, 1989), who emphasizes the importance of both the Augustinian and Erasmian traditions in forming the modern idea of the self. In his account, their influence combines with others to give rise to the modern condition in which self-exploration, self-control and personal authenticity are exalted above adherence to social conventions, traditions and rituals. This encourages mutual identification of individuals (we are all human whatever our place or rank of birth or achievement) against segmental bonding and in-group identification; the belief that each person has the right and duty to explore and follow their own unique path in life; and a spirit of liberalism.

Third, what about Alexis de Tocqueville (1988), whose reflections on the revolution in America single out religion, in this case Christianity of various hues, as a vital ingredient in the success of American liberal democracy? Focusing on religious mores (what he famously refers to as 'habits of the heart') and voluntary associations, de Tocqueville documented religion's role in sustaining the voluntarist, egalitarian, and democratic ethos and civil and political institutions of the USA.

The story of the continuing role of various forms of religious liberalism, Hindu, Jewish, Buddhist, Muslim and Christian, as well as those inspired by alternative forms of spirituality, has been less well told in the social sciences (for readings from and about liberal religion see Woodhead and Heelas, 2000: 70–109). This occlusion feeds illiberal secular sentiment. It denies the existence of support for religious freedom, tolerance and equal human dignity in Islam (Kamrava, 2006; Kurzman, 1998). It neglects the role of Hindu liberals – from Rammohun Roy to Gandhi (not to mention Theosophists like Blavatsky in India and Olcott in Ceylon) – in the struggle for Indian and Sri Lankan independence (e.g. Kopf, 1979). It forgets the important role of Judaism in the struggle for tolerance in Europe (Walzer, 2006). It is blind to the significance of Christian groups, alternative spiritualities and reforming Protestantism in the struggle for women's rights (e.g. Ginzberg, 1990). It forgets the role of Christian democratic parties in post-fascist Europe, of the Civil Rights movement in America and the Roman Catholic Church under John Paul II in the struggle against communism and support for human rights in communist countries (Woodhead, 2004). It never mentions the role of 'cults' like the Jehovah's Witnesses in extending the boundaries of religious freedom in Europe, especially in former communist countries (Beckford and Richardson, 2007). And it seems to have no sense of the key role of liberal Protestantism in the creation of the British style of liberal democracy. In relation to the latter, for example, it is worth remembering that it was the Church of England which supported relaxation of the law on abortion, divorce and homosexuality in the 1960s and 1970s (McLeod, 2007). The deeper point is that liberalism is more than political doctrine alone, and that religious liberalism has been important in the process whereby it has managed to carry popular conviction, not least through the role of sensibility-shaping myths, rituals, symbols, religious and quasi-religious practices (Ammerman, 1997).

Given this historical legacy, and given the fact that religion adapts to, as well as shapes, wider culture and society, it is no surprise that most religion in Britain today is broadly tolerant in its attitudes, open to rational debate and affirming of liberal democracy. This is as true of most Muslims in Britain as it is of Christians and of the large numbers of people who do not belong to an organized religion at all, but still call themselves spiritual, and believe in God. It is simply an unfounded prejudice to equate *all* religion with conservative, illiberal extremes. A recent survey of British Muslims finds that many even tend towards a moderate secularism: 60 per cent agree that religion is a private matter which should be kept out of public debates on socio-political issues, 54 per cent disagree that it is proper for religious leaders to influence voting of individuals and two-thirds acknowledge basic truths in many religions.[4] And a recent report by Demos, which analyses several surveys, including the Citizenship Survey, finds that religious people *in general* in the UK are more politically progressive than non-religious people (Birdwell and Litter, 2012).

There are, of course, plenty of counter-examples – not only of religious illiberalism but of overt religious hostility to liberalism, both past and present. A striking historical example which the Roman Catholic Church today would probably rather forget comes from as late as 1864: the *Syllabus of Errors*, Pope Pius IX's list of what the church considered to be the errors of the modern world:

Syllabus of the principal errors of our time ...

15 Every man is free to embrace and profess that religion which, guided by the light of reason, he shall consider true ... 24 The church has not the power of using force, nor has she any temporal power, direct or indirect ... 44 The civil authority may interfere in matters relating to religion, morality and spiritual government ... 77 In the present day it is no longer expedient that the Catholic religion should be held as the only religion of the State, to the exclusion of all other forms of worship ... 80 The Roman Pontiff can, and ought to, reconcile himself, and come to terms with progress, liberalism and modern civilization. (Quoted in Bettenson, 1989: 273–4)

---

[4] www.brin.ac.uk/wp-content/documents/Field-Muslim-opinions-and-opinion s-of-Muslims-Dec-2010.pdf.

Clearly religion can be illiberal, abusive, violent and despotic. Secularism has often been an essential corrective, and the creation of secular spaces has at certain points been crucial in the struggles of minority groups – for example, for much second-wave feminism and for gay liberation movements. But it is as distorting to identify secularism with liberalism as to identify religion with oppression, and it is as easy to draw up a list of secular wars, atrocities, genocides and organized oppressions as religious ones, despite the much shorter historical sway of secular polities, whether fascist or communist or 'liberal-democratic'. Selective readings of history have always been important in supporting secular modern projects, but their motivation and their consequences are illiberal.

Britain is not secular

A third proposition can be stated simply and quickly: Britain does not have a secular state, and it is not a secular society. As we have seen, radical secularism runs the two together by claiming that religion should be a purely private matter, outside both politics and public life. The fact that Britain is neither is therefore significant. This state of affairs does not imply the corollary: that Britain is a religious society with a religious state. My argument is that both forms of framing, with their simple binaries, are inadequate to the more complex, interesting and mixed reality they describe. There is insufficient space to gather the evidence to justify these statements here, and I have marshalled it elsewhere (Woodhead and Catto, 2012), but some of the main points can be briefly summarized.

The British state is not straightforwardly secular. Radical secularism prescribes an absence of religion from politics and its severance from the state. But there is an established church in England and a quasi-established church in Scotland. Religion continues to enjoy certain constitutional privileges. Moreover, the state funds and supports religion in a variety of arenas, including education, healthcare, prisons and the armed services. This remained true even during the so-called period of secularization/decline of public religion. In recent years both the current coalition government and the past New Labour governments have increased rather than decreased the state's reliance on 'faith-based organizations' to deliver certain state services. Far from being confined to a private sphere as radical secularism requires, religion also continues to play an important role in public life and debate – which is why the National Secular Society and the British Humanist Association are more active than ever, and have their work cut out for them. Examples include the role of the churches in education, prisons and welfare delivery; the rise of spiritually inspired complementary and alternative healthcare; religious voices in ethical debates.

British culture is religious as well as secular – including in funda- mental respects, like the calendar (the shape of the week and of the year with its festivals and holidays); the built environment, includ- ing the political heart of cities and the social heart of villages and smaller towns; persistent values, mores and collective and life-course rituals. Religion continues to matter a lot in many areas which affect us most: birth, death, marriage, personal and communal griefs and tragedies, memorialization and the underlying codes, symbols, images and stories which order experience (Frye, 1982; Martin, 2002). In per- sonal beliefs, British people are neither straightforwardly religious nor secular, either as individuals or as a society. In the 2001 census, for example, 77 per cent of the population identified as religious, and 23 per cent as 'no religion' or 'not stated'.[5] Only a minority of people are actively religious, and belief in a personal God has fallen significantly since the 1950s; but belief in 'a spirit or life-force', in the soul, and in the afterlife has grown (at least 60 per cent believe in some sort of God), and the majority of people are engaged on at least an annual basis in some form of religious or spiritual event.[6] Minority ethnic

[5] In a 2000 ORB survey commissioned by the BBC's *Soul of Britain* programme, when asked, 'which of these would you say you are?' (not exclusive options), the following percentages replied:

a spiritual person   31%
a religious person   27%
an agnostic person   10%
not a spiritual person   7%
not a religious person 21%
a convinced atheist   8%
don't know   5%.

[6] For a compilation of all the statistics on these points see www.brin.ac.uk/ figures/#ChangingBelief. Looking at church attendance alone: one in three of the British population attends church at Christmas and one in five at Harvest Festival. One in eight has visited a church to seek a quiet space in the last year and one in four has attended a normal Sunday service (Barley, 2003). Over half the British population have attended a funeral connected to a church over the past year, 39 per cent a wedding and 29 per cent a baptism (Barley, 2003).

groups are particularly religious: the Home Office Citizenship Survey (2001) finds that 17 per cent of whites say religion is important to self-identity compared with 44 per cent of black and 61 per cent of Asian respondents (O'Beirne, 2004: 18). Conversely, it is interesting that the same survey finds that 99 per cent of those who identify with 'no religion' are ethnically white.

The law of England and Wales, of Scotland and Northern Ireland is not straightforwardly secular. The common law tradition has religious roots and continuing influences. There are plural legal systems in operation, most notably Anglican canon law (other forms of law, including Roman Catholic law and Jewish law, are also operative in parallel to 'secular' law for their followers, and may be taken into account in some legal cases, for example, in relation to disputes over wills and inheritance). It is also interesting that human rights law recognizes that both 'religion or [secular] belief' deserve equal protection because of their analogous nature. Both are fundamental, identity-shaping commitments, which are often socially reinforced. Thus the recent ruling that Tim Nicholson, the 'green martyr', had a right for his secular beliefs to be afforded the same protection as religious beliefs is telling.

So to ask what place religion has in a liberal society, where that implies that it *has* no place, since this is a *secular* liberal society, is misleading. British people, like other Europeans – even the French – do not live in a straightforwardly religious society nor in a secular one. They live in a much more interesting mix, which neither of these categories can contain. It is a messiness which should be honoured: a historically shaped, pragmatic and time-won set of arrangements and compromises, which is likely to result in better outcomes for *all* its citizens than the neat ideologies which constantly strive to replace it with a more 'rational' system.

Secularism benefits from religious criticism, and religion benefits from secular criticism

My final proposition is that far from being afraid of religious criticism and opposition, secularism should welcome it, for it brings many

In other words, around half of Britons attend church at least annually for an 'occasional office' and around a third for a religious festival, particularly Christmas.

benefits: it keeps it on its toes; reminds it of its inbuilt limitations; and prevents it from becoming illiberal. Conversely, religion benefits from secular critique. When either one becomes too powerful and unopposed it degenerates; each requires the constant checks and critiques which are best supplied by the other.

At least three persistent lines of theological critique seem to have a constant relevance for liberalism. I take these chiefly from Christian theology, though the lines of argument find parallels in other religious traditions.[7]

First, theological critique reminds the liberal that mere freedom of choice is empty, for moral value is *given* – or at least recognized – rather than chosen and conferred. Liberal voluntarism easily overlooks this. As endless theological and religiously inspired critiques remind us (Iris Murdoch's *The Sovereignty of Good* (Murdoch, 1970) is one example, the work of John Milbank and Charles Taylor another), an anthropology of the self as will alone is a peculiarly empty one, which severs will from reason, fact from value and individuals from the world and one another. Liberalism is right that the fact I chose something is a good, but wrong that the fact that I chose it makes it a good.

Second, from the point of view of transcendence, liberal societies do not represent the end of history, and the liberal nation state is not the kingdom of heaven. In other words, religion is essential for warning liberalism against political messianism and detaching it from its easy alliance with doctrines of inevitable progress. It is mistaken to imagine that the abolition of religion will bring to an end visions of a perfect society: in fact, it is more likely to bring about a transfer of such visions to this world. Certainly the events of the twentieth century chastened liberalism, and put an end to liberal assumptions about its rightful place in the vanguard of civilization, but such social, ethical and political progressivism has, worryingly, given way to economic and technological progressivism, as has been evident in both left-wing and right-wing political programmes. Religion is an important counter. And it is interesting to note that it is not only forms of religion with 'high' transcendence which offer powerful critiques: the burgeoning green movement, with its elements of eco-spirituality and neo-paganism, offers another corrective (R. Taylor, 2009).

---

[7] This analysis is indebted to Robert Song's *Christianity and Liberal Society* (Song, 2006).

Finally, religion reminds liberalism that individuals and individual-ism are constituted by situation and connection and not just by personal choice. Moreover, this situatedness powerfully affects choices. In mak-ing this point, religion joins with socialism, feminism, post-colonialism and other 'critiques by the unequal' to remind liberalism that the sov-ereign individual is a social product, and that 'he' (as he is most likely to be) should not blind himself to the privilege which allows his will to count. Religion adds the reminder that he should also remember that he is a finite, dependent, and nurtured creature. It may extend its reminder of the web of connections back to the ancestors and spirits which surround him, the unborn who come after him, the God or gods who made him, the traditions which shape him and the natural order which sustains him. Where liberalism corrects religion by seeking to throw off the shackles of over-burdening and restrictive tradition and authority, religion corrects liberalism by preventing it from wholly disengaging from ends, obligations, contingencies, dependencies and dependants.

Conclusion

If these arguments – or even some of them – are right, then the con-clusion is that we should change the way we frame issues and prob-lems currently facing liberal society. In fact, not doing so is ferociously counterproductive, because framing *all* religion as a problem for lib-eralism creates a problem where none exists, and focusing only on conservative and illiberal forms of religion generates intolerance and division. The question is not: does religion have a place in liberal soci-ety? Or, what place does religion have in secular society? Or, how should liberal society treat religion? But: how should liberal states and societies deal with pluralism and conflict and, in particular, with intoler-ance, anti-democratic ideologies and movements and illiberalism?

Put like this, it is much more obvious that we are not today dealing with a new problem. The challenges posed by even the most militant religious groups of the contemporary world, let alone by women wear-ing *niqab*, are small by comparison with those posed by the totali-tarian movements of the twentieth century. By changing the terms of the debate in this way, we also stop stigmatizing certain vulnerable groups, and pull down a fantastical Aunt Sally of secular imagining. Illiberalism cannot be so neatly contained – as if our civil liberties were only under threat from religion. The danger of a radical secular ideology is not only that it mislocates the problem of illiberalism, but that in doing so it contributes to it. A richer understanding of a free society is not one in which either religion or secularism has a monopoly and seeks to exclude the other, but one in which both religious and non-religious people and institutions are able to choose, contribute, belong, express their opinions, debate and contest. If we embrace such a vision, we are more likely to remember that liberals can be religious as well as secular, and that illiberalism is by no means the prerogative of the former.

References

Ammerman, N. 1997. 'Golden Rule Christianity: Lived Religion in the American Mainstream', in David D. Hall, ed., *Lived Religion in America. Toward a History of Practice*. Princeton University Press, 196–216.

Asad, T. 1993. *Genealogies of Religion: Disciplines and Reasons of Power in Christianity and Islam*. Baltimore: Johns Hopkins University Press.

Bader, V. 2007. *Secularism or Democracy? Associational Governance of Religious Diversity*. Amsterdam: IMISCOE/Amsterdam University Press.

Balangangadhara, S. N. 1994. *The Heathen in His Blindness: Asia, the West and the Dynamic of Religion*. Leiden: Brill.

Barley, L. 2003. 'Believing without Belonging'. Research and Statistics Department, Archbishops' Council, London. Unpublished lecture handout.

Beckford, J. A. and Richardson, J. T. 2007. 'Religion and Regulation', in James Beckford and N. J. Demerath III, eds., *The Sage Handbook of the Sociology of Religion*. Los Angeles: Sage, 396–418.

Bettenson, H., ed. 1989. *Documents of the Christian Church*. Oxford University Press.

Birdwell, J. and Litter, M. 2012. *Faithful Citizens: Why Those Who Do God, Do Good*. London: Demos.

Cantwell Smith, W. 1962. *The Meaning and End of Religion*. London: Macmillan.

Cavanaugh, W. 2009. *The Myth of Religious Violence: Secular Ideology and the Roots of Modern Conflict*. New York: Oxford University Press.

Dawson, L. L. 2006. *Comprehending Cults: The Sociology of New Religious Movements*. Oxford University Press.

de Tocqueville, A. 1988. *Democracy in America*, trans. George Lawrence and ed. J. P. Mayer. New York: Harper Perennial (first published: vol. I, 1835, vol. II, 1840).

Dunn, J. 1979. *Western Political Theory in the Face of the Future*. Cambridge University Press.

Eccleshall, R., Geoghegan, V., Jay, R. and Wilford, R. 1984. *Political Ideologies*. London: Hutchinson.

Elias, N. 1978. *The Civilizing Process. The History of Manners*. Oxford: Blackwell.

Frye, N. 1982. *The Great Code: The Bible and Literature*. London: Routledge and Kegan Paul.

Ginzberg, L. D. 1990. *Women and the Work of Benevolence*. New Haven, CT: Yale University Press.

Harris, S. 2004. *The End of Faith: Religion, Terror and the Future of Reason*. New York: Free Press.

Heelas, P. and Woodhead, L. 2005. *The Spiritual Revolution: Why Religion is Giving Way to Spirituality*. Oxford: Blackwell.

Hitchens, C. 2007. *God is Not Great. How Religion Poisons Everything*. London: Atlantic Books.

Kamrava, M., ed. 2006. *The New Voices of Islam. Reforming Politics and Modernity: A Reader*. London and New York: I. B. Tauris.

Kopf, D. 1979. *The Brahmo Samaj and the Shaping of the Modern Indian Mind*. Princeton University Press.

Kurzman, C. 1998. *Liberal Islam: A Sourcebook*. New York: Oxford University Press.

McGoldrick, D. 2009. 'Muslim Veiling Controversies in Europe', in J. S. Neilsen, S. Akgönül, A. Alibašić, B. Maréchal and C. Moe, eds., *Yearbook of Muslims in Europe*. The Hague: Brill, 427–75.

McLeod, H. 2007. *The Religious Crisis of the 1960s*. Oxford University Press.

Mann, M. 1993. *The Sources of Social Power, vol. II, The Rise of Classes and Nation States 1760–1914*. Cambridge University Press.

Marsden, G. M. 1982. *Fundamentalism and American Culture. The Shaping of Twentieth-Century Evangelicalism 1870–1925*. Oxford University Press.

  1987. *Reforming Fundamentalism: Fuller Seminary and the New Evangelicalism*. Grand Rapids, MI: Eerdmans.

  1991. *Understanding Fundamentalism and Evangelicalism*. Grand Rapids, MI: Eerdmans.

Martin, D. 1992. *Does Christianity Cause War?* Oxford University Press.

  2002. *Christian Language and its Mutations: Essays in Sociological Understanding*. Aldershot: Ashgate.

Marty, M. and Appleby, R. S., eds. 1991. *Fundamentalisms Observed*. The Fundamentalism Project 1. University of Chicago Press.

1993. *Fundamentalisms and Society: Reclaiming the Sciences, the Family, and Education*. The Fundamentalism Project 2. University of Chicago Press.

1993. *Fundamentalisms and the State: Remaking Politics, Economies, and Militance*. The Fundamentalism Project 3. University of Chicago Press.

1994. *Accounting for Fundamentalisms: The Dynamic Character of Movements*. The Fundamentalism Project 4. University of Chicago Press.

1995. *Fundamentalisms Comprehended*. The Fundamentalism Project 5. University of Chicago Press.

Murdoch, I. 1970. *The Sovereignty of Good*. London: Routledge and Kegan Paul.

Nussbaum, M. 2008. *Liberty of Conscience: In Defense of America's Tradition of Religious Liberty*. New York: Basic Books.

O'Beirne, M. 2004. *Religion in England and Wales: Findings from the 2001 Home Office Citizenship Survey*. Home Office Research Study 274. London: HMSO.

Okin, S. M. 1999. *Is Multiculturalism Bad for Women?* Princeton University Press.

2005. 'Multiculturalism and Feminism', in Avigail Eisenberg and Jeff Spinner-Ialev, eds., *Minorities within Minorities: Equality, Rights and Diversity*. Cambridge University Press, 67–89.

Plant, R. 2011. 'Religion, Identity, and Freedom of Expression', *Res Publica*, 17, 7–20.

Riis, O. and Woodhead, L. 2010. *A Sociology of Religious Emotion*. Oxford University Press.

Rummel, E. 2006. *Desiderius Erasmus*. London: Continuum.

Smith, J. Z. 1988. *Imagining Religion: From Babylon to Jonestown*. University of Chicago Press.

Song, R. 2006. *Christianity and Liberal Society*. Oxford University Press.

Stringer, M. D. 2008. *Contemporary Western Ethnography and the Definition of Religion*. London and New York: Continuum.

Taylor, C. 1989. *Sources of the Self. The Making of the Modern Identity*. Cambridge University Press.

Taylor, R. 2009. *Dark Green Religion: Nature, Spirituality and the Planetary Future*. Berkeley and Los Angeles: University of California Press.

Walzer, M. 2006. *Law, Politics and Morality in Judaism*. Princeton University Press.

Woodhead, L. 2004. *An Introduction to Christianity*. Cambridge University Press.

2009. 'The Muslim Veil Controversy and European Values', *Swedish Missiological Themes*, 97, 1, 89–105.

Woodhead, L. and Catto, R., eds. 2012. *Religion and Change in Modern Britain*. Abingdon: Routledge.

Woodhead, L. and Heelas, P. 2000. *Religion in Modern Times*. Oxford: Blackwell.

5 | *Moderate secularism in liberal societies?*

DEREK MCGHEE

In this chapter I will examine one symptom of what José Casanova describes as the emergence of new historical developments associated with 'a certain reversal of what appeared to be secular trends' in that 'religions across the world are entering the public sphere and the arena of political contestation' (Casanova, 1994: 6). These developments are taken by some to be evidence of the advent of 'post-secular societies' (Habermas, 2006: 46), which is having particular effects in terms of the necessity of fostering the willingness to communicate (Habermas, 2010: 16) between what Habermas calls 'secular citizens' and 'religious citizens'. There are obvious problems associated with the inference (in the prefix 'post') that secularization is a linear and homogenous process (Reder, 2010: 38). Reder and Schmidt attempt to downplay 'the post-secular' as epochal shift and instead refer to it as a term that (1) acknowledges the continuing social role religions play in societies and (2) has become synonymous with examples of increasing engagement (that is, 'constructive dialogue') between faith communities and governments (Reder and Schmidt, 2010: 1). With regard to the latter, Dinham and Lowndes have stated that: 'academics, policymakers and practitioners are grappling with the emphatic return of faith to the public realm of policy making, and seeking to make sense of its implications' (Dinham and Lowndes, 2009: 1).[1] This chapter is an example of these 'grappling' activities. I will be examining a particular question in this context which is directly linked to questions raised by Raymond Plant's chapter, namely: to what extent are religious identities and arguments being included in the public political culture? By so doing I will examine two high-profile contributions that attempt

---

[1] The terms 'faith', 'faiths' and 'faith (or religious) communities', and 'people of faith' are all in their various ways problematic. The author is aware of the dangers of homogenizing and essentializing a number of incommensurable phenomena and diverse varieties of 'faith-designated groups' when using these terms (Bretherton, 2006: 373).

to make sense of religious identities and religious arguments in the public realm, and that make recommendations with regards to their place, role and significance. That is, the characteristics of moderate secularism as found in Tariq Modood's recent writings and Jürgen Habermas's proposals for creating inclusive spaces for dialogue (and complementary learning) in the political public culture in what he calls post-secular societies.

In this chapter I employ Dinham's metaphor of 'the public table' (Dinham, 2009: 3) as both a means of focusing on 'policy' debates and for 'spatializing' the central questions and problems to be explored here with regard to the continuing relevance of secular norms in the institutions of the social-political public sphere (Kooiman, 2005: 38).[2] On the whole this is a theoretical exploration of moderate secularism in and through Habermas's recent writings on post-secular societies. The particular focus of the chapter is on the institutional opportunities and constraints as well as the processes of self-censorship, interpretation and 'translation' that might occur at such 'public table' encounters.

Multiple secularisms and the emergence of moderate secularism

In this chapter I follow Levey's lead when he suggests that the narrow or negative meaning often attached to secularism, that is, as an ideological opposition to religion, or a delimited or principled exclusion of religion, is unhelpful if one is attempting to understand 'what the secular state was, is and should be' (Levey, 2009: 4). There are many different types of secular settlements across the world. Levey offers a comprehensive yet succinct summary of examples of these different secularisms, or secular settlements, with regards to organized religions:

Some liberal democracies continue to have state or established churches, though protect the religious freedoms of other communities (e.g. England, Greece and Denmark); some have official ties to a particular faith, such as the Catholic concordat in Spain, Portugal and Italy; while others honor religious neutrality by supporting or accommodating many religions (e.g.

[2] Dinham's metaphor of the public table is useful as it indicates 'the coming together of sometimes unlikely table-fellows' (Dinham, 2009: 3).

Germany, Sweden and India) or by privatizing all religion (France, the United States). (Levey, 2009: 5)

If the relation between religion and the state in liberal democracies today is the product of the protracted sectarian conflicts in early modern Europe (Levey, 2009: 1), then, what will be examined in this chapter, namely the alleged modification of the liberal secular settlement, is the product of the recognition that Britain, Europe and other parts of the world are facing new types of conflicts, new challenges to national solidarities and loyalties as a consequence of the multicultural and multi-faith diversity brought about by, for example, immigration. In this context religious organizations are being reconceived as organizations that can foster either integration or separatism; therefore, in the current climate, religious organizations are a significant component (and target) of government strategies. It is worth noting that the increasing significance of religion within the public domain is a source of contention and political debate not only for those who consider this a breach of secular values, but also those concerned about the increasing interference in the regulation of faith groups by the state, and those concerned by the potentially fragmentary effects of the focus on religious difference for the achievement of ethnic and racial equality.

It is in this context that I will draw on Modood's observation with regard to certain shifts in the secular settlement in countries such as the United Kingdom. According to Modood, at the heart of what has come to be viewed as secularism in Britain is a distinction between the public realm of citizens and policies and the private realm of beliefs and worship (Modood, 2007: 72). The spatialization that accompanies this designation of different types of activities into their 'public' and 'private' realms is not merely the neutral act of facilitating an ideal forum for 'rational debate': the public sphere. For Asad, this spatialization and separation sets up an exclusionary space which is articulated by power (Asad, 1999: 180). However, Asad reminds us that we should view liberalism or what he calls the 'myth of liberalism', following Casanova, as 'a project to be realized' (Asad, 2003: 59) which during its history has excluded (and eventually included) certain kinds of people: women, subjects without property and members of religious minorities (Asad, 1999: 180). Just as liberalism should be viewed as an 'unfinished' project open to modification, so should secularism. I advocate a reconceptualization of 'secularism' as secularisms, that is, different variants of secularism (and hence liberalisms) that can exist simultaneously in the form of 'modern hybrids' (Asad, 1999: 179).

It is in this context that Modood has described the emergence of a variant of secularism, namely moderate secularism. According to Modood, moderate secularism is a renewal or adaptation running in parallel with existing secularisms in North-Western Europe. What I find useful about Modood's term moderate secularism is its central characteristics: (1) it involves the inclusion of religious identities and organizations in the public realm; (2) it replaces the notion of secular 'neutrality'; and (3) it replaces a strong public/private divide (Modood, 2007: 78–9). For Modood, the emergence of moderate secularism is in part the result of evolutionary institutionalized adjustments (Modood, 2010) on a pragmatic case-by-case approach. This is associated with the demands for recognition by the holders of religious identities, who insist that they be recognized alongside other minority groups, for example, ethnic, gender and sexual minorities (Modood, 2007: 68–70). The strength of Modood's 'contextualist approach' is that it does not lead to the analysis of an abstract principle of secularism; rather it leads to the analysis of 'the actual practices and institutional forms of secularism in particular countries' (Lægaard, 2008: 161). In this chapter, Modood's depiction of these characteristics will be critically examined through exploring Habermas's recent writings on the necessity (in a post-9/11 world) of including religious identities and religious utterances in the public political culture and his recommendations with regard to how this inclusion can be achieved. Thus, Modood's characterization of moderate secularism will be examined through the critical investigation of Habermas's recommendations with regard to how political institutions should accommodate faiths. However, the central question that will be explored here is whether, in fact, Habermas's proposals offer a replacement of both the private/public divide and secular neutrality and can be understood as a blueprint for instituting a variant of secularism akin to Modood's moderate secularism.

This chapter will examine what the recent writings of Habermas (as well as Rawls, Baggini and Audi) offer us in terms of 'challenges for politics' set out in Raymond Plant's chapter. That is, does Modood's depiction of moderate secularism or Habermas's suggested institutional adjustments in what he calls post-secular societies adequately rise to the political challenges (which Plant attributes to Nagel and

Appiah) associated with the creation of spaces for the satisfaction of impersonal and personal values in political public culture in contemporary societies?

Habermas: the inclusion of religious identities and utterances in the public political sphere

Political theorists and sociologists have been critically engaging with the idea of the post-secular society since Habermas introduced the term in his 'acceptance' speech (entitled 'Faith and Knowledge') as winner of the German book trade Peace Prize in October 2001. In Habermas's depiction of 'post-secular societies' we find two aspects: empirical observations and normative arguments (Cooke, 2007: 227). With regard to empirical observations Habermas lists three interrelated social phenomena, each of which he attributes to a 'change of consciousness' in modern 'already secularized' societies: (1) the broad perception of global conflicts presented as 'hinging on religious strife' leads to a change in public consciousness; (2) the growing influence of religion not only worldwide but also within national public spheres in that churches and religious organizations are assuming the role of 'communities of interpretation' in the public arena of secular societies which also leads to a change in public consciousness; and (3) the expansion of religious diversity resulting from the presence of communities of immigration from countries with 'traditional cultural backgrounds' is the third stimulus for a change of consciousness in European populations (Habermas, 2008: 20). I agree with Hans Joas (Joas, 2008), who questions whether the term 'post-secular' is the right term for describing such alleged shifts in consciousness. Joas points out that the new relevance of religions in the post-9/11 world and more particularly the opportunities for 'complementary learning' found in Habermas's recent work is less about the secular state being overcome, but is, rather, a modification of certain states' 'secularist self-image' (Joas, 2008: 107). According to Joas, what Habermas is describing when he refers to these alleged shifts in consciousness is a situation whereby 'the secular State and/ or the general public' seem to have changed their attitude, or, perhaps more accurately, Habermas believes that they ought to have changed their attitude, toward the continued existence of religious communities and, more importantly for the purpose of this article, 'the ideas generated by them' (Joas, 2008: 107). However, what Joas does not elaborate on is what Habermas suggests should happen in terms of the 'institutional adjustments' (Bader, 2009: 135) necessary to accommodate the 'new' political relevance of religions in 'post-secular' societies. This is what I intend to focus on in this chapter. I will examine the potential for new types of political engagement associated with what Cooke refers to as the normative aspects of Habermas's writings on post-secular societies (Cooke, 2007: 227).

Habermas's recent work follows the later Rawls, in that both of them reconsidered their original positions on the exclusion of particularist identities and vocabularies in 'the public realm'. What we find in Habermas's writings on post-secular societies and in the later Rawls is an acceptance of the legitimacy of these identities and these vocabularies in 'the public realm', which is simultaneous with their recognition of the potential contribution these previously excluded speakers and discourses could make. However, it should be noted that both Habermas and Rawls are referring to particular types of engagement in particular fora located in a particular sphere of the 'public realm', namely, what Habermas calls the political public culture (rather than the formal institutions of state), and what Rawls refers to as the public political culture viewed widely as opposed to the more restricted institutional settings (for example, parliament and the judiciary) of the public political culture viewed narrowly (Riordan, 2004: 183). For the later Rawls, contributions made by the representative of 'comprehensive doctrines' (for example religions) in the public political culture should be permitted but only *under the proviso* that their 'religious arguments' will be translated into an appropriate secular discourse. In Habermas we find similar processes. However, Habermas is a little more detailed in his reasons for advocating why 'religious citizens' should not be expected to 'split' their identities or censor the 'religious' aspects of their contributions in the 'public realm'. For Habermas, this is a matter of preserving the integrity of what he calls the 'pious citizen' and recognizing that the elitist assumptions and asymmetrical burdens that lie behind these requirements assume that all participants are 'poly-glottal' and thus potentially exclude what he refers to as 'mono-glottal' citizens (Habermas, 2006: 10) who might not have the capacity to express themselves in multiple discursive registers. For Habermas, the strict demands of secular neutrality made by, for example, Robert Audi (see below) that 'religious persons' should be willing to engage in self-censorship in order to achieve what Audi calls 'theo-ethical equilibrium' in their 'public realm' participation (Audi, 2000: 130) should only fall on, for example, politicians and civil servants, who in carrying out their responsibilities in state institutions should remain neutral (Habermas, 2006: 9–8; 2010: 21).

In many ways, what is significant about Habermas's recent writings is that they are a direct challenge to the aims of a liberal public philosophy which sets out to define a standard common to all citizens regardless of their beliefs. For Habermas, the demands of secular neutrality or a Rawlsian 'duty of civility' should not be placed on 'religious citizens' as many of them 'would not be able to undertake such an artificial division within their own minds without jeopardizing their existence as pious persons' (Habermas, 2006: 8). For Habermas this is not just a matter of avoiding the violence of 'splitting' or the elitism of assumed poly-glottism, it is a matter of also avoiding the requirements of what he views as an artificial process expected of 'religious citizens' that calls for a 'flimsy switchover of religiously rooted political convictions onto a *different* cognitive basis' (Habermas, 2006: 8). By so doing Habermas has made the connection between procedural exclusions and substantive exclusions (Cohen, 1996; Parekh, 2000) in that he recognizes that the exclusion of 'religious arguments' from certain aspects of the public sphere is not only unfair, it can also 'sever secular society from important resources of meaning' (Habermas, in Chambers, 2007: 214).

In Habermas we find a dismissive approach to what he views as the over-exaggerated fears in political liberalism with regards to the presence of religious arguments in the public realm. As such there are some parallels here with I. M. Young's (2000) decentred view of democratic processes associated with the enlargement of the conception of political communication. In his writings on 'post-secular' societies Habermas has challenged what he calls the 'strict impartiality' vis-à-vis the state and religious communities in Rawlsian political liberalism. The latter has resulted, according to Habermas, in 'an overly narrow, supposedly secularist definition of the political role of religion in the liberal frame' (Habermas, 2006: 6). Habermas is intent on persuading the liberal state that it has 'an interest in unleashing religious voices in the political public sphere and in the political participation of religious organizations as well' (Habermas, 2006: 10). Habermas has proceduralist and substantive objections to the prohibition of 'religious arguments' in 'the public realm' which he also shares with Parekh. For Parekh the latter can lead to disenfranchisement, oppressive consequences and political violence (Parekh, 2000: 204), but can also 'deprive political life' in two further ways: (1) with regard to the valuable insights religion offers, and (2) the moral energies that religions can mobilize for just and worthwhile causes (Parekh, 2000: 324). According to Habermas (as for Parekh), the unleashing of religious voices and discourses in the political public culture requires certain institutional modifications. Whereas Parekh's emphasis is more on the bottom-up and spontaneous creation of spaces for 'intercultural dialogue' in civil society (Parekh, 2000: 223 and 306), Habermas's institutional adjustments are more top-down; they are a matter of introducing new spaces in the pre-parliamentary political public culture that will facilitate the processes of 'double' or 'complementary' learning between what he calls 'secular' and 'religious' citizens and 'secular' or 'religious' mentalities (Habermas, 2003, 2005, 2006, 2008, 2010). For Habermas, these complementary learning processes have the potential for facilitating understanding and recognition across difference, whereby

secular citizens or those of other religious persuasions can under certain circumstances learn something from religious contributions; that is, for example, the case that they recognize in the normative truth content of a religious utterance hidden intuitions of their own. (Habermas, 2006: 10)

From this we can see that there is common ground between Modood's moderate secularism and Habermas's proposals for introducing new institutional spaces for facilitating dialogue and complementary learning, especially in terms of suggesting 'inclusive spaces', which in turn represents a deprivatization of religious identities. However, the question remains – does this add up to a replacement of secular neutrality as depicted by Modood?

The translation and containment of religious utterances

When we consider the recent developments associated with the inclusion of religious identities and organizations in the public realm we can be seduced into thinking that the secular settlement has shifted from benign neutrality (Glazer, 1975, 1983) or benign neglect (Kymlicka,

1996) to a practical engagement on a number of different levels. However, despite these developments, the institutional constraints on discourse during these encounters must be considered. Thus in this section I will ponder the question whether Habermas's recommendations will lead to a replacement or continuance (in the form of institutional constraints) of liberal secular neutrality.

There are in existence a number of what will be called 'guidelines' that can be found in the literature for the purpose of instructing how what are referred to as 'people of faith' or 'believing subjects' should conduct themselves in the 'public realm'. These 'guidelines', in turn expose for analysis how particular authors perceive the negotiation of the transcendent/immanent divide when people of faith are called to the public table. According to Baggini, in order to avoid having one's contribution deemed irrelevant, the 'test' in a Rawlsian sense is for people of faith at 'the public table' to use 'reasonable comprehensive doctrines' only when they are supported by 'proper political reasons' and not simply reasons that stem solely from comprehensive doctrines (Baggini, in Furbey, 2009: 36). Baggini's Rawlsian test, therefore, necessitates, for example, 'the representatives' of faith communities finding ways of expressing their beliefs in universalistic rather than particularistic terms (Baggini, 2006: 210). The 'trick', therefore, is for the speaker to employ universalist and immanent terms and frameworks in order for their contribution to enter 'the secular debate' even though their commitments (and contributions) remain 'rooted in religion' (Baggini, 2006: 210). For Baggini:

Secularism does not deny people the right to be motivated by and to live by their religious beliefs. Nor does it even prohibit them from bringing these commitments to the secular sphere. All that it prohibits is that the debate itself is not couched in sectarian terms. (Baggini, 2006: 210)

What Baggini is alluding to is what Audi describes as 'the achievement of theo-ethical equilibrium' whereby 'a rational integration between religious deliverances and insights and, on the other hand, secular ethical considerations' is achieved (Audi, 1997: 21). According to Audi, when people of faith are invited to the public table, especially when they are invited to participate on matters of public morality or of political choice, they 'have a *prima facie* obligation ... to seek equilibrium between those considerations and relevant secular standards of ethics and political responsibility' (Audi, 1997: 37). Audi's 'toolkit' for the achievement of theo-ethical equilibrium includes recommendations that people of faith season their 'public realm' contributions with: 'a knowledge of many facts, say medical facts about the population needing help and sociological facts concerning their patterns of life. Here one may properly seek an equilibrium that yields a socio-political judgment which is at once morally and religiously sound and scientifically informed' (Audi, 1997: 37).

In contrast to Habermas, what we find in Audi is an appreciation of poly-glottal dexterity whereby the 'representatives' of faith communities who find themselves at the public table are thought to be proficient in a number of discursive registers. However, what this amounts to in Audi is an injunction that the 'representative' of faith communities at the public table should adopt a tactical approach that involves speaking to the policy-makers 'in their own language', that is, co-opting scientific-factual frames of reference which in turn relegates, through self-censorship, their reliance on unpredictable (in terms of their vulnerability of being deemed irrelevant) religious frames of reference. Audi's self-censorship model for neutralizing 'religious' from 'political' considerations is organized around two principles: the principle of secular rationale and what he calls the lesser principle of secular motivation (Audi, 2000: 86 and 96). According to Audi, these principles allow 'those with high standards grounded in their religious commitments' to harmonize religious and political commitments (Audi, 2000: 86). The principle of secular rationale is linked to Audi's stipulation that people of faith do not, in particular contexts, 'advocate or support any law or public policy that restricts human conduct, unless one has and is willing to offer adequate secular reasons for this advocacy or support' (Audi, 2000: 86).[3] Audi clarifies the latter by suggesting that 'if my only reason is to promote my own or other distinctively religious ideals, then I would not satisfy this principle' (Audi, 2000: 87). The lesser (and more porous) principle of secular motivation is a supplementary device for the person of faith to employ when participating at

---

[3] Audi defines a 'secular reason' as 'roughly one whose normative force, that is, its status as a prima facie justificatory element, does not evidentially depend on the existence of God (or on denying it) or on theological considerations, or on the pronouncements of a person or institution qua religious propositions' (Audi, 2000: 89).

the public table.[4] According to this principle, 'one has a (*prima facie*) obligation to abstain from advocacy or support of a law or public policy that restricts human conduct, unless in advocating or support-ing it one is sufficiently motivated by (normatively) adequate secular reasons' (Audi, 2000: 96).

Habermas also provides details in his recent writings of to how 'safe-guards' and 'parameters' can be instituted in the context of including religious identities and arguments in the public political sphere. It is here that Habermas relies on what he calls the 'institutional trans-lation *proviso*' following the later Rawls (Habermas, 2006: 10). For Habermas the institutional translation *proviso* becomes the filter through which 'religious arguments' may pass from what he describes as 'the confused din of voices in the public sphere' into 'the formal agendas of State institutions' (Habermas, 2008: 28). It is through this process of filtration, that the 'raw' 'truth content' contained in religious arguments found in 'the pre-parliamentarian domain' (Habermas, 2006: 10) can enter into 'the institutionalized practice of deliberation and decision-making' in the 'formal proceedings within political bodies' (Habermas, 2006: 10). Rather than 'translators' act-ing 'in due course' and in 'good faith' (as vaguely stipulated in the later Rawls) what Habermas advocates is a creative, dialogic interpretative task for particular 'official' (for example, representatives of govern-ment) 'secular citizens' who are expected to 'open their minds to the possible truth content of these presentations and enter into dialogues from which religious reasons then might well emerge in the trans-formed guise of generally acceptable arguments' (Habermas, 2006: 11). Habermas also suggests a particular arrangement between his proposed new fora in the political public culture and the institutions of the state. In his formulation the institutions of state must be both distanced in terms of procedure, yet in their willingness to 'learn' they must remain 'osmotically open' to the substantive aspects of compre-hensive doctrines (including religions) 'without relinquishing [their] independence' (Habermas, 2003: 105).

---

[4] According to Audi, since an argument can be tacitly religious (evidentially or motivationally) without being religious in content, the individual in question might fail to adhere to the secular motivation principle even when offering arguments that on their face are neither religious nor fail to provide an adequate secular reason for their conclusion (Audi, 2000: 97).

What are the consequences of this for Modood's characterization of moderate secularism? In Habermas, as in Modood, engagement and inclusivity are taken as positive developments that either are or should be happening; also, the spaces in which these developments are or should be happening are positively endorsed by both. Furthermore, in Modood and Habermas these developments have or will lead to a deprivatization of religious identities. However, I would not go as far as to say that the existence of these characteristics replaces existing secularism or replaces secular neutrality. Perhaps the most we can say is that these observed characteristics (Modood) and recommendations (Habermas) with regard to these new opportunities for engagement seem to be running in parallel (as suggested by Modood) with existing secularism in North-Western Europe. However, what we can say with some confidence is that their occurrence does not and will not disrupt the secular neutrality of the institutions of the state, mainly because these encounters are and will be relegated to the pre-parliamentary spaces of the political public culture widely defined.

Inflexible and essentialist 'religious' identities

In many ways, the insights of the theorists discussed above are crucial for our academic understanding of what we might call the moderate secularist encounter across the public table where religious identities are being deprivatized. Modood does not examine how these 'deprivatized' individuals are to conduct themselves in these new spaces. As noted above, other theorists have given this a great deal of thought. In Audi we find 'believing subjects' who have the agency and the reflexivity to self-censor and thus modify their contribution 'as needs be' depending on the audience, especially if this results in the maintenance (at all costs, for Audi) of liberal secular neutrality. The same cannot be said for Habermas. There are numerous examples in which Habermas's distinction with regard to the encounter between 'unbelieving' and 'believing citizens' is problematic. In Habermas, we find the presentation of rigid, essentialist identities, and these identities are assigned a 'mentality' by Habermas, that is as having either a 'secular' or a 'religious' mentality (Habermas, 2006: 47). This promotes binary thinking, which in reality might not be sustainable. For example, a devout Christian MP might be able to switch from one 'mentality' to another, and blur both 'mentalities' on occasion when making a strategic moral compromise (Spencer, 2008: 23).

What this boils down to is the question of the extent to which these 'believing subjects' or 'pious citizens', as Habermas calls them, are able to incorporate a degree of 'ethical hybridity' in their utterances at the expense of what Wolterstorff calls 'ethical wholeness' (Wolterstorff, 1997: 105) at the public table. According to Wolterstorff, this 'separation' could be a problem for those individuals who are striving for 'wholeness, integrity and integration in all aspects of their lives' and therefore the separation of their 'religious convictions' from their social and political existence 'is not an option' (Wolterstorff, 1997: 105). When taken to its logical conclusion, this line of argument leads to the question of whether 'people of faith' (both in government and the representatives of faith communities) who are called to the public table are able or willing, to 'bifurcate their lives between what they are committed to religiously and what they are, or could be, committed to non-religiously' (Sterba, 2000: 40). Again there is a degree of inflexibility here, which suggests an absolute separation between realms, mentalities and identities. Perhaps this would be an issue for a small minority of 'fundamentalist' individuals but not for the vast majority of the representatives of faith communities who are called to the public table at various junctures in their professional lives, whether at the local, regional or national level. Warner *et al.* (2010) make a similar point when they refer to Charles Taylor's observations in *A Secular Age* with regard to the great many people who have been 'cross-pressured', that is, pulled in both directions, caught somewhere between an 'open' and 'closed' perspective on the world to different degrees in different milieus (Warner *et al.*, 2010: 8–9). According to Warner *et al.*, Taylor suggests that 'in the midst of such pulls and pressures, with draws and demands on both sides' (Warner *et al.*, 2010: 8), there are individuals who are able to stand in what Taylor calls the 'open space where you can feel the winds pulling you, now to belief, now to unbelief' and can thus 'feel some of the force of each opposing position' (Taylor, 2007: 549).

What I have uncovered in this chapter is a lack of appreciation and connection with established ways of understanding social identities in many of the established literatures examined here (for example, Rawls and Habermas). To take Charles Taylor's eloquent observations above further, what I suggest is actually *missing*, especially from Habermas's recent work on 'post-secular encounters', is an appreciation of the multiple subject positions 'pious citizens', and indeed everyone else, can occupy and the intersectional nature of all identities. Poststructuralists from across the social sciences and humanities have taught us to think of individuality and identity as dynamic phenomena produced and reproduced in social interaction. According to Stuart Hall, identity is not one thing for any individual; rather, each individual is both located in, and opts for a number of differing and, at times, conflicting identities depending on the social, political, economic and ideological aspects of their situation. Viewed in this way 'identity' emerges as a kind of unsettled space in between a range of intersecting identities (Hall, 1991: 10). What is missing from Habermas's contributions is an appreciation of the multiple subject positions that individuals can occupy and the various discursive repertoires that they have at their disposal in different contexts. The social category 'monoglot' is useful for countering some of the elitist assumptions associated with the requirements of poly-glottal discursive dexterity. Yet this social category is also patronizing and potentially constraining because it does little to acknowledge that the 'representatives' of 'faith communities' are not some otherworldly 'species' of human able to communicate only from a transcendent realm, but rather, like everyone else, they are 'in the world' and as such will have to communicate at a number of different levels and in different ways in response to their various roles, situations and responsibilities.

Conclusion

Just how neutral and inclusive is the new moderate secularism? According to Audi, Baggini, Habermas and Rawls there are four potential options for 'believers' in these encounters: (1) self-censorship in the form of the sanitization of 'non-secular reason'; (2) mimicry of the discourses of policy-makers, thus co-opting the language and delivery of scientific facts; (3) continuing to contribute through explicitly referencing their particular comprehensive doctrine's discursive framework, thus risking their contribution being deemed 'unreasonable' and/or irrelevant; and (4) continuing to contribute through explicitly referencing their particular comprehensive doctrine's discursive framework in the hope that their contribution could be subjected to processes of 'translation' or 'interpretation' into 'secular' discourse which will result in their contribution being granted entry, in modified form, into the order of (public) discourse. However, much of the established contemporary literatures that recommend, for example, option (4) (waiting for translation or interpretation, especially in the case of Habermas and Rawls) are actually built upon problematic assumptions with regard to essentialist, reified and inflexible identities and associated 'mentalities' that these authors assume exist across the so-called immanent and transcendent divide that allegedly structures so-called 'religious' and 'secular' encounters across the public table.

In terms of the question of the extent to which religious identities and arguments are being included in the public political culture, I have much sympathy with Modood's observations of moderate secularism, and with Habermas's recommendations for the institutional adjustments to facilitate greater inclusion of what he calls 'religious citizens' in political public culture. However, on closer inspection, when we explore both Modood's and Habermas's recent writings together we see that although Habermas's recommendations with regard to the creation of new inclusive spaces in the public political culture somewhat disrupts the 'strong public/private divide', it does not replace 'the notion of secular neutrality' in the institutions of state. In a sense then, we can see that it is not only, in Raymond Plant's terms, the 'liberalized form of that religion' that is to be included in the new institutional spaces proposed by Habermas. Nor does Habermas insist that 'religious citizens" beliefs be held 'in a liberal way' (see Plant, this volume). However, what is clear is that the beliefs, arguments, experiences and insights 'religious citizens' proffer in the new institutional spaces proposed by Habermas are to be 'neutralized' through the processes of interpretation and translation. It is only through these processes that the 'pre-parliamentary' utterances of the 'religious citizens' included in these new spaces can be allowed to penetrate the osmotically protected institutions of state.

References

Asad, T. 1999. 'Religion, Nation-State, Secularism', in P. van der Veer and H. Lehmann, eds., *Nation and Religion: Perspectives on Europe and Asia*. Princeton University Press, 178–96.

2003. *Formations of the Secular: Christianity, Islam, Modernity*. Stanford University Press.

Audi, R. 1997. 'Liberal Democracy and the Place of Religion in Politics', in R. Audi and N. Wolterstorff, eds., *Religions in the Public Square*. Lanham, MD: Rowman & Littlefield, 1–66.

2000. *Religious Commitment and Secular Reason*. Cambridge University Press.

Bader, V. 2009. 'Secularism, Public Reason or Moderately Agonistic Democracy?', in G. B. Levey and T. Modood, eds., *Secularism, Religion and Multicultural Citizenship*. Cambridge University Press, 110–35.

Baggini, J. 2006. 'The Rise, Fall and Rise Again of Secularism', *Public Policy Research*, 12, 14, 204–12.

Bretherton, L. 2006. 'A New Establishment? Theological Politics and the Emerging Shape of Church–State Relations', *Political Theology*, 7, 3, 371–92.

Casanova, J. 1994. *Public Religions in the Modern World*. University of Chicago Press.

Chambers, S. 2007. 'How Religion Speaks to the Agnostic: Habermas on the Persistent Value of Religion', *Constellations*, 14, 2, 210–23.

Cohen, J. 1996. 'Procedure and Substance in Deliberative Democracy' in S. Benhabib, ed., *Democracy and Difference*. Princeton University Press, 95–119.

Cooke, M. 2007. 'A Secular State for a Postsecular Society? Post-metaphysical Political Theory and the Place of Religion', *Constellations*, 14, 2, 224–38.

Dinham, A. 2009. *Faiths, Public Policy and Civil Society*. Basingstoke: Palgrave Macmillan.

Dinham, A. and Lowndes, V. 2009. 'Faith and the Public Realm', in A. Dinham, R. Furbey and V. Lowndes, eds., *Faith in the Public Realm: Controversies, Policies and Practices*. Bristol: Policy Press, 1–20.

Furbey, R. 2009. 'Controversies of "Public Faith"', in A. Dinham, R. Furbey and V. Lowndes, eds., *Faith in the Public Realm: Controversies, Policies and Practice*. Bristol: Policy Press, 21–40.

Glazer, N. 1975. *Affirmative Discrimination: Ethnic Inequality and Public Policy*. Cambridge, MA: Harvard University Press.

1983. *Ethnic Dilemmas 1965–1982*. Cambridge, MA: Harvard University Press.

Habermas, J. 2003. *The Future of Human Nature*. Cambridge: Polity Press.

2005. 'Pre-political Foundations of the Democratic Constitutional State?', in F. Schuller, ed., *Joseph Cardinal Ratzinger and Jürgen Habermas. Dialectics of Secularization: On Reason and Religion*. San Francisco: Ignatius Press, 19–52.

2006. 'Religion in the Public Sphere', *European Journal of Philosophy*, 14, 1, 1–25.

2008. 'Notes on Post-secular Society', *New Perspectives Quarterly*, 25, 17–29.

2010. 'An Awareness of What is Missing', in J. Habermas, N. Brieskorn, M. Reder, F. Ricken and J. Schmidt, *An Awareness of What is Missing: Faith and Reason in a Post-Secular Age*. Cambridge: Polity Press, 15–23.

Hall, S. 1991. 'Ethnicity, Identity and Difference', *Radical America*, 23, 4, 9–20.

Joas, S. 2008. *Do We Need Religion: On the Experience of Self-Transcendence*. Boulder, CO: Paradigm Publishers.

Kooiman, J. 2005. *Governing as Governance*. London: Sage Publications.

Kymlicka, W. 1996. *Multicultural Citizenship*. Oxford University Press.

Lægaard, S. 2008. 'Moderate Secularism and Multicultural Equality', *Politics*, 28, 3, 160–8.

Levey, G. B. 2009. 'Secularism and Religion and a Multicultural Age', in G. B. Levey and T. Modood, eds., *Secularism, Religion and Multicultural Citizenship*. Cambridge University Press, 1–24.

Modood, T. 2007. *Multiculturalism: A Civic Idea*. Cambridge: Polity Press.

2010. 'Moderate Secularism, Religion as Identity and Respect for Religion', *Political Quarterly*, 81, 1, 4–14.

Parekh, B. 2000. *Rethinking Multiculturalism: Cultural Diversity and Political Theory*. Basingstoke: Palgrave Macmillan.

Reder, M. 2010. 'How Far Can Faith and Reason be Distinguished? Remarks on Ethics and the Philosophy of Religion', in J. Habermas, N. Brieskorn, M. Reder, F. Ricken and J. Schmidt, *An Awareness of What is Missing: Faith and Reason in a Post-Secular Age*. Cambridge: Polity Press, 36–50.

Reder, M. and Schmidt, J. 2010. 'Habermas and Religion', in J. Habermas, N. Brieskorn, M. Reder, F. Ricken and J. Schmidt, *An Awareness of What is Missing: Faith and Reason in a Post-Secular Age*. Cambridge: Polity Press, 1–14.

Riordan, P. 2004. 'Permission to Speak: Religious Arguments in Public Reason', *Heythrop Journal*, 45, 178–96.

Spencer, N. 2008. *Neither Private nor Privileged: The Role of Christianity in Britain Today*. London: Theos. http://campaigndirector.moodia.com/Client/Theos/Files/NPNP.pdf.

Sterba, J. P. 2000. 'Rawls and Religion', in V. Davion and C. Wolf, eds., *The Idea of a Political Liberalism*. Lanham, MD: Rowman & Littlefield, 34–45.

Taylor, C. 2007. *A Secular Age*. Cambridge, MA: Belknap Press of Harvard University Press.

Warner, M., Vanantwerpen, J. and Calhoun, C. 2010. 'Editors' Introduction', in M. Warner, J. Vanantwerpen and C. Calhoun, eds., *Varieties of Secularism in a Secular Age*. Cambridge, MA: Harvard University Press, 1–31.

Wolterstorff, N. 1997. 'The Role of Religion in Decision and Discussion on Political Issues', in R. Audi and N. Wolterstorff, eds., *Religions in the Public Square*. Lanham, MD: Rowman & Littlefield, 67–120.

Young, I. M. 2000. *Inclusion and Democracy*. Oxford University Press.

6 Excluded, included or foundational? Religions in liberal-democratic states

VEIT BADER

As we know, the status of religion in public and political life in liberal democracies has been heavily contested for centuries. In recent philosophy and politics, the focus of this debate has been rather narrowly on reasons, arguments and doctrines (i.e. principles, values and norms) or symbolic universes. We can discern three possible positions. First position: religions in this narrow sense should be *excluded* from public or political debate in political society, from democratic debate or discourse, from elaborating alternatives for democratic decision-making and, particularly, from legislative decision-making, implementation of laws and regulations and from adjudication (different varieties of *exclusivist secularism*, *ethical secularism* and *foundational secularism*). Second position: religions should not be restricted to private life or civil society but should be allowed to play a fair and equal role in public discourse, in civil society and in democratic debates and deliberation on all issues without being allowed a privileged role, let alone a foundational or monopolistic role (different varieties of *inclusivist secularism* or, in my terminology, public and political religions compatible with priority for liberal-democratic constitutionalism). Third position: religions, or more narrowly one religion, claim a *foundational status* over competing religions or against non-religious morals, reasons, arguments or doctrines. This is usually combined with 'cultural' and 'political' but also 'legal' and 'constitutional' establishment.

In earlier publications (Bader, 1999; 2007a: ch. 3; 2009a) I have dealt extensively with the first two positions and there is no need to repeat the arguments in detail by adding an updated version to this ever-growing body of literature. My aim here is, instead, to discuss 'foundationalism' or 'non-foundationalism' in more detail (in the first section of this chapter) and, particularly, to inquire whether, and if so in which ways, religions in a wider sense – including cultural framing,

This chapter is dedicated to the memory of my daughter Ruth Bader.

135

upbringing and learning minimally 'decent' civic attitudes, virtues and practices and/or more demanding 'liberal and democratic' ones – can be said to be necessary and irreplaceable pre-constitutional conditions of liberal-democratic constitutionalism (LDC) or, even more broadly, of 'liberal and democratic societies' (third and fourth sections). This broader meaning of religion and this claim, which has been ignored in recent philosophical discussions on 'public reason restraints', was already at the core of debates amongst the American founding fathers, in de Tocqueville's writings and in the long tradition of civil religion contributions since then (Bader, 2007a: 122f.). It has been particularly strong in Germany since the Second World War and it seems to gain momentum in current debates on religion as a public good that has to be publicly financed exactly like other public goods.

In my discussion in this chapter I take debates amongst German constitutional lawyers and theorists as an example (following Willems, 2004) for the following reasons.[1] While the constitutional regulation of the religion–politics relation in the Weimar Republic was characterized more by 'indifference' of the state, the state in the constitution of the German Federal Republic in its early phases could even be characterized as a tolerant Christian state (*christlicher Toleranzstaat*) which only slowly and inconsistently developed towards a plural and liberal republic. The constellation of political power after the Second World War had changed in favour of religious collective actors. The huge majority of the population still belonged to the Lutheran and Catholic churches; the Big Churches were perceived, rather amazingly, as uncontaminated by the Nazi regime and hence were accredited with a comparatively huge moral authority, accompanied by an astonishing revival of 'natural law'; the two interconfessional parties (CDU and CSU) viewed the Nazi regime as a consequence of radical Enlightenment secularization – particularly of the principle of moral/ethical individual autonomy – and strived for a *Rechristianisierung* of politics and society, for as large as possible a political space for the two Big Churches, for a thorough religious impregnation of public schools and for privileges for faith-based Christian organizations in

---

[1] Space and my limited knowledge prevent my comparing Italy and particularly England, Norway and Denmark with Germany in this regard because, and this would be my hunch, one would find quite similar arguments amongst constitutional lawyers in countries with established Anglican and Lutheran Churches (see Christoffersen *et al.*, 2010 for Denmark).

care for children, youth, social services and the elderly. Changes in the political constellations as a consequence of secularization, pluralization and 'modernization' in the 1960s and even the impact of a considerable number of Muslim immigrants in the 1970s and 1980s did not result in changes in the regulation of the intense and massively biased cooperation between the state and the Big Churches. The established consensus in religion–politics and the high degree of juridification of the remaining political conflicts are reflected in the paramount role of the German Constitutional Court and of academic *Staatskirchenrecht*, which, as through a prism, expresses the *changing legitimations* for the rather unchanged legal/constitutional situation even in *Religionsverfassungsrecht* (Grimm, 2009; Ladeur, 2009).

Doctrinal foundationalism or priority of liberal-democratic constitutionalism

Let me briefly sketch what I mean by liberal-democratic constitutionalism (LDC) in legal and institutional terms. 'Liberal democracy' has been a historically late and contested compromise in theory and politics and so is LDC. 'Liberal constitutionalism' connotes the core or rock-bottom elements of any form of modern constitutionalism: the full list of civic rights against violation by states and all others, rule of law, separation of powers, minority-protection against simple majoritarianism, written or factual constitutions, constitutional courts and judicial review. It contains inherent tensions, for example between life/security and civil freedoms. 'Democratic constitutionalism' connotes free and equal political rights (freedom of political communication, voting and representation), democratic elections of parliaments and governments, governmental responsibility, democratic majoritarianism and fairly limited powers for constitutions and constitutional review, if any. More specifically, I defend minimalist conceptions of LDC in opposition to thick international human rights maximalism and more demanding concepts of 'thick' participatory, egalitarian democracy, and a moderately agonistic, pluralist liberal democracy in opposition to deliberative consensus democracy. LDC is a meta-legal and meta-constitutional ideal of rights and basic institutions, abstracted from the huge variety of liberal-democratic constitutions, non-Western ones (such as India) amongst them. It should not be confused with 'liberalism' as a contested political philosophy or an even more contested and contradictory political ideology (Bader, 2009a, 2010, 2011b; see Bhargava, 2011).[2]

From the perspective of LDC, I have criticized exclusivist and foundational secularism. 'Ethical secularism' (leading an autonomous, self-chosen, fully transparent life) is incompatible with reasonable pluralism concerning the good life. All political liberals and all defenders of political secularism share this basic argument. Still, many political liberals remain committed to 'secularism' on a second-order level when it comes to philosophical or doctrinal foundations or justifications of LDC. Defenders of an independent, secular political ethics from Bayle, Spinoza and Kant to Audi and Habermas in his earlier and also in his most recent writings claim that LDC has to be and can only be based on 'secular' reason or rationality. In my view, they cannot resolve the paradox of second-order secularism that 'secularism presents itself as the solution after all other voices have spoken' (paraphrasing Anne Phillips). It cannot be decoupled from more comprehensive ethical secularism, moral liberalism and the demanding values of procedural or substantive autonomy and rationality or reasonability. As the contributions to this volume by Raymond Plant and Derek McGhee point out, the late Rawls, in developing the strategy of a wide and deep 'overlapping consensus' – a 'non-foundational', 'freestanding', 'political-not-metaphysical' approach – goes some way in relaxing these requirements. He rejects the requirement of a commonly held foundation, recognizing from the outset that there cannot be a universally agreed basis, independent or religious, for the principles of political justice or for LDC. He himself has eventually criticized the identification of 'public' reason with 'secular' reason, while Habermas still sticks to the requirement that religious reasons have to be 'translated' into 'secular' reasons. He has also softened but not abandoned the 'reasonability restraints' (extensive criticism in Bader, 2009a: 112f. and 115–34; 2012a).

Yet all these 'secularist' approaches are at least in tension with or even incompatible with basic tenets of LDC in three regards. First, the *philosophical meaning*, if any, of priority for LDC is a radicalization of

---

[2] In his contribution to this volume, Raymond Plant does not clearly distinguish between liberal-democratic constitutions, LDC as a meta-legal and meta-constitutional ideal and the different varieties of philosophical liberalism. I focus on a non-foundationalist treatment of LDC; his main focus is a criticism of 'liberal philosophical justifications and foundations'.

the idea of a really 'freestanding' conception. Principles and practices of decent polities or of LDC are more important than the whole variety of conflicting philosophical or religious foundations. Fortunately, the validity of minimal political morality and of liberal-democratic political morality, minimally understood, does not depend upon the truth of any of the competing moral theories. This is what is meant by 'priority of rights over theories of rights', 'priority of institutions over institutional theories', 'priority of right action over (competing theories of) right motivation'. Such a considered commitment to non-foundationalism has been described as 'philosophical shallowness' (Hunter, 2009) or 'epistemological and moral abstemiousness' (Geuss, 2002: 333). Modern, pluralist democracy is best conceived as an open project. The political form of a society is not and should not be perceived as the realization of a transcendent vision (Lefort, 1999). Its centre may be described as 'empty', 'hollow' or better as 'overcrowded'. Pluralist democracy rejects any monopolistic symbolic – religious or philosophical – *Letztbegründung* (final justification) or any one 'archimedean point' (Willems, 2004). Instead of privileging or instituting one *Weltanschauung* it thrives on many lively, competing and often incompatible symbolic universes in so far as these accept – for whatever reasons – minimal morality and the more demanding morality of LDC, minimally understood.

Second, secularist approaches are at odds with one of the core features of LDC, with moderately contestational or agonistic democracy, in particular an extensive interpretation of 'freedoms of political communication', including: freedom of opinion, information, print/media of mass communication, assembly, propaganda and demonstration, association or organization and petitions and hearings (Frankenberg and Rödel, 1981: 331). These freedoms cannot guarantee idealized models of grassroots democratic deliberation, guided by 'public reason' and strictly separated from negotiations and power asymmetrics. Instead, they are meant to guarantee crucial minimal preconditions for actual democratic debate (deliberation-cum-negotiation) and decision-making. They do not, and should not, discriminate between 'secular' and 'religious' opinions; on the contrary, they encourage as many voices as possible to be raised, listened to and responded to. In this regard, it is astonishing that philosophers of political liberalism have tenaciously defended issue-, content- and reasonableness-restraints at all, let alone worried especially about 'religious' reasons and arguments.

Freedoms of political communication, like all other human rights, are obviously not 'absolute', but the two well-known restrictions – public order/civic peace and anti-discrimination – apply or should apply equally to religious and secular speech (Bader, 2009a: 114; see my criticism of Turkish and Indian Supreme Court secularist restrictions in this regard: Bader, 2010).

Third, modern LDC requires that all opinions and voices, ultimately expressed as votes, have to count equally when it comes to final decision-making, even if paternalistic elites think, perhaps with good reason, that they are not 'reasonable', uninformed, misinformed, false, morally wrong, disgusting and so on. This third core element, a specific, egalitarian, anti-paternalistic mode of decision-making, requires that all defenders of 'truths', whether religious or secular (philosophical, scientistic or professional/'expertocratic') have to learn to resolve their respective 'fundamentalist dilemma'. Since 'error has the same rights as truth', fundamentalist interpreters of religions certainly have (had) to learn to resist the temptation of 'theocracy' or, more precisely, the rule of the earthly representatives of God, gods or the Transcendent, which is different from claiming that religions have to liberalize (see below). This is still nicely captured by the old phrase indicating the shift from God's to popular sovereignty: *vox populi vox dei*. Yet the same holds for philosophers and all kinds of scientific and professional experts: they have to learn to stem the philosophical 'conquest of democratic politics' (Barber, 1988) and the temptation of expertocracy (Bader, in press). In my view, it is crucial not to misunderstand or phrase the conflict between political absolutism (of all sorts) and LDC in terms of 'religious fundamentalism' or 'religious piety' versus 'secularism' (Bader, 2012a; Jansen, 2011).

In opposition to the remnants of elitist cognitivist rationalism – even in the writings of the late Rawls – it is increasingly seen that reasons should not be reduced to (clearly and propositionally articulated) arguments, that they should be fully open not only to theoretical but also to practical knowledge, that they should not exclude emotions and passions, that homogeneous views of public reason (singular) have to be rejected and that the plurality or multiplicity of perspectives has to be explicitly recognized (see similarly, Stepan, 2010). 'Public reason' does not guarantee, and public reasoning does not result in, consensus. Even 'reasonable reasons' are not reasons 'that might be *shared by all citizens as free and equal*' (Rawls, 1999: 138; italics added) or reasons with which we all can agree. They should be 'understandable', 'comprehensible', 'intelligible' or 'accessible', but it is crucial to resist the – often unrecognized – slide from the requirement of a moderate threshold of understanding to the demanding requirement of agreement. Such a slide is systematically exploited in Habermas's formal pragmatics, for example, and trades on the ambiguity of the German term *Verständigung*. So liberal attempts to restrain public reason, in the end, do not seem to exclude much. Reasonable conceptual, moral, theoretical and empirical disagreement continues unabated. And the criteria of exclusion ultimately seem to boil down to *attitudes or virtues such as moderation and self-restraint* (see below) and *good practices of liberal democracy.*

The phrase 'acceptance of priority for LDC' by religions should not be confused with something like 'liberalization of religion'. Rather, it is a shorthand formula including, first of all, constraints by *minimal morality* (basic security and subsistence and respective 'rights', due process, minimal or decent respect and collective toleration), second, more demanding constraints by liberal morality minimally understood (individual toleration and freedom of conscience, equal civic rights, equal respect) and, third, constraints by minimal democratic morality (equal political rights and freedoms of political communication).[3] In line with the criticisms of Raymond Plant and John Milbank in this volume, LDC explicitly does not require all religions to 'liberalize' in the following senses. (i) To liberalize their *doctrines* or give up their transcendent truth-claims in favour of some secular worldview or some relativistic or scepticist position (yet no truth-claims should be enforced on others and all defenders of truth have to accept that error has the same right as their truths in democratic decision-making; see above). (ii) To liberalize their *practices and customs* or to accept

[3] See Bader, 2007a: ch. 2 for an elaboration of my concept of differentiated morality. In a substantive perspective, my version of moral minimalism is fairly similar to Plant's version of 'natural law' (agency, basic human needs or 'interests' and protection against 'basic harm'). In a procedural perspective, my moderate universalism (like Plant, it is opposed to 'relativism' and 'absolutism') highlights more the necessity of an open trans-cultural dialogue as part of an open 'common ground strategy' in order to find out what 'human nature' or 'central human goods' are and how they can be interpreted and weighed, particularly in cases in which they conflict. In addition I would highlight much more that 'moral pluralism' is not restricted to trans-cultural differences and tensions but is also a paramount feature of LDC itself (see Bader, 2011a).

principles and rights of liberal and democratic morality in the internal life of their families, groups, associations, organizations. Quite to the contrary, LDC guarantees strong collective and associational autonomy or 'maximum accommodation (also for ultra-orthodox religions) within the confines of minimal morality'.[4] (iii) To privatize, subjectify, individualize or secularize religion or religiosity. So clearly, priority for LDC is not to be confused with a 'Protestantization of Catholicism', of Lutheranism (Herberg, 1960; Handy, 1976: 211; Miller, 1985: 274) or of Islam, and certainly not as a 'secularization of religion' (see extensively Bader, 2011c).

In my view, there is a crucial distinction between processes of religious change due to the mere fact that orthodox non-liberal but peaceful religions live in modern societies and under conditions of liberal-democratic constitutional states, on the one hand, and intentional policies to liberalize religions, on the other hand. Living under such conditions, which are fairly radically at odds with their own cultural practices, inevitably impacts on conservative isolationist religions even if the state tries to let them live alone as much as possible, as a liberal state should, in my view (see Bader, 2007a: 213f.). It may lead to an unrecognized, slow acculturation, to intended reforms from within these religions, even without state policies to seduce them or to impose liberalization on them, or to a reactive, intentional purification of their traditional ways of living and practising.

Is liberal-democratic constitutionalism unthinkable without doctrinal religious backing?

If non-liberal religions liberalize even without being aware of it, or if they have learned to accept liberal democracy from the inside, this may be interpreted, from a perfectionist or 'conservationist' position, as a regrettable flattening of genuine pluralism (Shah, 2000: 129), or it may be praised from the perspective of more or less 'comprehensive' moral liberalism. Independent of the way in which one wants to evaluate or judge this development, it is clear that it becomes increasingly unfair

---

[4] See extensively Bader, 2007a: ch. 4 and ch. 5. See Swaine, 2006 for an extensive attempt to explain to 'theocrats' why they should endorse LDC or, in Plant's terms, 'what it is that gives liberalism such authority'.

to reproduce the secularist distrust of all religions as being inherently fundamentalist (see below).

Now it is time to look at the other side of the coin and defend priority for LDC against the main religious and theological challenges claiming that LDC, or more broadly liberal-democratic society, is impossible, unstable or cannot flourish without religious backing (Galanter, 1966: 289f.; Stoltenberg, 1993). In analysing these charges we have to broaden the understanding of religion from doctrine/belief to include ethos (habits, virtues) and religiously impregnated cultural practices and political/legal institutions. Only then can we critically analyse the full scope of these challenges. In earlier writings I have discussed six overlapping but analytically distinct challenges. First, LDC is said to be doctrinally impossible or its public morality is unstable without backing by religious morals and virtues. Second, religion(s) are needed as an antidote to consumerism, egotism, materialism or moral decisionism inherently connected with modernity and secular morality. Religion(s) are also supposed to provide an antidote to, third, absolutist state sovereignty; fourth, rationalist modernity; and, fifth, nationalism. All three antidotes are assumed to be inherent threats or necessary consequences of modern and purely secular morality. Finally, it is claimed that priority for LDC cannot claim universal validity nor can it be fair or neutral. I have refuted all these charges (by, amongst others, Parekh, 1996, 2000; Thiemann, 1996; Wolterstorff, 1997) in other texts (Bader, 2007a: 122–5) and space prevents me from even summarizing my criticisms in this chapter. Here I focus on the first challenge, which may be the most fundamental one.

This challenge comes in two basic versions, one focusing on *doctrine*, the other on *habits*, *virtues* and *good practices*. Before discussing the latter, which in my view is the core problem, we should briefly address the doctrinal charge. This allows me to deal with the second foundationalist strategy, the religious *common-ground strategy* (Bader, 2007a: 107, with Taylor, 1998). In a world of usually fairly restricted religious diversity and rival religious doctrines, the strategy consists of searching for and finding some common ground that is or can be shared by these religions. This strategy assumes that 'everyone shares some religious ground' (Taylor, 1998: 35); it is inherently limited because it excludes non-religious grounds and it is also tempted to treat religious reasons within traditions as given and fixed, neglecting internal dissent. To the extent to which the common-ground strategy privileges or even monopolizes (i) one religion over all other religions or alternatively (ii) in the more inclusive version 'religious reasons' over 'secular reasons', it is as incompatible with LDC as is foundationalist secularism, and for exactly the same reasons. It violates the three core requirements of LDC spelled out above (see also Modood, 2010: 8f., against 'religion as truth').

The first, more exclusivist, doctrinal version is characteristic of the Christian tradition. It was first developed by Pufendorf, Locke and Leibniz; it has been 'rather Christian in spirit' excluding Judaism and Islam but also Roman Catholicism and Orthodox Christianity. Christianity had to undergo a long and contested learning process (Bader, 2007a: 119ff.; 2011c) in order to come to terms with internal religious diversity, with the modern state and with emerging liberal and democratic constitutionalism. This learning included doctrinal learning: to see peace, stability and public order not only as strategic, but also as moral values. In order to make religion peaceable, Grotius and Coornhert amongst others started to replace dogma and creed with a morality oriented to social peace (Galston, 2002; Shah, 2000; *adiaphora*, priority for tolerance). Learning toleration started to tame fundamentalist theological doctrines and also opened ways to replace parochialist, dogmatic and sectarian conceptions of Christianity by a more universal Christian doctrine and ethics, a rather general, non-denominational or non-sectarian Christianity, biblical theism or post-Enlightenment deism. Only during the last century did the Christian common ground become more inclusive and ecumenical (e.g. in the writings of Hans Küng). Even more importantly, in this long and contested process doctrines became less important than attitudes, habits, virtues and cultures/practices of toleration. Making Christianity peaceable or compatible with 'decent polities' or minimal morality, however, is different from learning to endorse LDC from the inside. It took centuries of contestation before Protestantism in some of its varieties, and much later and less firmly Catholicism and Orthodoxy, eventually did so.

Non-Christian traditions developed the second variety, more inclusive common-ground strategies and habits, virtues and practices of toleration much earlier and more decisively. Ashoka, the third monarch of the Mauryan dynasty in India, was crowned in 274 BC. He vastly expanded the borders of the empire and eventually conquered the kingdom of Kalinga in a battle in 262 BC in which tens of thousands

lost their lives. This massacre convinced him to apply Buddhist principles to the administration of the vast empire till his death in 232 BC.
This can be seen as the first attempt to develop a Buddhist polity in an
ethnically and religiously incredibly diverse empire (Dhammika, 1993:
5). In this regard, there was 'no reason for Ashoka to discuss Buddhist
philosophy' for his reform of the judicial and political system.[5] This
broad and benevolent religion served as a 'symbol of a new imperial
unity and a cementing force to weld the diverse and heterogeneous
elements of the empire'.[6] Being an 'enthusiastic Buddhist, he was not
partisan towards his own religion or intolerant of other religions. He
seems to have genuinely hoped to be able to encourage everyone to
practise his or her own religion with the same conviction that he practised his':

[T]here should be growth in the essentials of all religions ... [this] can be
done in different ways, but all of them have as their root restraint in speech,
that is not praising one's own religion, or condemning the religion of others
without good cause. And if there is cause for criticism, it should be done
in a mild way. But it is better to honour other religions for this reason. By
doing so, one's own religion benefits, and so do other religions, while doing
otherwise harms one's own religion and the religions of others. Whoever
praises his own religion, due to excessive devotion, and condemns others
with the thought 'Let me glorify my own religion', only harms his own
religion. Therefore contact (between religions) is good. One should listen
to and respect the doctrines professed by others. Beloved-of-the-Gods,
King Piyadasi, desires that all should be well-learned in the good doctrines
of other religions. (Rock Edict No. 12 in the translation by Dhammika,
1993: 8)[7]

---

[5] This can be understood as non-foundationalism *avant la lettre*. In the words of
Edward D'Cruz, he wanted to instigate 'a practice of social behaviour so broad
and benevolent in its scope that no person, no matter what his religion, could
reasonably object to it'.

[6] This is a remarkable example of the 'institutional logics' of empires (Bader,
2007a: 195f., and 2003; for recent comparative historical research on the
Ottoman, Habsburg and Russian empires: Barkey, 2009). Here the effects of
'religion' on 'social cohesion' and 'political unity' (see Delfiner, 1965: 313–16)
are the core issue: 'diversity within unity' is required for the stability of
multi-ethnic, -national and or -religious polities (from empires to the EU).

[7] Quoted by Jacobsohn, 2003: 14, n. 21; and Sen, 2009: 75–7, n. 40, in divergent
translations.

In this explicitly duty- or virtue-based common-ground strategy, one finds a long list of public or state morals that is repeated in different varieties in many rock and pillar edicts: 'compassion, moderation, tolerance and respect for life' and 'mutual respect'; do no or 'little evil'; 'non-injury, restraint and impartiality to all beings' (Rock Edict 13); 'act with impartiality', 'non-anger and patience' versus 'envy, anger, cruelty, hate, indifference, laziness or tiredness' (Kalinga Rock Edict 1; see The Seven Pillar Edicts 3). This common ground has important consequences for public policy domains such as foreign policy (peaceful coexistence), the reform of the judicial system (more fair, less harsh, less open to abuse, 'uniformity in law and uniformity in sentencing' (Pillar Edict 4)), public works, inspection of administrators and judges, welfare/happiness of all and protection of animals, forest and wildlife reserves. It is accompanied and backed by a long and equally varied list of individual morals: respect (towards parents, elders, teachers, friends, servants, ascetics and Brahmins), generosity and harmlessness towards all life and qualities of the heart, such as kindness, gentleness, self-examination, truthfulness, gratitude, purity of the heart, enthusiasm, strong loyalty, self-control, love of the Dhamma. Limitations of space prevent me from presenting the much more elaborate – and much better known – duty- and virtue-based common-ground strategy of Mahatma Gandhi (Madan,1998, 2008; see Eisenlohr, 2006 for Mauritius) or the political ethos of Confucianism from the 'Eastern traditions'.

If one clearly sees that learning toleration or minimal morality and liberal and democratic constitutionalism in 'the West' has been a rather conflictive, complicated, lengthy and still unfinished process, then a self-critical reflection on this process provides an excellent basis for interreligious and intercultural dialogue and for understanding such learning in 'the Rest', particularly for Islam. The fashionable, endlessly repeated statement that Islam is inherently incapable of learning the same lessons that Christian churches and denominations eventually and painfully learned is really astonishing.[8] There is insufficient

---

[8] Repeated also by Habermas (2008a, 2008b) and Grimm (2009), who still thinks that 'particularly' the Islamic tradition has 'not undergone the process of historicization and contextualization of God's revelation' so that 'it is difficult for them to bridge the incompatibility of religious dogmas by a spirit of tolerance vis-à-vis believers of a different faith' (Grimm, 2009: 2370), while

space even to summarize the well-known doctrinal and institutional counter-arguments (see my summaries in Bader, 2007a: 120ff., and more extensively 2011c). As in the case of Christianity, theoretical and practical learning depends on institutional conditions, most prominently on the presence or absence of liberal-democratic constitutional states. LDC emerged in the West, not in countries with Islamic majorities, for historically contingent reasons.

Two points are important here. First, it should now be obvious that habits, cultures, virtues, duties and practices of toleration, moderation and self-restraint, or more broadly of minimal morality (Bader 2007a: 72ff. and 180ff.), are not specific, if indeed they adhere at all, to 'the West' or the Christian tradition and also that they are not in need of an exclusivist secular foundation. Second, the more demanding principles and cultures/practices, habits, virtues and duties of LDC do not follow logically or by any historical necessity from the minimal morals of a decent polity. LDC needs no exclusivist secularist foundation, but it certainly needs no exclusivist religious foundation or, more specifically, no Christian foundation, neither doctrinally, as has been claimed by Huntington and many others falling prey to the 'fallacy of unique founding conditions' (Stepan, 2000, 2010), nor as a practical ethos.

Both exclusivist Christian foundational claims have been articulated under the heading of 'The Cultural Importance of Christianity of German Constitutionalism' (Willems, 2004). They have been repeated by many German constitutional lawyers for a long time (their very peculiar way of learning lessons from the Nazi regime) and are still aggressively defended in the recent context of simultaneous ongoing 'secularization' and perceived threats by the old and new other of Christianity: Islam. Christianity is perceived as a core, constitutive element of German (and European) culture and history and its constitutional orders and legal principles (Huber, 2001; Link, 1999), which cannot even be understood without Christian thinking, Christian ethics and Christian law. Christian heritage includes human dignity based in *Gottesebenbildlichkeit*, freedom, equality and brotherhood; justice and solidarity based in Christian *Nächstenliebe*; checks and balances; *Amtsethos*, principles of representation and majority; the concepts of

conceding that 'peaceful coexistence' and 'progress in the West' 'took a long time' (Grimm, 2009: 2371).

corporation (*Körperschaft*) and *Anstalt*; the separation of secular and spiritual powers, of religion and politics (see also Plant, this volume, for criticism). Following the long and misleading tradition of 'secularization', this 'heritage' is not problematized; only the Christian or transcendent foundations are said to be replaced by secular and immanent ones. This then serves to legitimize a very specific Christian education in value-guided behaviour (*zu wertbestimmtem Verhalten*: Heckel, 1996) or in values and norms that have been crucially formed by Christianity; 'als Erziehungsziel vorgegebene christliche Wertordnung' (a Christian value-order that is pre-given as the aim of education) in all their well-known consequences for the German education system: confessional schools (*Konfessionsschule*), Christian public schools (*christliche Gemeinschaftsschule*), crosses in classrooms, Christian bias in history lessons and so on. Attempts to pluralize this Christian, church-bias have been caricatured as 'mascots'.[9]

---

[9] Bishop Huber of the Lutheran EKD Brandenburg has proposed placing a picture of Mecca beside the cross. This has been ridiculed by Isensee as follows: 'Consequently, all world-religions should have to be taken into account, eventually also all civil-religious emblems and private-religious mascots [*privatreligiöse Maskottchen*] ... a bazaar of religious arbitrariness [*Bazar religiöser Beliebigkeiten*].' The result is a reckless defence of all privileges for the old, established Big Churches, also as a consequence of the 1995 decision of the Federal Constitutional Court (BVerGE 93.1) leaving wide margins of discretion to the German *Länder*. See Willems's excellent criticism of these monopolistic claims that Christianity serves as the sole and exclusive legitimation of the liberal constitutional state. See *Lautsi* v. *Italy* and the divergent interpretation of the cross as a 'cultural' versus 'religious symbol' by the Veneto Administrative Court (March 2005), the Italian Consiglio di Stato (April 2006) and the ECtHR in November 2009 (Lautsi I: incompatible with the pupil's freedom not to be subjected to religion) and March 2011 (Lautsi II: 'within the margins of appreciation left to the respondent State'). The stunning results are not only completely contradictory and opportunistic rulings but, more importantly, the Grand Chamber sacrificed the protection of basic principles ('neutrality' even in its relational or inclusive interpretation) in favour of a doctrine of wide margins of appreciation that does not guarantee minimalism in this as in other religion cases (see my criticism in Bader, 2010: 33–5). My own first requirement of LDC is nicely phrased by Schlaich, a critical German constitutional lawyer: 'From a constitutional perspective ... The modern state lacks a prescribed philosophical/ religious foundation [*verbindliche weltanschauliche Grundlage*] ... Access to accepting the state should not be philosophically/ religiously narrowed [*darf nicht weltanschaulich verengt werden*]. Also in this regard the state has to be the "home of all citizens" [*Heimstatt aller Bürger*]. The secular state determines itself without deeper metaphysical references' (Kirchhof, 1994: 130).

Is liberal-democratic constitutionalism impossible or unstable without religious morals and virtues?

The second – only analytically distinct, intuitively more plausible and more important – meaning of the exclusivist, monopolistic claim is that LDC is impossible or unstable without Christian virtues and moral behaviour. Many religious believers and some theologians still think 'that a person cannot be solidly moral without being religious' (William Bennett, criticized by Audi, 1989: 290f.). Implicitly or explicitly, they claim that secular morality in general is impossible or at least unstable. The argument that religion has to be the 'ultimate guarantor of liberty' was shared by the American founding fathers.[10] For Jefferson, religion is the 'only firm basis' of the 'liberties of the nation' that are perceived as 'a gift of God' and 'are not to be violated but with his wrath' (Jefferson, 1955: Query XVIII). For Washington 'religion and morality are indispensable supports'. They are 'great pillars of human happiness' and the 'firmest props of the duties of men and citizens'. 'And let us with caution indulge the supposition that morality can be maintained without religion … reason and experience both forbid us to expect that national morality can prevail in exclusion of religious principle' (Washington, 1796). For Adams religion is 'the only true foundation of morality'. With minor variations, these statements have been repeated until today. For de Tocqueville 'despotism may govern without faith, but liberty cannot'. The 'Declaration of Common Beliefs' (1942, by Protestant, Catholic and Jewish representatives) states: 'God's will is the only ultimate sanction of human morality and

---

[10] See Forst, 2004: 12f. for 'Locke's fear'. See Delfiner (Delfiner, 1965: 316ff.) for the 'effects on liberty' for their negative answers to the question 'whether purely secular values are sufficient to carry forward the ideals and purposes of American Constitutionalism' (Drinan, quoted in Delfiner, 1965: 319). Arendt also is convinced that the loss of the 'trinity of religion, authority and tradition' (Arendt, 1961: 125), particularly the 'loss of authentic religion – good morals sanctioned by the Fear of Hell' (Arendt, 1961: 135), 'public life was bound to lose the religious sanction of transcendent authority' (Arendt, 1961: 135) – are specific characteristics of 'modern' societies and the 'modern state', intimately connected to the 'separation of Church and state' (Arendt, 1961: 126). See McConnell, 2002: 90–3, for the felt moral challenge of disestablishment. See Woodhead (this volume) for the 'historically constitutive' role of Christian liberalism. This historical argument that 'liberal democracies need some sort of religious or mythical grounding in order to be formed' (anonymous reviewer for Cambridge University Press) does not demonstrate that this would also be a condition of their further existence and development ('*Genese ≠ Geltung*').

man's freedom and happiness depend on his obedience to it' (quoted from Stokes, 1950: 505f.). In his criticism of the 'religious advocates of a public secularism', Herberg argues that 'a society, and the state … remain "legitimate", "righteous" and "lawful" only in so far as they recognize a higher majesty beyond themselves … Beyond which there is nothing, it becomes totalitarian: in effect, it divinizes itself' (quoted in Delfiner, 1965: 320). Max Huber (judge in the Permanent Court of International Justice, 1934) maintains that 'religion served to correct a double hubris: the tendency of liberty of individuals or of the state from becoming absolute and that of authority and of the community becoming an absolute', referring to Müller-Armack· the 'loss of religious faith leads to the substitution of idols for faith', the only choice is 'serve either God or idols (national, racial, social and political values)'.[11] The frequent reference to God in preambles of constitutions

---

[11] This argument is shared by Arendt: revolutions are 'the only solution which the Roman-Western tradition has provided for emergencies' (Arendt, 1961: 141) but all revolutions 'have gone wrong' and 'authority [is] nowhere being re-established' because there is no 'concomitant awareness that the source of authority transcends power and those who are in power'. According to her we are condemned to live without the 'religious trust in a sacred beginning and without the protection of traditional and therefore self-evident standards of behaviour for the elementary problems of human being-together' (Arendt, 1961: 141). The argument that religion or Christianity is the only guarantee against totalitarian temptations of rationality and politics in modernity is also shared by German constitutional lawyers (such as Kirchhof, 1994; Stein, 2001) postulating the necessity to symbolically express 'the non-negotiability of the core values of the constitution such as human dignity or basic and human rights' ('*die Unverfügbarkeit der zentralen Wertauffassungen der Verfassung wie der Menschenwürde oder der Grund- und Menschenrechte insgesamt*') through a transcendence relation, e.g. through '*Gottesformeln in den Verfassungen*' (appeals to God in the constitutions). The limitation of politics and rationality cannot itself be the product of political decisions and they can only be effective if backed by religious fundaments (or other metaphysical *Letztbegründungen*). Some claim such backing for rather particularistic and contested interpretations such as specific Christian understanding of marriage and family life (Lenk) or bioethical (abortion, euthanasia) and bio-technological issues, while others (Stein) see that they – as a result of 'philosophical state neutrality' – cannot be imposed or obligatory. Willems (2004) has argued convincingly that cultural and religious pluralization and individualization has undermined the basis of all monologically constructed programs of civil religions. If the symbolic proclamations of the obligation of self-limitations of the political are seen as necessary they can only be effective if they acknowledge 'all those traditions that share this conviction'.

of nation states (but also the failed one of the EU) and to religious oaths (see Markoff and Regan, 1987: 168ff.) is also inspired by arguments that 'laws of humankind' cannot command the same intensity and reliability.

The exclusivist, monopolistic variety of this argument – Christianity as a necessary pre-political foundation of liberal-democratic polities or pre-constitutional condition of German constitutionalism – is again very prominent amongst German constitutional lawyers.[12] This is a much stronger claim for two reasons: first, it is not only a historical or genetic claim but a general claim that 'modern, free societies' depend inherently on a political culture that they and their state are unable to produce or even reproduce, and, second, that only religions, particularly Christianity, are able to provide for these 'meta-legal and pre-political foundations' (Heckel, 1996: 468). The argument comes in two versions, a rather conservative one and, only at first sight astonishing, a 'postmodernist' one.

Let me start with the conservative one. In the famous wording of Böckenförde: freedom, the core idea of modernity, provides 'no further-reaching social and political guiding ideas able to work as connecting orientations and powers for the use and regulation of freedom' enabling a common and communal life; to the contrary, the central ideal of human rights even propels the process of pluralization and individualization (Böckenförde, 1995: 722; 725). For pragmatic and normative reasons, the state cannot produce such attitudes without losing its liberal character. Religions traditionally provide for such resources and binding forces but 'these basic ethical attitudes, ethos-impregnated life forms, and cultural traditions need to be cared for, awakened and handed down by upbringing/education and have to be buttressed by what goes for public order' (Böckenförde, 1995: 724). In sweeping statements by Kirchhof, these arguments are used to defend the privileged and exclusive role of Big Churches, both Protestant and Catholic:

The Basic Law gives the Churches, because they cannot be missed [*Unverzichtbarkeit*] for communal life, a place in public life and thus opposes a process of secularization which relegates belief and religion solely to the

---

[12] Tariq Modood's conservationist argument that it might be possible to 'pluralize and multiculturalize' even Anglican 'weak establishment' may be a bit over-optimistic (see Modood, 2010: 6f.) but if so, it would be one possible 'way of institutionalising religious pluralism' (Modood, 2010: 7).

private intimacy/subjectivity [*Innerlichkeit*] of individuals and wants to declare them irrelevant for public life ... The Churches develop and inspire the spiritual culture in which the political community is rooted, they care for the foundations of the rule of law and democracy in their holistic order of Truth, Values, and Virtues ... Hence the Church is an institution that works in parallel with the state and is provided by the constitution with a compact ... guaranteeing privileges [*Hoheitsrechte*], protects her spiritual and *gemeinnützigen* [in the public interest, welfare, charitable] sphere of activity, and provides organizational and financial help. (Kirchhof, 1994: 655)

Again and *in principle* I share the main points of criticism expressed by Willems (2004): the exclusivist and monopolistic claim inevitably fails because of cultural and religious pluralization and individualization. It is based on the assumption of a homogeneity, claiming that societies can be integrated only on the basis of a common, shared culture and ethos (*Sittlichkeit*) which threatens constitutional freedoms. If we need pre-political foundations of liberal-democratic politics, the exclusive public stimulation and funding of religions or even of Christianity is either incompatible with or cannot provide civic-democratic virtues and orientation towards the public interest. If the exclusivist and monopolistic claim is rejected or waived, however, the issue becomes a comparative empirical and much more complex one: which traditions (secular, humanist, various religions) and which institutions (families, schools, etc.) are more effective in creating citizens that have habitualized the core virtues of moral minimalism and the more demanding but still minimalist ones of liberal democracy, minimally understood (see below)?

In a slightly different, more postmodern way Ladeur (2009) – in an article dealing with 'the return of Religion as a Postmodern Phenomenon' and 'the recent evolution of constitutional doctrine and court practice' (from *Staatskirchenrecht* to a more individualist *Religionsverfassungsrecht*) – refers to 'the collective dimension of the constitutive character of religion, which shapes the identity of individuals by paradoxical societal means', underwriting Linbeck's assumption that 'open societies' need religious communities in the process of inculcating 'moral abstraction' in individuals, which is paradoxically necessary for the preservation of the openness and plurality of society (Ladeur, 2009: 2457). Both allude to the biblical (in particular, the Jewish) tradition for the 'foundation of an opening towards the

Excluded, included or foundational?

Other, the strangeness, as the reference to a "universality in becoming"' (see Ladeur, 2009: 2464). He claims that Möller's argument against Böckenförde – 'that the plurality and ambivalence of religious forms (their potential destructive side) tended to be ignored' – 'is itself erroneous; the openness and plurality of the Judeo-Christian tradition is not an impediment … On the contrary, it is the form that gives historical viability to the paradox of the collective venture of founding individual freedom' (Ladeur, 2009: 2458). Obviously, he argues not in favour of establishment of one church or for a state religion, but, when it comes to 'religion as culture' (those elements that extend beyond 'belief') – literature, history, morality or symbols – the 'privileged position of the established Christian denominations' is legitimate because we 'cannot separate religion from culture':

The impact of religious traditions on the common culture and the reproduction of a shared knowledge basis in state schools is a consequence of the inscription of the trans-subjective element of the symbolic-linguistic forms of life, which must be inculcated in the process of the cultural reproduction of a society. The tendency towards a decoupling of religion and society is equivalent to an 'exculturation' of religion, or alternatively a reduction in the meaning of culture. (Ladeur, 2009: 2460)

Hence no 'formal equality of religions' can be expected or established, only something like a 'structural tolerance' in the public sphere. He concedes that this inculcation is possible 'not only through religion' but assumes 'that an alternative is not easy to formulate, which is demonstrated by the irritating and uncertain role of state schooling in postmodern fragmented societies', ending with the hypothesis that 'it is difficult to renounce the contribution of religion to the formation of identities by schools in liberal societies. This is why one can, in fact, speak of the role of established religious denominations in a collective culture as being a "precondition of the constitution"' (Ladeur, 2009: 2461), to wit of 'mainly an unconscious character'.

In three respects, I agree with some of the basic claims in both varieties of these 'religion as culture' strands.[13] First, indeed, 'the state is no abstract neutrality [*kein wesenloses, abstraktes Neutrum*] but

---

[13] See Olivier Roy's project ReligioWest (2012) for a critical comparative analysis of 'Religion as Culture'.

a historically, politically, and culturally formed particularity which is also conditioned by religious elements and experiences' (Hollerbach, 1998: 31). In my own words, strict neutrality is a myth and/or a dangerous utopia (Bader, 2007a: ch. 2.3).[14] Second, neither strict separation of (organized) religion(s) and state/politics nor religion as private belief and politics of privatization and individualization is required by minimal or by liberal-democratic morality or LDC. Third, a 'strictly equal treatment' of all religions in all regards is impossible and also not required.[15]

Yet, regimes of 'selective cooperation' between state and organized religion(s) – as defended in the existing corporatist variety in Germany by both conservative and postmodernist defenders of majority bias and church privileges (in tax administration, public funding of churches and faith-based organizations, privileges in labour law, privileges in education, public symbols, etc.) – have to live up to reformulated principles, such as 'relational', 'inclusive' or 'benevolent neutrality' and 'fairness as even-handedness'. These regimes are compatible with LDC only if they can be reasonably and plausibly defended in contexts of broad and rapidly changing

[14] While Plant refers to criticism of 'difference-blind' conceptions of neutrality he ends up advocating 'a difference-blind type of politico-legal system such that threats and potential harms to any of the basic goods of agency are to be regarded as coercive irrespective of questions about identity'. This 'turning back' is motivated by a criticism of 'any kind of legal recognition of religion in identity terms' which I mainly share but would extend to all 'identity' terms, including 'race, sex, gender, ethnicity'. The issue should not be 'recognition of identity' but fighting misrecognition of religious cultures, groups, associations and organizations as well as striving for fairness as even-handedness (instead of 'fairness-as-hands-off') in matters of ethno-religious cultures (see Bader, 2007b for a similar criticism of Brian Barry). His eventual reproduction of the myth of a religiously difference-blind state is a practical consequence of his conceptual and theoretical neglect of cultural practices as a 'basic good' and, hence, his neglect of deep-seated cultural inequalities, of 'cultural harm'.

[15] In all these three regards, I agree with Modood, who phrases these arguments in terms of 'religion as identity' on 'the public or civic level' of a polity or country:

We are a Christian country and so Christianity should be taught in schools or be referred to in the constitution and so on. This does not have to be a particularly conservative argument. The same logic is present in the following: We are no longer a Christian country and have to re-make the national identity to reflect new inclusions, or we need to have multi-faith schools or a plurality of schools within the state system and reflected in the national curriculum. (Modood, 2010: 11)

religious diversity and the burden of proof is on religions claiming such exclusive privileges (Bader, 2007a: ch. 7). In this respect, the defences quoted above fail blatantly in the recent German context (for the reasons given by Willems, summarized above). The treatment of so-called 'alien' or 'new' religions, alluding to 'Islam' and to the pejorative meaning of 'sects', by the German Constitutional Court has been scandalous. Ladeur is also critical in this regard (Ladeur, 2009: 2468). In addition, it is certainly not the business of a liberal state to meddle with individual and collective identities (Bader, 2013, critical of Modood), nor, clearly, to privilege a very specific and in itself highly contested understanding of Judaism, Christianity or the 'Judeo-Christian' tradition, either in the conservative or in the 'po-mo' variety. Finally, regarding education, LDC certainly does not require a monopoly for governmental schools, indeed, but allows for, and favours, in my view, mixed educational systems and public funding of non-governmental schools, religious schools amongst them, under specified conditions (Bader, 2007a: ch. 10). Yet the German system – which gives such huge privileges to Protestantism and Catholicism regarding religious instruction in public schools – in teaching religious education, history, literature, etc. without pluralizing the curriculum and at the same time not publicly financing any Islamic schools is clearly indefensible on all accounts.

To sum up, all these claims 'betray their lack of respect for humanist ethics with assertions like "secular morality is no morality" ... In other words they fear that in the absence of divine sanction and divine authority ethical life is impossible' (Kulananda, 1996: 68, from a Buddhist perspective). The exclusivist claim that a non-religious morality would be impossible is so obviously untenable and has been so often convincingly refuted that I refrain from repeating the arguments: morality does not, structurally or conceptually, depend on religion. In the Western tradition it was refuted powerfully for the first time by Pierre Bayle in his *Pensées* (1683) with the courageous idea that a 'society of atheists would be possible – and possibly be even more peaceful than religious societies' (Forst, 2004: 13). Much earlier, Michel de l'Hospital clearly stated that 'it is possible to be a citizen without being a Christian' (quoted in Saunders, 2007: 74; see Audi, 1989: 290f.). The monopolistic claim that only Christianity, or the 'Judeo-Christian tradition', would provide for such a public morality is equally untenable, as demonstrated above.

If, and to the extent to which, the arguments for the importance of a religious backing of the principles and the culture, habits, virtues and practices of decent polities and/or liberal-democratic morality and LDC lose their exclusivist and monopolistic character, they gain in strength and plausibility. For a start, it is quite clear that institutions of LDC cannot work and flourish below a certain threshold of habitualized liberal-democratic culture and a certain quantity of virtuous citizens and political leaders (Bader, 2007a: ch. 6.1). Whether a non-religious public morality can be stable depends not on religious or secular foundations and backings but on the question whether religious or non-religious institutions are more creative seedbeds of minimally required civic and liberal-democratic attitudes and virtues.[16] The issue, then, is no longer one of 'in principle' but a practical and a comparative one, as should be expected from my perspective of contextualized morality, which draws heavily on empirical social sciences, particularly on comparative institutionalism (see Bader, 2012b). This may be disappointing for people who expect one clear-cut and generalizable answer to questions whether liberal democracies need some sort of religious or mythological grounding in order to be formed or to be stable and flourishing.

As we know, 'virtuous citizens do not fall from heaven, nor are they the inevitable side effect of shared principles. They also do not flow quasi-automatically from living in appropriate institutional settings ... They have to be learned and acquired' (Bader, 2007a: 183). This happens, if at all, in four overlapping settings; in primary and secondary socialization (i.e. upbringing in 'families' and education: intentional schooling), in democratic (political) institutions, in many associations of civil society and in everyday interactions with demographically widely heterogeneous people. The questions then are: do (which?) religious families fare better, equally or worse compared with (which?) non-religious families? Do (which?) religious schools fare better, equally or worse compared with (which?) non-religious schools, governmental schools amongst them? Do (which?) religious associations fare better compared with the whole variety of non-religious

---

[16] See Bader, 2007a: ch. 6.2. I also refute the myopic and self-congratulatory charge that a 'secular' or 'rational ethics' would be achievable only for elites, religion to be the only stable foundation for decent and democratic attitudes of the 'masses'.

associations? Do (which?) religions foster or hinder heterogeneous everyday interactions (bonding and bridging)? As we also know, these are theoretically and empirically contested, highly contextual (in which countries, times?) issues that are very hard to research and difficult to answer.[17] Some religions in some countries at some time may do well, even better than non-religious institutions/relations, but others perform less well or even do no good at all in all or some of these regards.[18] The little and very shaky evidence with regard to learning civic and democratic virtues in schools, for instance, is slightly favourable for religious schools compared with governmental schools in European countries and North America (Bader 2007a: 271f. with references). These findings, which may back up some of the statements by Ladeur quoted above, certainly irritate defenders of 'public education only' and should temper the high hopes of civic republicans that public schools are the most important 'schools of democracy'.

[17] See Bader, 2007a: ch. 9.3–9.6 and 10.3 and 10.4 for some indications. See also Bader and Maussen, 2011. A consequence from the broadly shared scepticism of the effectiveness of 'civic-democratic education' could be to focus more explicitly at more modest aims that are still very difficult to achieve: teaching and learning toleration and basic civic virtues (see also Vogt, 1997).

[18] Here I disagree with Modood's much too general treatment of 'respect for religion': first, one should take much more seriously the fact that some religions have been and still are 'mutually intolerant' (Modood, 2010: 15) and even his claim that 'respect for the religion of others' has been 'the prevalent view in the Middle East and South Asia' is uncritically over-optimistic. Second, doing so makes it impossible to generally speak of 'religion as a good in itself', 'a fundamental good', 'an ethical good' and to deplore 'the closing down of any religion (as) a loss of some sort' (indeed a very strong, undifferentiated, perfectionist or 'conservationist' argument). Instead, religion in itself is neither good nor bad: it depends! The weaker, more plausible version would be that 'a society, a culture, a country would be poorer' not without it, but without any religions. The claim that religion 'is part of good living' (Modood, 2010: 16) is as untenable as the reverse claim that any good life has to be a 'secular' one. In my view, there is no need to 'go beyond toleration, and freedom of religion, but also beyond civic recognition' (Modood, 2010: 17, 16). Modood and I share the 'worry about an intolerant secularist hegemony' (Modood, 2010: 17) but in order to defend 'a more genuine pluralism' we should defend only those religions that are compatible with minimal morality and/or more demanding with minimalist LDC, not just 'religion'. To repeat: religion can be a public bad, an evil, and is not just a 'public good' that should be privileged and publicly financed. It can indeed be seen 'as a potential public good or a national resource ... which the state can in some circumstances assist to realise' (Modood, 2010: 6), but this presupposes that one draws the lines and stops talking about religion in the abstract (actually this has been the core of my criticism of Bhiku Parekh's treatment of religion, see below).

In sum: as in the case of doctrinal foundations of LDC, where the important thing is not for which reasons – religious or non-religious ones – people 'subscribe', the important thing here is that people learn the minimally required civic and democratic virtues, and not in which institutional settings, religious or non-religious, this learning is taking place. And the disturbing findings of the poor record of public schools in some countries and inner cities (but not in Scandinavian countries!), compared to the slightly better but still meagre results of religious schools, should lead to concerted efforts to improve the teaching and learning of civic-democratic virtues in both.

Conclusion

Let me draw some brief conclusions on the role of religions in liberal-democratic states. First, I hope to have shown that some religions may play an important role in public and political debates and also in contributing to the stabilization and flourishing of civic-democratic cultures, virtues and practices. But this claim must be freed from exclusivist claims that only religion can deliver all these goods or from even stronger monopolist claims that only a certain religion, such as Christianity or the 'Judeo-Christian tradition', can do so. Second, we should urgently stop talking about religion in general or in the abstract, because religions then and now certainly have not done all these beneficial things but have done and do serious wrong and evil. Entering religion x at time t in space s and polity p – i.e. contextualizing religions as well as liberal-democratic constitutionalism – is, at least for the moderately contextualist morality and political theory I am defending, not the same as parochialism, relativism or conservatism. We can compare, we can learn and we can distinguish better from worse religions, institutions and practices. Third, if we defend existing regimes of selective cooperation between state and (organized) religion(s) against aggressive secularists propagating privatization of religion and 'strict separation' (Sajó, 2008; see, critically, Bader, 2010), we should also criticize these regimes in all cases in which they do not live up to the demands of relational neutrality and fairness as even-handedness, particularly in their treatment of old and new minority religions. And we should not hesitate to argue for better, alternative institutional designs and policies, such as *associational governance* (Bader, 2007a: Conclusions; see also 2008 and 2009b). In this regard, Modood's plea for 'moderate secularism' is needlessly conservative and lacks any perspective of realist utopias (see Bader, 2011b).

References

Arendt, H. 1961. *Between Past and Present*. New York: Viking Press.

Ashoka. 1993. *The Edicts of King Ashoka*, trans. Ven. S. Dhammika. Kandy, Sri Lanka: Buddhist Publication Society.

Audi, R. 1989. 'The Separation of Church and State and the Obligations of Citizenship', *Philosophy and Public Affairs*, 18, 259–96.

Bader, V. 1999. 'Religious Pluralism. Secularism or Priority for Democracy?' in *Political Theory*, 27, 5, 597–633.

2003. 'Religious Diversity and Democratic Institutional Pluralism', *Political Theory*, 31, 2, 265–94.

2007a. *Secularism or Democracy? Associational Governance of Religious Diversity*. Amsterdam: IMISCOE/Amsterdam University Press.

2007b. 'Defending Differentiated Policies of Multiculturalism', *National Identities*, 9, 3, 197–215.

2008. 'How Should Liberal-Democratic States Accommodate Religious Diversity?' *IMISCOE Policy Brief* 8, March.

2009a. 'Secularism, Public Reason or Moderately Agonistic Democracy?', in G. B. Levey and T. Modood, eds., *Secularism, Religion and Multicultural Citizenship*. Cambridge University Press, 110–35.

2009b. 'Reply. Review Symposium: Historic Settlements and New Challenges: Veit Bader, Secularism or Democracy? Associational Governance of Religious Diversity', *Ethnicities*, 9, 566–70.

2010. 'Constitutionalizing Secularism, Alternative Secularisms or Liberal Democratic Constitutionalism? A Critical Reading of Some Turkish, ECtHR and Indian Supreme Court Cases on "Secularism"', *Utrecht Law Review*, 6, 3, 8–35.

2011a. 'Religion and the Myths of Secularization and Separation'. RELIGARE Working Paper 5, 31 March, www.religareproject.eu/content/religion-and-myths-secularization-and-separation.

2011b. 'Beyond Secularisms of all Sorts', *The Immanent Frame: Secularism, Religion and the Public Sphere*, 11 October, www.blogs.ssrc.org/tif/2011/10/11/beyond-secularisms-of-all-sorts.

2011c. 'Religions, Toleration, and Liberal Democracy. A Theory of Doctrinal, Institutional, and Attitudinal Learning', in Monica Mookherjee, ed., *Democracy, Religious Pluralism and the Liberal Dilemma of Accommodation*. Dordrecht: Springer Netherlands, 17–46.

2012a. '"Post-Secularism" or Liberal-Democratic Constitutionalism?', *Erasmus Law Review*, 5, 1, 5–26 www.erasmuslawreview.nl/files/Volume05Issue01-Bader.

2012b. 'Normative or Empirical Comparisons?', *The Immanent Frame: Secularism, Religion and the Public Sphere*, 9 January, www.blogs.ssrc. org/tif/2012/01/09/normative-or-empirical-comparisons.

2013. 'Moral Minimalism and More Demanding Moralities. Some Reflections on "Tolerance/Toleration"', in Jan Dobbernack and Tariq Modood, eds., *Tolerance, Intolerance and Respect: Hard to Accept?* Basingstoke: Palgrave Macmillan, 23–51.

In press. 'Sciences, Politics, and Associative Democracy. "Democratising Science" and "Expertising Democracy"', *Innovation: The European Journal of Social Sciences Research*, 26, 3.

Bader, V. and Maussen, M. 2011. 'Comparative Report on Religious Schools. Introduction', in *The Embodiment of (in)Tolerance in Discourses and Practices Addressing Cultural Diversity in Schools*. ACCEPT Pluralism Project, http://cadmus.eui.eu/bitstream/ handle/1814/20955/ACCEPT_2012_01_WP3_ComparativeReport. pdf?sequence=1.

Barber, B. 1988. *The Conquest of Politics*. Princeton University Press.

Barkey, K. 2009. *Empire of Difference. The Ottomans in Comparative Perspective*. Cambridge University Press.

Bhargava, R. 2011. 'Beyond Moderate Secularism', *SSRC Blogs*, 16 September, www.blogs.ssrc.org/tif/2011/09/16/beyond-moderate-secularism.

Böckenförde, E. W. 1995. 'Erfolge und Grenzen der Aufklärung', *Universitas*, 50, 720–6.

Christoffersen, L., Iversen, H. R., Petersen, H. and M. Warburg, eds. 2010. *Religion in the 21st Century*. Farnham: Ashgate.

Delfiner, H. 1965. 'Church–State Relations and Religious Instruction in the Public Elementary Schools of Switzerland, West Germany and the United States'. Unpublished Ph.D. thesis.

Dhammika, Ven. S. 1993. 'Introduction', in *The Edicts of King Ashoka*. Kandy, Sri Lanka: Buddhist Publication Society.

Eisenlohr, P. 2006. 'The Politics of Diaspora and the Morality of Secularism: Muslim Identities and Islamic Authority in Mauritius', *Journal of the Royal Anthropological Institute*, 12, 305–412.

Forst, R. 2004. 'The Limits of Toleration', *Constellations*, 11, 3, 3, 12–25.

Frankenberg, G. and Rödel, U. 1981. *Von der Volkssouveränität zum Minderheitenschutz*. Frankfurt: EVA.

Galanter, M. 1966. 'Religious Freedoms in the United States: A Turning Point', *Wisconsin Law Review*, 217–96.

Galston, W. 2002. *Liberal Pluralism: The Implications of Value Pluralism for Political Theory and Practice*. Cambridge University Press.

Geuss, R. 2002. 'Liberalism and its Discontents', *Political Theory*, 30, 3, 320–38.

Grimm, D. 2009. 'Conflicts between General Laws and Religious Norms', *Cardozo Law Review*, 30, 2369–82.

Habermas, J. 2008a. 'Die Dialektik der Säkularisierung', *Blätter für Deutsche und Internationale Politik*, April, 33–46.

  2008b. *Between Naturalism and Religion: Philosophical Essays*, trans. Ciaran Cronin. Cambridge: Polity Press.

Handy, R. T. 1976. *A History of the Churches in the United States and Canada*. Oxford: Clarendon Press.

Heckel, M. 1996. 'Das Kreuz im öffentlichen Raum', *Deutsches Verwaltungsblatt*, 111, 9, 453–82.

Herberg, W. 1960. *Protestant – Catholic – Jew*. Garden City, NY: Doubleday.

Hollerbach, A. 1998. *Religion und Kirche im Freiheitlichen Verfassungsstaat*. Berlin: de Gruyter.

Huber, W. 2001. *Rechtfertigung und Recht: Über die christilichen Wurzeln der europäischen Rechtskultur*. Baden-Baden: Nomos.

Hunter, I. 2009. 'The Shallow Legitimacy of Secular Liberal Orders', in G. B. Levey and T. Modood, eds., *Secularism, Religion and Multicultural Citizenship*. Cambridge University Press, 27–55.

Jansen, Y. 2011. 'Postsecularism, Piety and Fanaticism; Reflections on Jürgen Habermas' and Saba Mahmood's Critiques of Secularism', *Philosophy and Social Criticism*, 37, 9, 977–98.

Jacobsohn, G. 2003. *The Wheel of Law. India's Secularism in Comparative Perspective*. Princeton University Press.

Jefferson, T. 1955. *Notes on the State of Virginia*. Chapel Hill: University of North Carolina Press.

Kirchhof, P. 1994. 'Die Kirchen und Religionsgemeinschaften als Körperschaften des öffentlichen Rechts', in *Handbuch des Staatskirchenrechts der BRD*, vol. I. Berlin: Duncker and Humblot, 651–87.

Kulananda, D. 1996. 'A Buddhist Perspective', in T. Modood, ed., *Church, State and Religious Minorities*. London: Policy Studies Institute.

Ladeur, K. H. 2009. 'The Myth of the Neutral State and the Individualisation of Religion', *Cardozo Law Review*, 30, 2445–71.

Lefort, C. 1999. *Fortdauer des Theologisch-Politischen?* Vienna: Passagen Verlag.

Link, C. 1999. 'Der Einfluß christlicher Werte auf die deutsche Verfassungsordnung', in *Vom christlichen Abendland zum multikulturellen Einwanderungsland?* Bad Homburg: Herbert Quandt Stiftung, 18–23.

McConnell, M. 2002. 'Educational Disestablishment', in S. Macedo and Y. Tamir, eds., *Moral and Political Education*. New York University Press, 87–146.

Madan, T. N. 1998. 'Secularism in its Place', in R. Bhargava, ed., *Secularism and its Critics*. New Delhi: Oxford University Press, 297–320.

2008. 'Indian Secularism: A Religio-Secular Ideal'. Conference paper, Istanbul, 6–9 July.

Markoff, J. and Regan, D. 1987. 'Religion, the State and Political Legitimacy in the World's Constitutions', in T. Robbins and R. Robertson, eds., *Church–State Relations, Tensions and Transitions*. New Brunswick, NJ: Transaction Books, 161–82.

Miller, W. L. 1985. *The First Liberty*. New York: Alfred A. Knopf.

Modood, T. 2010. 'Moderate Secularism, Religion as Identity and Respect for Religion', *Political Quarterly*, 81, 1, 4–14.

Parekh, B. 1996. 'Religion in Public Life', in T. Modood, ed., *Church, State and Religious Minorities*. London: Policy Studies Institute, 16–23.

2000. *Rethinking Multiculturalism: Cultural Diversity and Political Theory*. Basingstoke: Palgrave Macmillan.

Rawls, J. 1999. *The Law of Peoples*. Cambridge, MA: Harvard University Press.

Roy, O. 2012. *ReligioWest*. Florence: European University Institute, www.eui.eu/Projects/ReligioWest/.

Sajó, A. 2008. 'Preliminaries to a Concept of Constitutional Secularism', *International Journal of Constitutional Law*, 6, 605–29.

Saunders, D. 2007. 'France on the Knife-Edge of Religion', in G. B. Levey and T. Modood, eds., *Secularism, Religion and Multicultural Citizenship*. Cambridge University Press, 56–81.

Sen, A. 2009. *The Idea of Justice*. London: Penguin.

Shah, T. S. 2000. 'Making the Christian World Safe for Liberalism', in D. Marquand and R. Nettler, eds., *Religion and Democracy*. Oxford: Blackwell, 121–39.

Stein, T. 2001. 'Im Bewußtsein der Verantwortung vor Gott … "Christliches Menschenbild und demokratischer Verfassungsstaat"', in *Säkularisierung und Reskralisierung in westlichen Gesellschaften*. Wiesbaden: Westdeutscher Verlag, 185–201.

Stepan, A. 2000. 'Religion, Democracy, and the "Twin Tolerations"', *Journal of Democracy*, 11, 37–57.

2010. 'The Multiple Secularisms of Modern Democratic and Non-democratic Regimes', in Craig Calhoun and Mark Juergensmeyer, eds., *Rethinking Secularism*. New York: SSRC Press, 114–44.

Stepan, A., Linz, J. J. and Yadav, Y. 2010. *Democracy in Multinational Societies: India and Other Polities*. Baltimore and London: Johns Hopkins University Press.

Stokes, A. P. 1950. *Church and State in the United States, vol. II*. New York: Harper.

Stoltenberg, N. M. 1993. 'He Drew a Circle That Shut Me Out', *Harvard Law Review*, 106, 581–667.

Swaine, L. 2006. *The Liberal Conscience*. New York: Columbia University Press.

Taylor, C. 1998. 'Modes of Secularism', in R. Bhargava, ed., *Secularism and its Critics*. New Delhi: Oxford University Press, 31–53.

Thiemann, R. F. 1996. *Religion in Public Life*. Washington, DC: Georgetown University Press.

Vogt, W. P. 1997. *Tolerance and Education*. Thousand Oaks, CA: Sage Publications.

Washington, G. 1796. Farewell Address, 19 September, www.millercenter. org/president/speeches/detail/3462.

Willems, U. 2004. 'Weltanschaulich neutraler Staat, christlich-abendländische Kultur und Säkularismus' in M. Walther, ed., *Religion und Politik*. Baden-Baden: Nomos, 303–28.

Wolterstorff, N. 1997. 'Why We Should Reject What Liberalism Tells Us about Speaking and Acting in Public for Religious Reasons', in P. J. Weithman, ed., *Religion and Contemporary Liberalism*. University of Notre Dame Press, 162–81.

7 | Justificatory secularism

CÉCILE LABORDE

Over the last two decades or so, secularism in Europe has often been mobilized as a legitimate public language for the expression of fears about Islam in contemporary societies (Laborde, 2008). But is there a core truth – or a grain of truth – in secularism, and if so, what is it? When we criticize the ideological uses of secular ideology, do we do so from an anti-secularist position, or from an alternative (untheorized) secularist standpoint? Here one could develop two distinct research projects. The first would be interpretative: it would lay bare the implicit normative basis of existing critiques of secularism. The second would be straightforwardly normative: it would seek to go back to first principles and identify the sense (if any) in which secularism can be articulated as a defensible position. In this chapter I pursue the latter strategy, and attempt to salvage a version of secularism that is both conceptually precise and politically plausible. Such desiderata commend themselves as inescapable for any academically sound theory of secularism. The term has become hopelessly inflated in public discourse and associated – by both its friends and foes – with a bewildering array of positions: separation between church and state,

I dedicate these remarks to my friend Emile Perreau-Saussine, who died prematurely, aged thirty-eight, when I began working on this text. The argument was directly inspired by the many friendly yet passionate discussions we had about secularism, religion and Rawls, in a Turkish restaurant in north London, over several years. Emile would no doubt have strongly disagreed with some of the views expressed here, and would have forced me to think again. I miss his intelligence, his faith, his patience and his generosity. Early drafts of this piece were presented at the Zutshi–Smith Symposium on 'Religion in a Liberal State' in Bristol (May 2010), as an Inaugural Lecture at UCL (June 2010), at the Social Sciences Lunchtime Seminar of Princeton's Institute for Advanced Study (September 2010) and at the Political Theory Workshop of Columbia University (March 2011). I am grateful to participants in those events, as well as to the editors of this volume, particularly Tariq Modood, for their constructive criticisms. My stay at the Institute for Advanced Study, where this piece was completed, was funded by the Florence Gould Foundation.

political rationalism, the privatization of religion, the embrace of stat-ist modernity, Western imperialism, republican citizenship, women's emancipation, Islamophobia, colonial and neo-colonial authoritarian-ism, and so forth. The ideological inflation is such that it is often dif-ficult to ascertain what advocates and critics of secularism are exactly arguing about. This chapter is part of a wider project that seeks to identify a minimalist – indeed deflationary – definition of secularism and tease out its normative implications. Generally, I take secularism to be a political position about the proper relationship between the state and religion and, more specifically, one which singles out religion for both special protection and for special restrictions. Normative dis-putes about secularism can then be interpreted as disputes about what is 'special' about religion (in relation to other categories such as class, race, culture, ideologies, etc.) and whether such features justify specific constitutional, legal or political treatment. The conception of secular-ism that I favour is conceptually minimalist – it narrows down the set of relevant questions to be asked – as well as being normatively defla-tionary. My view is that, for many purposes, religion does *not* deserve special treatment.

In this chapter, I attempt to identify one of the (few) senses in which religion remains relevantly special. It has to do with the justifi-cation of political power, and underpins what I shall call *justificatory secularism*. Broadly speaking, I follow philosophers such as John Rawls and Jürgen Habermas in positing that state officials and polit-ical representatives should not justify their actions, laws and policies by appeal to conceptions of religious truth. This is one important, indeed inescapable, value implicit in the secular ideal of 'separation' or 'non-establishment' of religion. In a society characterized by eth-ical pluralism, state-authorized coercion needs to be justified, and it needs to be justified to the people – to all of us, despite the differ-ences that divide us. Here the question is: when our representatives seek to justify the common laws that should govern us all – laws about education, health care, public order, foreign policy, the civil laws of marriage and procreation and so forth – can they appeal exclusively to religious reasons? Is it legitimate, morally speaking, to 'talk God' in democratic politics? More precisely, what role should religious reasons play in the public justification of laws and policies? I understand justificatory secularism to provide an answer to just this question.

I have three tasks in this chapter. First, the chapter attempts to provide a definition of the core claims of, and rationale for, justificatory secularism by articulating what I call a 'non-imposition norm'. Second, it provides a preliminary account of what is special about religion in relation to this norm. Third, it surveys a number of common critiques of secularism and shows that justificatory secularism is not vulnerable to them. I hope to show not only that justificatory secularism, as I define it, is essential to liberal legitimacy and democratic deliberation, but also that religious believers have good reasons to be secularist in my sense. This is because secularism, understood as a mode of justification of democratic coercive laws, need not exclude, marginalize or neglect religion, and it is compatible with recognition of a prominent place to religion in the secular state. A secular state, I suggest, is not defined by its substantive commitments, institutional settlement or specific policies. Rather, it is defined by the type of justification it offers for them. If my argument is correct, it is a plausible response to the charge that the liberal secular state is necessarily committed to a comprehensive, substantive liberalism – a version of which appears in Raymond Plant's thoughtful and provocative chapter in this volume.

The non-imposition norm

Let me begin with an extract from a legal opinion from a justice from the South Dakota Supreme Court in 1992, concerning a dispute between former spouses over visitation rights regarding their two children, where the point in dispute concerned the non-custodial mother's homosexuality. About this woman the judge wrote:

Until such time that she can establish, after years of therapy and demonstrated conduct, that she is no longer a lesbian living a life of abomination (see Leviticus 18:22), she should be totally estopped from contaminating these children. (Levinson, 1997: 81)

Many of us recoil at such public expression of homophobic sentiment and at the suggestion that lesbians cannot be good mothers. But in the instinctive secularist rejection of conservative religious argument, do we object to the sentiment itself, or to the way in which it is justified? Let us take a less biased example.

A South African judge in the 1980s, influenced by the anti-apartheid sermons of Archbishop Desmond Tutu, made a ruling about equal rights for Black South Africans by appealing to the status of human beings as 'made in the image of God'.

Here, clearly, it is not what the judge says but how he says it that is at issue. Few people would fail to be moved by the sentiment, nor would they fail to grasp the rhetorical power of this biblical reference among white and black South Africans alike. Yet I would like to suggest that the secularist suspicion of the validity of public appeal to religious reasoning should hold in both cases – the homophobic and the anti-racist case. The thought here is that what is wrong with religious argument as official justification is not that it is not 'rational' or 'true' (about these matters judges must be publicly agnostic) but rather that, at least in pluralistic Western societies with a history of religious conflict, it is controversial and divisive in a particular way. When officials seek to justify laws and policies, they should exercise religious restraint and appeal solely to secular grounds for their rulings and decisions. For example, the view that all human beings are equal regardless of their skin colour is an ideal that is accessible to all citizens, whether or not they believe that there is a God who created all human beings in his image. So I understand secularism to be a *meta-theoretical* position about modes of political justification, rather than a *normative, substantive* position about the particular ends and values that citizens should pursue. Justificatory secularism tells us not what we can think, do or say, but, rather, how the state should justify its laws and actions. So, it is compatible with secularism for religiously minded officials to argue against homosexual parenting rights (for example) provided they seek to find grounds that others can comprehend and either accept or reject through the use of their common reason – references to the best interests of children, not to the book of Leviticus. One may think this is a self-evident, almost trivial, proposition. Yet others – a growing number of critics of secularism – take this as evidence of the naïvely rationalistic and perversely anti-religious bias of secularism. Before I assess the charge, let me explain in more detail what I think justificatory secularism precisely entails.

The foundational values underpinning justificatory secularism can be grasped from an interpretation of the ideal of 'non-establishment' and the functional differentiation between temporal and spiritual spheres that it rests upon. Such differentiation is one of the defining features of the secular age, to use Charles Taylor's phrase (Taylor, 2007). While critics of the teleological 'secularization thesis' have convincingly demonstrated that the secular age implies neither the decline nor the privatization of religion, they have stressed that some kind of differentiation between 'temporal' and 'spiritual' spheres is an inescapable feature of contemporary societies (Casanova, 1994: 212). Roughly speaking, the state is a temporal authority, concerned with the provision of temporal goods, and it should leave the management of spiritual affairs to religious institutions or individuals themselves. Even if such separation of jurisdictions proves elusive and contested, it meets important normative desiderata, provided it is carefully accounted for. The view advanced here is that the most important mode of separation between state and religion is *justificatory*. This means that there are a variety of permissible institutional church–state settlements, but what matters is that they are not justified by state officials by appeal to the truth of religion (Laborde, 2011).

The prohibition of such (justificatory) establishment of religion by the state can be explained by reference to four features of (what we have come to understand as) religion in Western societies. First, the state is *incompetent* in religious matters. Pronouncements on religious truth are not the province of democratic majorities, bureaucratic experts or constitutional judges. Second, religion has long been the site of deep and profound political *conflict*, notably in Europe since the seventeenth-century wars of religion. Third, religious disagreements are profound and intractable, because they touch on matters of *ultimate concern* to individuals – the good life, the meaning of death, prospects of salvation and so forth. Fourth, religious categories have acquired a specific salience in social life, often acting as markers of *insider/outsider status*. Taken separately, these four features are, arguably, not unique or special to religion. Consider: the state is also incompetent in matters of scientific truth; class conflict has been as, if not more, salient in European history; matters of ultimate concern to individuals do not necessarily take a religious form; and gender, race and sexuality are also salient categories of exclusion and discrimination. For many legal and political purposes, therefore, religion can be usefully compared with analogous categories, be they class, race, gender, science or political ideologies. In many areas, the category of religion is special but not unique. And yet, taken together, the four features account for one unique characteristic of the politico-legal treatment of religion – namely, the justificatory norm of non-establishment. This asserts that there is something particularly wrong about the official imposition of religious views, *qua* religious, on citizens. Call this the Non-Imposition Norm (NIN). This requires the state not to appeal to, endorse or establish any religion. It is because religion has come to be associated with these four features that a norm of non-establishment or, more accurately, non-imposition (NIN) applies – uniquely – to it.

The site of justificatory secularism

It is important, however, to be clear about the site of justificatory secularism – who exactly it applies to. As with the US First Amendment clause, NIN primarily applies to the state and its officials. Because they have representative obligations – they speak in the name of all – and because state acts are particularly coercive, state officials are under a stringent obligation of religious restraint when they publicly justify their actions and policies. If they fail to find secular reasons for the policies they advocate or implement, they should refrain from enforcing their religious views through their rulings and decisions. No such obligation, I have argued elsewhere, falls on ordinary citizens. For example, the demand, made in the name of French *laïcité*, that state school pupils, or users of public services, show restraint in the expression of their religious beliefs is an illegitimate extension of the demands of secularism from the state to citizens. In fact, the state should be secular so that citizens do not have to be secular – non-establishment of religion by the state is what allows the latter freely to exercise the rights associated with freedom of conscience (Laborde, 2008). In civil society and in what Habermas calls the informal public sphere (Habermas, 2008: 130) where citizens exchange ideas and deliberate with others within churches, civil associations, universities and other public forums, they are not bound by justificatory secularism. To ask ordinary citizens to be constrained by NIN would be to misunderstand the very point of NIN: the reason why the state should not impose any religious view is precisely to allow citizens freely to exercise their democratic rights, including rights of free speech and of conscience. Theories of deliberative restraint which place stringent limits on what citizens can say in the public sphere violate basic democratic and liberal rights and, in effect, ask citizens to act, at all times, as if they were agents of the state.

Instead, justificatory secularism guarantees full rights of free expression to ordinary citizens in the opinion-making sphere, while imposing stringent obligations for state officials in the decision-making sphere. This deceptively simple distinction obscures an important intermediate sphere, where citizens act both as private citizens and as putative holders of political office. The question then arises: to what extent should citizens taking part in politics – say, as candidates for office or as party leaders – be expected to have internalized the norms of justificatory secularism? After all, they are positioned in between the 'narrow' decision-making sphere and the 'wide' opinion-making public sphere. If that is so, they should be expected to exercise some form of religious restraint. Citizen-candidates (as we may call them) should seek to support whatever religious views they have with suitable secular ones. This means that they have a role to play in translating and channelling religiously influenced ideas into the political process, and so should sincerely attempt to find and articulate secular arguments. They might not succeed in finding them, in which case (by contrast to officials and state representatives, who should always exercise religious restraint) they may solely appeal to their religious views. As we shall see below, in relation to some deep issues relating to the status of life and death, citizen-candidates might find it impossible to articulate their views in secular language. Yet for most political issues, citizen-candidates should seek to identify and articulate the secular values which best express and convey their deeper views.

It should be clear by now that justificatory secularism diverges from more demanding accounts of the role of public reason in political debate. Rawlsian philosophers, notably, argue that when citizens propose to use collective coercive power, they should put forward special kinds of reasons – reasons that are 'public' in the sense that they are not grounded in comprehensive, controversial conceptions of the good and draw, instead, on a shared political conception of justice (Quong, 2010: ch. 9). By contrast, justificatory secularism does not require that citizens appeal only to secular or public reasons, nor that they share a fixed, full conception of justice. Rather, it emphasizes the role of wide public deliberation in the identification of relevant principles of political justice. This is because general principles of public reason remain inconclusive and indeterminate unless and until they are interpreted, weighed and ranked in relation to the specific issues at stake (Laborde, 2011; Quinn, 1997: 149–52). And such weighing and ranking will, naturally, be done against the background of the deep, diverse non-public views which people bring to their deliberations. While we should expect that, in a well-ordered liberal democracy, public decisions will be justified by appeal to secular reasons (as per NIN), free deliberation about deeper 'reasons for reasons' is necessary for the evaluation and selection of appropriate secular reasons. Bringing all perspectives, including religious ones, into public debate has fundamental epistemic virtues in two ways. Citizens may not know, in advance of public deliberation with others, which of their religious views will be translatable into secular language; or they will not be able to justify to others why, in relation to particular laws or policies, one secular value should in their view carry more weight than another, *unless* they are able to explain how their comprehensive doctrines support the special importance of that secular value. So, by contrast to Rawls's theory of public reason, justificatory secularism does not assume that citizens share a fixed, coherently ordered conception of justice. Rather, there will be large reasonable disagreement between them about the ordering, content and implications of the general principles that they will converge upon during their deliberations. And reasonable disagreement about political justice is ultimately related to reasonable disagreement about broader conceptions of the good. Full and inclusive democratic debate is required to find out the particular shape and content of the public conception of justice.

To illustrate, consider two societies. Society A is largely secularized in outlook; religious groups play a limited role in public debate; and dominant conceptions of morality are secularized (perhaps post-Christian). Society B, by contrast, has a religious majority; religious groups are active in politics; and dominant conceptions of morality are influenced by religious norms. Society A has liberal laws on (say) abortion and homosexual rights; society B has more restrictive laws. Both sets of laws are justified by appeal to relevantly secular reasons. For example, legislators in society A appeal to women's rights and equality between sexualities; legislators in society B appeal to the right to life and the value of the traditional family. Both societies meet the demands of justificatory secularism, and the structure of the different conceptions of justice that they have adopted in relation to these two policies inevitably reflects the dominant comprehensive views held within those societies. Minorities in both societies will reasonably object to the particular conception of political justice dominant within their societies:

they will do so on political grounds (by appeal to political values) even though their values are informed by, and grounded in, their deeper beliefs and values. Such inter- and intra-society disagreements are part and parcel of normal democratic politics, and the meta-theory of justificatory secularism has no ambition to dissolve or resolve them.

What the theory does, however, is to identify three groups of citizens, with differentiated, scalar duties depending on their position on the opinion-making–decision-making continuum. As secular democratic debate is not insulated from the broader and deeper debates that take place in the wide public sphere, political parties and other political associations have a filtering and translating role. This, as suggested above, can be interpreted as a NIN-related duty for citizen-candidates, who should attempt to extract and articulate relevant secular principles from the multi-layered, rich, comprehensive debates about values held in the wide public sphere. So, in the wide public sphere, ordinary citizens have no duty of religious restraint; in the political sphere more narrowly construed, citizen-candidates have a limited duty of religious restraint; and state officials and representatives have a strict duty of religious restraint (see also Greenawalt, 1995). Officials, of course, may personally hold religious beliefs for their views, but – as the legislators and judges in society B in our example – they should refrain from presenting them as reasons for their actions and policies. Public reasons, *stricto sensu*, are sparse and 'metaphysically thin', to use Rawls's phrase: they appeal to fairly general principles (basic rights and liberties, public order and the like) and do not go deeply into 'reasons for reasons'. Yet deep reasons can and must be articulated and debated elsewhere in the democratic public sphere. Justificatory secularism, then, advocates less stringent limitations on legitimate democratic debate than Rawlsian theories of public reason. It narrows down the *site* of public justification: representatives rather than citizens are subjected to NIN. In addition, as I shall explain next, it narrows down the *object* of public justification: only religious justifications, *qua* religious, are within the constitutional scope of the NIN.

The object of justificatory secularism

So what is so special about religious as opposed to other forms of restraint? What is it about religious reasons that makes them the object of NIN? After all, much of our secularized moral vocabulary – including our political morality – is religious in origin, even if it now appears to us to be freestanding. And many of us draw our political beliefs from our faith: it may be our faith that grounds our belief in the political values of freedom, equality, human dignity, the value of relationships and love, charity, the rule of law and social justice. In the previous section, I began adducing some sceptical considerations about the way in which the categories of 'public' and 'non-public', 'religious' and 'secular' have been used in liberal political theory. While many liberal philosophers have singled out religious reasons as problematic for the purposes of public reasoning, few have identified the features in virtue of which it is wrong for the state to 'impose' religious views. One notable exception is Robert Audi, who has put forward an epistemic account of religious reasons: such reasons, by virtue of being ultimately grounded in God's nature or commands, are not intelligible in the way secular reasons are (Audi, 2000: 100). A more common approach has been to subsume religious reasons within broader categories of 'comprehensive conceptions of the good' (Rawls, 1996) or 'ethical worldviews' (Habermas, 2008). In all cases, secular reasons are public in so far as they appeal to potentially *shareable* principles – where the criterion of 'potentially shareable' refers to a partly epistemic and partly conventional account of accessibility. While these accounts of public reason have been subjected to probing and sophisticated criticisms (Chaplin, 2008; Eberle, 2002; Greenawalt, 1995; McGraw, 2010; Perry, 1997; Stout, 2004; Wolterstorff, 1997) it is my view that a version of them is tenable: one grounded in the values of non-establishment and NIN.

The theory, which I can only sketch here, would go as follows. There are three features of religious reasons that make them unsuitable as justificatory reasons for state actions and policies. Neither of them is, by itself, sufficient to ground NIN, yet, put together, they are necessary and sufficient to do so. These are: *comprehensive scope*, *controversial content* and *alienating form*. The first feature, drawn from Rawls's distinction between comprehensive and political doctrines, suggests that the state should not impose comprehensive views of the good life on its citizens; it should not tell people how to live but, instead, identify political principles of justice that are 'freestanding' and compatible with a variety of comprehensive doctrines. It is an important feature of some forms of religious reasoning that they are comprehensive in this sense. Yet, as we saw, secular reasons can be contained within comprehensive religious views, yet also be freestanding and therefore able to act as 'public reasons'. As Rawls himself suggested, religious believers can derive and extract from the web of their theological beliefs reasons that are publicly accessible and potentially shareable. New natural-law theorists, for example, have put forward Catholic perspectives in the publicly accessible, secular language of human dignity, the social importance of the family, duties of care and charity and so forth (George and Wolfe, 2000). Such values are public values in the sense that they can be discussed and debated politically and – for example in the case of gay rights and contraception – confronted with other public values such as rights of non-discrimination, women's rights, the value of loving relationships and alternative conceptions of human dignity. Likewise, public reasons can be detached from secular comprehensive views. Rawls argued that comprehensive secular doctrines such as utilitarianism could not ground public reasons. But he should have made it clear that some suitably public, metaphysically thin and non-comprehensive reasons could be extracted and detached from such doctrines too. Consider, for example, the utilitarian premise that all individuals are to count for one and not more than one: this is an appropriate public reason. By contrast, an officially invoked reason such as 'because there is no God' or 'because religion is metaphysical nonsense' would fall foul of the strictures of justificatory secularism, in so far as it is only understandable by reference to a comprehensive atheistic ethics, and therefore takes a controversial position on matters of faith. But what this means is that what (if anything) is special about religious views is not so much their scope as their content.

Second, then, some have argued that religious reasons are *controversial* in a particular way. On Audi's view, religious reasons have a radically different epistemic status from secular reasons. They are subjected to different evidential standards and are not rationally falsifiable: they cannot be contested, challenged or debated through ordinary human reasoning. While it is true that religious justification often relies on reasons that appeal to a particular experience that cannot be shared (e.g. revelation) or to a particular text whose authority is contested (e.g. sacred scriptures), critics have rightly pointed out that any hard-and-fast distinction between religious and secular reason will be difficult to draw. Secular reasons – even widely shared postulates such as that of the moral equality of human beings – are as inaccessible or axiomatic as religious reasons. Conversely, there is a large amount of rational controversy and scholarly dispute about religious doctrine and interpretation. Both points can be readily conceded. Yet they do not entirely unsettle the special nature of religion. On the first point, public secular reasons are not as likely to touch upon matters of 'ultimate concern' as religious reasons do. And on the second point: while matters of religious doctrine are the object of public discussion and controversy, it is not clear that the state is the competent authority to adjudicate those disputes. As I suggested above, these two features of religion – the religious incompetence of the state and the fact that religion is of 'ultimate concern' to individuals – help account for the non-establishment norm. They explain why it is particularly wrong for the state and its officials to appeal to the truth of religion in the justification of coercive actions and policies. In sum, we can say that religious reasons belong to a category of views (ethically comprehensive and epistemically controversial) that are problematic as official justification for state actions. Yet we have conceded that while religious reasons may paradigmatically belong to such a category, they do not uniquely do so.

There is, however, a third and final feature of religion which has historically been crucial (in the West at least) in securing the special – and unique – place of religion as the focus of NIN. This is the fact that religious state speech is deemed to be divisive and alienating, because of a particular history of conflict whereby religious categories have acquired political and social, not only epistemic and ethical, salience. It is these two additional features of religion – the heritage of religious conflict and the persisting use of religion as a marker of discrimination and exclusion – which ultimately ground justificatory secularism. They explain why two public statements with the same propositional content, such as 'God asks us to treat all human beings as equals' (axiom A) and 'we must treat all human beings as equals' (axiom B), have a different status in public justification. It is neither the scope nor the content (putatively uncontroversial) of the injunction but, rather, the form of the statement that is problematic. In a society where religious categories still act as markers of insider/outsider status, the way the state speaks matters as much as what it says. If, in many religiously pluralistic societies, religious justifications cannot act as acceptable axioms, it is because of the historical legacy of the political import of religious divisiveness in such societies. This explains why, in Western societies in particular, religious reasons are on a different plane from other deeply controversial reasons.

This completes my sketch of justificatory secularism. To recap: a secular state in my sense is a state where officials refrain from appealing to religious views, and where citizen-candidates seek not to rely solely on such views when they engage in public debate about the justification of laws and policies. With this definition in mind, how are we to respond to the charges made against the ideal of the secular state? As anticipated, I will argue that justificatory secularism is not vulnerable to a range of critiques commonly levelled at secularism.

Defending secularism against its critics

In the quickly expanding critical literature on secularism (Bhargava, 1998; Levey and Modood, 2009; Stout, 2008) it is possible to identify three distinct charges against secularism: first, secularism *marginalizes* religion; second, it *excludes* believers; third, it *neglects* religion.[1] I will argue that, however pertinent these criticisms are of the actual practices of existing secular states, and of the comprehensive project of some secularist ideologies, they do not give us grounds to jettison the basic secular suspicion vis-à-vis certain forms of justification of political coercion in religiously diverse societies.

Marginalization of religion

The first charge is this. Secular states are complicit in the secularization of society. Two different types of examples are usually brought to illustrate this point. The first is that secular authoritarian states such as the USSR, Turkey or Iraq have engaged in highly repressive anti-religious policies; and the second is that some European secular states have deliberately relegated religion to a narrow, private sphere. It is easy to see how the plausibility of justificatory secularism is not affected by these real-world practices of secularism. Nothing in justificatory secularism suggests that the secular state should be committed to a comprehensive programme of secularization of society – to what

---

[1] A fourth charge, which I do not deal with in this chapter, is that the secular state is itself religious. This more fundamental critique, pressed by Talal Asad and his followers, challenges the very distinction between secularism and religion, in two ways: it asserts that secularism is an irreducibly Christian doctrine; and it asserts that Western legal and political secularism functions, for all intents and purposes, as a religion.

Ahmet Kuru calls an 'assertive secularism' (Kuru, 2009). Three main points can be made.

First, the fact that some authoritarian regimes have instrumentalized the rhetoric of secularism to curb dangerously politicized religious militancy does not discredit secularism as such, but only illiberal secularism. Illiberal secularism is a comprehensive political programme that equates religion (particularly, in the colonial and neo-colonial context, Islam) with obscurantism, uncivilized barbarism, political violence and the oppression of women. Secularism can and has been associated both with authoritarian and with liberal politics (and, more relevantly in colonial and neo-colonial contexts, with authoritarian projects of forcible modernization of society). Yet on the view that I present here, secularism tells us only something about the kind of reasons that can be put forward in justifying policies and laws. Secularism, and the non-imposition norm NIN, is a theory of justification that is derived from the liberal and democratic concern for the legitimacy of laws (although, admittedly, more needs to be said about how precisely justificatory secularism relates to liberal-democratic theory generally). In so far as illiberal, undemocratic secular states have had no such concern for democratic justification, they remain tangential to the philosophical ideal outlined here.

Second, it is undeniable that some societies, in particular in Europe, have undergone a profound and multi-faceted process of secularization, in the sense that religious belief has become residual, privatized and marginal to political identities. Yet it is not clear that self-proclaimed European secular states are responsible for the historical advent of the 'secular age' – nor, for that matter, is it clear that the reverse process of partial desecularization of those societies should be, in turn, traced back to the public philosophy and practices of such states. Consider, too, the counter-example of the USA, where official separation between church and state has historically gone hand in hand with the existence of a vibrantly religious civil society (Berger *et al.*, 2008). Generally, therefore, social secularization and the political form of the state do not necessarily cohere. And when some states (France is a good example here) have forcibly encouraged social secularization, it is because they have been committed, not to the meta-theoretical secularism about justifications and reasons that I advocate here but, rather, to a wide-ranging political programme of promotion of republican democratic citizenship, which has been set against and counter-posed to 'private' religious allegiances (Laborde, 2008). This, however, is in no way entailed or mandated by meta-theoretical secularism. In other words, existing secular states are not exemplars of justificatory secularism in my sense.

Third, and crucially, a state committed to justificatory secularism is not designed or exclusively suitable for de facto secularized societies (such as European societies). The secular state, rather, is a state suitable for any society where there is a level of religious and, more generally, ethical pluralism (and, we may add, a history of bitter and salient religious conflicts). So a secular state can theoretically preside over a highly religious civil society. Interesting, if different and complex, examples here might be the USA (with its strong non-establishment tradition) or India (Bhargava, 2009). Indian secularism includes both a meta-theoretical and a substantive political commitment. Politically, it signifies not so much strict, Western-style separation of state and religion, as roughly equivalent public support for the dominant religions of Hinduism and Islam. But the public philosophy that the Indian constitution upholds is a secular, albeit religion-friendly humanism which historically emerged as the shared language of politics within the context of religious pluralism in India. And so, India, despite being presided over by a secular state in my sense, has a vibrantly religious civil society. In sum, justificatory secularism does not marginalize religion. Is there, however, a more specific form of exclusion of religion that would seem to be implied by it?

Exclusion of believers

The claim here is this. Religious believers are excluded from public reason, and therefore from public debate, because of the demand of religious restraint. As no religious reason in favour of a law should be officially invoked unless suitably secular views are also put forward in support, those who are unable or unwilling to present their deeply held views in a secular form are thereby excluded (Eberle, 2002; Stout, 2004; Weithman, 1997; Wolterstorff, 1997). Clearly, this is a more pointed charge, and it deserves a careful response. The first thing to point out is that religious believers are *not* excluded from public debate under justificatory secularism. There is nothing wrong with believers freely engaging in religious advocacy in the wide public sphere, and forming, expressing and defending religiously inspired ideals about common laws and policies. It is only when citizens take on the more restricted positions of candidates for political office that they are expected to seek secular reasons for the coercive laws that they propose to advocate (and ultimately to enforce). Is this, however, an unreasonable demand? In requiring that religious arguments be at some point 'translated' into secular language, or else be deemed unsuitable for the purposes of public justification, can justificatory secularism be suspected of a secularist bias or a Christian bias (or both, given the Christian genealogy of secularism)? Although both charges cannot be answered fully within the scope of this chapter, let me say something brief about each in turn.

First, it is just not the case that religious groups and organizations have found it impossible to articulate their deepest values within secular policies. For example, Catholic groups in South America or the Islamic *Adalet ve Kalkınma Partisi* (AKP) in Turkey have been able to defend religiously inspired, socially conservative platforms by appeal to traditionalist secular values such as the family, the defence of public order and so forth. Generally, in most areas of public debate, justificatory secularism is able to provide the framework for vigorous public debate: this is true of classically 'political' controversies such as wealth distribution, social justice, foreign policy, the use of torture and so forth. And the whole gamut of debates about sex, homosexuality, education, faith-based associations, religious exemptions, free speech and so on can also be fought in terms of public reason. Religious believers, who hold profound, comprehensive beliefs about what the demands of morality entail in these cases, should be prepared, if they seek political office, to offer their fellow citizens secular reasons to justify their views in public. For example, they can invoke such values as the social good of marriage and reproduction, church doctrinal autonomy, the social role of religious charities, the wrongness of offensive speech, parents' rights and the particular harm suffered by citizens forced to act against their conscience, all of which are legitimate secular values. These values do not, however, automatically trump other democratic values, such as women's rights, children's rights, equality as non-discrimination, the social good of all loving relationships, freedom of speech and so on. So, by appealing to the justificatory structure of the secular state, we can locate recent controversies on the plane to which they belong: that of the legitimate and reasonable disagreement about citizens' rights and liberties in a democratic society, rather than an existential stand-off between 'secularists' and 'believers'. Even in the most controversial areas of bioethics, abortion and physician-assisted suicide, appeal has been made by religious citizens to the value of human dignity – a secularized version of the sacredness of human life.

Yet it must be conceded that when public policy touches on such controversial, metaphysical matters as the status of the human foetus or of clinically dead patients, secular reason shows its limits. Within democratic political culture, there is no freestanding, shared view of philosophical anthropology which could be endorsed by religious and non-religious citizens from the point of view of their own comprehensive premises. When public policy touches on questions deeply bound up with comprehensive questions about the meaning of life, it cannot require religious believers, even those seeking public office, solely to invoke impeccably secular principles. It is this possibility that was left open by the requirement, set out above, that the duty of civility implies that they 'seek to find' secular reasons, as opposed to 'succeeding' in finding them. So, they may sincerely seek secular reasons to justify their fundamental opposition to stem-cell research, abortion and physician-assisted suicide, but they may not find any (the secular ideal of human dignity is perhaps not robust enough) and they then might have to resort to appeal to their belief in the ineffable sanctity of all human life. In such fundamental ethical issues, which inevitably touch on the meaning of life and death, there may not be a shared language of secular reason, which would be relevantly agnostic about ultimate ends and commitments. In this case, the most we can perhaps require on the part of state representatives and officials is to exercise equal restraint in the expression of controversial religious *and* secular views – as much as this is compatible with the need to legislate in these highly contested areas of bioethics.

What of the second charge, that justificatory secularism, as a post-Christian ideology, is valid only for Western societies? I have already alluded to the historical connections between the political norm of non-establishment and the Western heritage of religious conflict. But, in my references to India and to contemporary Turkey (the AKP), I have also adduced considerations that imply that the ideals of justificatory secularism may have wider application. The question as to whether the 'deflationary' conception of secularism that I have presented here can be endorsed from non-Western comprehensive doctrines is still open. The secular norm of NIN, at the very least, is incompatible with theocracy – the imposition by the state of a comprehensive religious worldview. To deny this is to miss the force of secularism. Yet, admittedly, to say this is not to say much about the broader theological, historical, ethical and epistemological assumptions of justificatory secularism – this is a topic for another occasion.

Neglect of religion

Now, critics of secularism may then press a third, more subtle, last charge. They can point out that a secular state will unavoidably develop an anti-religious bias in its policies. This is because, by excluding substantive views about religion from its permissible justifications, it fails to take seriously the way in which religion is a good that needs to be supported and fostered by state institutions if it is to flourish in appropriate ways. A state that is agnostic about religion is, for all intents and purposes, a state that is incapable of grasping the importance of religion to people's lives. As a result, secular states – even states committed to my minimalist theory of justificatory secularism – would unavoidably, albeit non-intentionally, neglect religious needs and aspirations (Rosenblum, 2000; Weithman, 1997).

This charge would miss the point of secularism, and it is important to see why. This line of criticism confuses a meta-theoretical position about justification, a demand of restraint in invoking particular reasons, with a substantive policy prescription, a ban on state support of specific activities and forms of life, notably religious ones. Yet in a secular state, the state can and must protect religion, not by appeal to religious arguments but by appeal to good secular reasons. A state can support religious activities and practices, not because it endorses and affirms the good that they pursue but, for example, in the name of the public values of religious freedom or equality between citizens. Let me take some real-world examples. Even self-proclaimed secular states such as France and the USA subsidize chaplaincy services in state-controlled, enclosed spaces such as prisons and the army, to ensure that prisoners and military personnel are actually able to exercise the religious liberties available to other citizens in freely constituted civilian religious associations. And religious organizations providing public services such as health or social care, on the same terms as secular organizations, may also be recipients of public funds. In and by itself, secularism is a thin theory of justification, and does not tell us anything substantive about the relationship between the state and religious groups (Laborde, 2011). And, as the USA example more broadly suggests, even constitutional commitment to a 'wall of separation' between state and church and non-establishment is not incompatible with strong state support for (the conditions necessary for guaranteeing the actual) free exercise of religion. Secularism in politics – the injunction not to appeal to the truth of a particular religion or to the command of a particular God – is rooted in the ideal of respect for conscience. And freedom of religion is the one (and perhaps the only) conclusively justified principle in liberal political philosophy (Gaus, 1996: 160–70). Liberals typically assume that we all have a higher-order interest in following the dictates of our conscience, without being coerced or otherwise subjected to undue pressure. To be forced to live a life that does not speak to our most profound commitments, and specifically beliefs about the meaning of life and death and about our ultimate subjection to the will of God, would be, to use Rawls's phrase, to endure excessive 'strains of commitment' (Rawls, 1996). This explains why (in the anglophone liberal tradition) burdens on conscience are deemed to be more strenuous than obstacles to the pursuit of purely secular conceptions of the good, however comprehensive, principled and fundamental to the person's life these may be.

Given this special importance of freedom of conscience as a public value in liberalism, the charge that secularism neglects religion is, at least, overstated. For the secularist ban on public appeal to the truth of religion does not extend to a ban on appeal to the importance of religion for people themselves. And this has important implications for the nature and content of public debate in secular states. Imagine a religious believer who seeks to convince others that she should be granted an exemption to an otherwise publicly justified law on the grounds that the law unduly burdens her conscience. Note that this does not fall foul of the secular duty of civility, in so far as the argument takes the form: 'I believe that my God commands that I do X, and as the state is committed to free religious exercise, it should allow me to do X.' So the believer does not require that others believe or even understand X, but simply that they accept that their public commitment to free religious exercise may require them to allow her (the believer) to do X. So here we have an example of a private reason (my reason to do X) becoming a public reason (reasons for others to help me do X) via appeal to the widely accepted secular value of 'freedom of religion'. And secular courts, particularly countries with strong Christian Protestant traditions, have traditionally been deferential towards subjectively held, religiously based obligations, holding them to be weightier than secular commitments derived from general freedoms of thought and expression. The Free Exercise clause of the US First Amendment, for example, allows religiously motivated persons to be exempted from general laws when these unduly burden their conscience (such exemptions, however, are no longer constitutionally required – see *Smith*, 1990). This means that you can quit employment with 'good cause' (and full employment benefits) if your religion prevents you from meeting the demands of a particular job – for instance if you are a Sabbatarian and cannot work on Saturday (*Sherbert*, 1963, jurisprudence); and you can withdraw your children out of otherwise compulsory school at fourteen if you are a member of the Old Amish order (*Yoder*, 1972). Freedom of religion, then, is specially protected even in self-proclaimed separationist, secular states. In recent years, many countries have had to consider tricky cases of conflicts between freedom of religion and association on the one hand, and rights of non-discrimination (for women, gays and lesbians) on the other. Of course, claims of conscience by themselves cannot trump all other values, and courts must assess if and when such claims are rightful and should be accommodated. But the main point remains. The secular state may not talk about God but it talks about freedom of religion, and it often talks about it loudly.

Conclusion

I have suggested that justificatory secularism is not vulnerable to the standard charges levelled at secularism. The latter tend to rely on conflation between the meta-theoretical claims of justificatory secularism and more substantive commitments which are not entailed by it: a commitment to reduce religious influence in social life (*marginalization*), to silence religious voices in public debate (*exclusion*) or be indifferent towards the substantive claims of religion (*neglect*). A secular state, I suggested, should not be defined by its substantive commitments, institutional settlement or specific policies. Rather, it is defined by the type of justification it offers for them. I hope to have shown that the ideal of the secular state speaks both to believers and to atheists. It shows atheists and agnostics that not all 'religious' reasons are problematic for the purposes of public deliberation (only certain kinds of reasons with a specific content, source and form are), and that these are problematic only when they are put forward by officials who claim to speak in the name of all. It also shows that anti-religious sentiment can be as suspect a political justification as appeal to the truth of religion, in so far as it takes a substantive position on matters of faith. In turn, the ideal of justificatory secularism suggests to religious believers that, even though they may understandably resent the secularization of *society*, the secular *state* does not forbid them from defending their views and values in the private and public sphere. While the secular state is, by definition, anathema to theocrats, it should appeal to the great majority of believers of all faiths. And it should give defenders of secularism reasons for hope, as well as for restraint. In the current offensive against the secular state, secularists should stick to their guns, but not blaze them in all directions: religion has a legitimate place in the secular state.

This chapter, then, has begun to articulate what may be called a minimalist, *deflationary* theory of secularism. It does not conflate secularism with the comprehensive, oppressive, statist project rejected by critics, nor with the messianic future of emancipation and enlightenment promised by its defenders. In line with the liberal tradition broadly conceived, I take secularism to be a thin theory of justification of political power. As such, it does not commit us to the range of positions and ideologies with which it is often tightly associated in popular and academic discourse. In closing, let me highlight – and disprove – three of these common conceptions. First, it is a mistake to see secularism as the antonym of religion and as an anti-religious position. Contra eulogists of the 'secularization thesis', there is no need to identify secularism with rationality, progress and modernization, and religion with irrationality, faith and conservatism. Justificatory secularism requires only a basic distinction between temporal and spiritual authority, and a public commitment to the non-establishment of religion by the state. Second, it is a mistake to claim that secularism offers a substantive interpretation of what equality, or freedom, or women's rights or social justice requires. Contra the progressive protagonists in the US Culture Wars, secularism cannot by itself generate the 'correct' (i.e. egalitarian, individualistic) answers on issues of bioethics, sexual and gender justice. It is not impermissible for religiously minded groups to seek to influence public debate on these matters, as on many others. To refute their arguments, appeal to norms of religious restraint will not be sufficient: substantive egalitarian views need to be defended, not simply assumed to follow from 'secularism'. Third, it is wrong to view secularism as a comprehensive ethic to be endorsed by citizens in liberal-democratic states. Contra some republican and public-reason theorists, secularism is, for the most part, a set of constraints on official state actions and speech, not an individual disposition and virtue. In fact, on the view that I defend, the state must be secular so that ordinary citizens do not, themselves, have to be secular.

References

Audi, R. 2000. *Religious Commitment and Secular Reason*. Cambridge University Press.

Berger, P. L., Davie, G. and Fokas, E. 2008. *Religious America, Secular Europe? A Theme and Variations*. Aldershot: Ashgate.

Bhargava, R. 2009. 'Political Secularism: Why It Is Needed and What can Be Learnt from its Indian Version', in G. B. Levey and T. Modood, eds., *Secularism, Religion and Multicultural Citizenship*. Cambridge University Press, 82–109.

Bhargava, R., ed. 1998. *Secularism and its Critics*. New Delhi: Oxford University Press.

Casanova, J. 1994. *Public Religions in the Modern World*. University of Chicago Press.

Chaplin, J. 2008. *Talking God. The Legitimacy of Religious Public Reasoning*. London: Theos.

Eberle, C. J. 2002. *Religious Conviction in Liberal Politics*. Cambridge University Press.

Gaus, G. 1996. *Justificatory Liberalism: An Essay on Epistemology and Political Theory*. Oxford University Press.

George, R. and Wolfe, C., eds. 2000. *Natural Law and Public Reason*. Washington, DC: Georgetown University Press.

Greenawalt, K. 1995. *Private Consciences and Public Reasons*. New York: Oxford University Press.

Habermas, J. 2008. *Between Naturalism and Religion: Philosophical Essays*, trans. Ciaran Cronin. Cambridge: Polity Press.

Kuru, A. T. 2009. *Secularism and State Policies toward Religion*. Cambridge University Press.

Laborde, C. 2008. *Critical Republicanism. The Hijab Controversy and Political Philosophy*. Oxford University Press.

2011. 'Political Liberalism and Religion: On Separation and Establishment', *Journal of Political Philosophy*, 21, 1, 67–86.

Levey, G. B. and Modood, T., eds. 2009. *Secularism, Religion and Multicultural Citizenship*. Cambridge University Press.

Levinson, S. 1997. 'Abstinence and Exclusion: What Does Liberalism Demand of the Religiously Oriented (Would-Be) Judge?', in P. J. Weithman, ed., *Religion and Contemporary Liberalism*. University of Notre Dame Press, 233–55.

McGraw, B. T. 2010. *Faith in Politics. Religion and Liberal Democracy*. Cambridge University Press.

Perry, M. 1997. *Religion in Politics. Constitutional and Moral Perspectives*. New York: Oxford University Press.

Quinn, P. L. 1997. 'Political Liberalisms and their Exclusion of the Religious', in P. J. Weithman, ed., *Religion and Contemporary Liberalism*. University of Notre Dame Press, 138–61.

Quong, J. 2010. *Liberalism without Perfection*. Oxford University Press.

Rawls, J. 1996. *Political Liberalism*. New York: Columbia University Press.

Rosenblum, N. L. 2000. *Obligations of Citizenship and Demands of Faith. Religious Accommodation in Pluralist Democracies*. Princeton University Press.

Stout, J. 2004. *Democracy and Tradition*. Princeton University Press.

2008. '2007 Presidential Address: The Folly of Secularism', *Journal of the American Academy of Religion*, 76, 3, 533–44.

Taylor, C. 2007. *A Secular Age*. Cambridge, MA: Belknap Press of Harvard University Press.

Weithman, P. J., ed. 1997. *Religion and Contemporary Liberalism*. University of Notre Dame Press.

Wolterstorff, N. 1997. 'Why We Should Reject What Liberalism Tells Us about Speaking and Acting in Public for Religious Reasons', in P. J. Weithman, ed., *Religion and Contemporary Liberalism*. University of Notre Dame Press, 162–81.

8 | *What lacks is feeling: mediating reason and religion today*

JOHN MILBANK

Plant's contribution to this volume raises a question about the nature of religion in public discourse, especially in the context of a post-metaphysical philosophy. In this chapter I will ask whether Habermas (and inevitably Kant) can be questioned about the very presuppositions that guide the framing of such a question.

Was fehlt?, asks Jürgen Habermas in the course of his now famous debate about post-secularity, faith and reason with the Munich Jesuits (Habermas *et al.*, 2010). *What lacks* to us today, in an age supposedly governed by reason? Here Habermas takes up the post-religious lament of Brecht and Adorno: how do we supply the role that religion once fulfilled?

But he takes it up in a very different key, because he is newly aware, in the early twenty-first century that, far from going away, religion is if anything returning – in terms of numbers in the Third World, and in terms of public influence in the West. This return is by no means always benign: religious extremism is returning also. Yet in a new combination, secular extremism has reached a new pitch of intensity and we are also seeing the rise of an increasingly militant naturalism. Both these phenomena Habermas understandably regards as threatening to a reasonable humanism. In the face of this threat he wishes to defend and refortify its neutral, secular ground. However, he continues to be haunted by the Brechtian lack. And in the face of this lack he no longer suggests merely a novel substitute for lost faith, but rather that reason must continue to draw upon faith's resources. Religion is not going to go away and we need not only reasonable forms of religion but also a rational respect for faith if human beings and the planet are to have a sane future.

This seems immediately compelling. However, I shall argue below that what is problematic about Habermas's proposals is the sharp divide that he assumes between faith and reason, on the basis of a presumed non-surpassability of the post-metaphysical era inaugurated by Kant. He understands both Pope Benedict's revival of a metaphysical

187

mediation between faith and reason *and* newly over-extended onto-logical naturalism to be violations of the 'limits of pure reason'. I shall further contend that Habermas is already outdated in the face of a manifest revival of metaphysics and that both a revived blend of Greek reason with biblical faith and an ambitious naturalism are coherent, though rival programmes. Either idiom, I shall suggest, permits a much greater mediation between faith and reason than Habermas allows and does so especially in terms of the role given to *feeling*. Moreover, if we read David Hume aright (which is to say in a drastically revisionary fashion) we shall see that such a perspective is by no means entirely alien to the Enlightenment legacy, to which Kant need not, after all, be regarded as the primary witness. In this respect, I also want to problematize the terrain presented by Plant.

I shall try to show that when faith and reason are mediated by feeling they are actually less likely to take sinister forms than when they are corralled against each other. Finally I shall suggest that Habermas's own pragmatized transcendentalism, far from being a bulwark against anti-humanist reduction, is entirely subject to such reduction. By contrast, the right sort of naturalism can lend itself to a spiritualizing elevation. *Was fehlt?* I shall therefore claim, in an inter-linguistic play on verbal affinities, is 'feeling' – which is both the lack of one for the other and the urge towards that other.

Habermas and the lack within reason: the debate with Ratzinger and the Munich Jesuits

Habermas's approach to our current global dilemmas is sensitive, even anguished, and highly acute. As he observes: 'At the level of elementary interactions, a gap seems to be opening up between a prickly moral consciousness and the impotence in the face of the structurally imposed switch to strategic conduct' (Habermas, 2010b: 74).

Exactly so: one has here a kind of sterile oscillation between a ruling ruthlessness on the one hand and impotent moralistic whining on the other. The ruthlessness is the result of the ever-greater submission of more and more spheres of human life to an instrumentalist and capitalist logic, which Habermas fears is now more and more driven by a revived social Darwinism. In the face of this ruthlessness, moral reserve retreats into the private domain and takes the form of a stuttering series of complaints that too often are merely about the supposed restriction of certain individuals and groups from full participation in the mass instrumentalizing process.

It is a considerable tribute to his intellectual integrity that Habermas sees that perhaps the greatest exception here are religious groups who continue to foster impulses towards moral action on a collective scale. For this reason one has to ask, what is it which they provide that is otherwise 'lacking'? Habermas's answer, broadly speaking, is that they provide vivid pictures and motivating stories for individuals, and above all that they provide images of community that are compelling ('the body of Christ' and so forth) but which exceed the bounds of the mere nation state – thereby opening up a universal and global loyalty.

Habermas is clear that human solidarity now needs these religious resources if it is to fight both religious and naturalistic fanaticism. However, he asks to what extent it is legitimate for religious people to speak in terms of their religious visions in the public domain – and at times his questioning here is in excess of his answering. Yet on the whole he supplies a rather uncompromising kind of reply: although secularity must continue to draw, like Hegel, on religious resources, it must eventually translate these resources into strictly rational terms for the sake of official legislative debate and usage. And by rational terms Habermas means the terms of Kantian critical reason, which render out of court any totalizing and cosmological metaphysical claims.

In order to sustain such a demand, two more protocols must be observed. First, religions must be required to accept this need for translation, along with the secular neutrality of the state, the monopoly over 'fact' of scientific discourse and the monopoly on public morality of the norms of communicative action in terms of free access to conversation and the intention of publicly verifiable truth. But secondly, this acceptance must be no mere reluctant resignation. To the contrary, religions must be required so to modify their dogmas (if they are not already so compliant) as to find specifically internal, theological ways of embracing the absoluteness of these secular norms (Habermas, 2010a).

Yet correspondingly, secular reason must be required to admit that it has no remit when it comes to determining the truth or otherwise of faith. So the trade-off, one might say, for outlawing the metaphysics of Joseph Ratzinger would be that we would equally outlaw the scientism of Richard Dawkins. A question, of course, arises about the dubious practicality of such proposals. But more theoretically, questions arise about their coherence. Everything in fact depends for Habermas upon the absoluteness of the Kantian revolution, which, by banishing metaphysical mediation, finally gave secular consecration to the Protestant separation of reason and faith. But in that case, is Habermas covertly engaging in a new sort of *Kulturkampf*?

One could argue that this is indeed so. He is prepared to admit that the great metaphysics of East and West are of a single axial birth with the world religions. However, he wishes to say that later 'a division of labour' between metaphysics and Christian theology was worked out. Yet this is immediately to admit that what we are faced with here is an explicitly Christian event, and the question arises as to its possible ideological contingency rather than logical necessity. Habermas quite wrongly chides Ratzinger with a deficient historicism, but Ratzinger is the far more prodigious historicist on precisely this point. For Ratzinger would ascribe to the view that the dogmatic separation of philosophy from theology is the paradoxical result of the dubious creation of a category of 'pure nature' by a theology concerned for theological reasons sharply to divide nature from grace. Equally he would ascribe to the view that a metaphysics independent of all theology is the result of a specifically theological establishment after Duns Scotus of being as univocal and so as comprehensible outside the Neoplatonic logic of participation in God (Rowland, 2010).

The fact that the issue between Habermas and Ratzinger turns in part on this question of genealogy is clearly confessed by Habermas himself at the end of his essay in the Munich debates (Habermas, 2010a: 22–3).[1] There he alludes to the contingent shifts just mentioned, but says: (1) that Scotism and nominalism were preconditions for the rise of modern science; (2) that Kant's transcendental turn was required for 'our modern European understanding of law and democracy'; (3) that historicism was the precondition for a proper cultural pluralism, besides an improper relativism. Finally and crucially, he identifies these three stages as ones in a progressive 'de-Hellenization'.

But these claims are historically dubious. First, the medieval rebirth of Greek science preceded the advent of univocity and nominalism, and one could even argue that they led physics initially in an over-mechanistic direction which more Neoplatonic and Hermetic

---

[1] For an earlier debate between Habermas and Ratzinger, see Habermas and Ratzinger, 2006.

influences later corrected, beginning with Isaac Newton. Second, the French and American, to say nothing of older British, Scandinavian and Swiss, contributions to European constitutionalism have got simply nothing to do with Kant whatsoever! Third, historicism only implies an irreducible pluralism if one disallows the more radically historicist idea – as admitted by Ratzinger – that events can uniquely disclose truths.

Meanwhile the approbation of 'de-Hellenization' is revealing. For this phenomenon cannot be prised apart from a claimed (but arguably spurious) greater fidelity to the biblical legacy, sundered from Greek metaphysics, which is traceable through Scotus, nominalism and the Reformation. Clearly Habermas cannot rationally be seen to be assenting to this tendency in theological, or a fortiori Protestant theological terms. Yet here arises most acutely the question about the status of his proposed 'translation' of theological into secular terms.

For evidently the above-cited remarks show that at least some of the theology he wants to translate is Scotist, Ockhamist and Protestant. But in that case, do the secular variants really struggle entirely free of a specifically religious origin? And is it not strange that the translations which *all Christians* are asked by Habermas to sign up to are translations of positions at variance with those of most mainstream Catholic intellectuals? Thus in order to ascribe to these translations they would have first to switch their allegiance from theologically metaphysical positions, which, according to Habermas, are *not translatable into the terms of reason at all.*

In order to make such a drastic requirement of Catholic Christians, Habermas would have to show that, far from his Kantian philosophy being rooted in certain older theologico-metaphysical assumptions, these assumptions were rather initial adumbrations of a truly critical philosophy. This would be to accord with the position of the fine intellectual historian Ludger Honnefelder, for whom Scotus' writings were the beginning of a critical turn which asked first about the capacities of human reason as an instrument rather than first about the division of being.[2]

However, the suspicion must lurk that Ratzinger might be able to trump Habermas metacritically at this juncture. Is Scotus the

[2] Honnefelder's complex genealogy is most accessible in his short book based on lectures given in Paris: Honnefelder, 2002.

anticipator of Kant's reasons or is Kant still the prisoner of Scotus' and Ockham's theology? It is after all clear to historians that univocity of being, nominalism and voluntarism were all taken up for reasons that were as much theological as philosophical. And all three positions can be and are contested within perfectly respectable contemporary theology and (more decisively) philosophy. So if, as many historians of philosophy (Honnefelder included) have now claimed, the Kantian critical turn assumes the validity of these positions, then its absolute historical hiatus can be questioned.

The point is not here to adjudicate on this issue, but rather to throw into doubt Habermas's rather blithe (and surely now rather provincial) assumption that those who cannot accept our 'post-metaphysical' situation have somehow failed to follow certain ineluctable arguments. To the contrary, it was rather the octogenarian Benedict XVI who (unusually amongst contemporary Germans) looked 'cool', who seemed to 'get' the post-postmodern *Zeitgeist*, without trying, like Habermas, to retreat into a modern humanist comfort zone that is no longer sustainable (see the following section). Hence Ratzinger might well counter to Habermas that to embrace 'de-Hellenization' from a secular vantage point is to fall victim to a theologically exegetical error that is outright factually wrong. For Hellenic influence is indeed present within the New Testament from the outset, nor do contemporary biblical critics (outside Germany, at least) any longer subscribe to nineteenth-century Lutheran delusions about a vast gulf between the Hellenic and the Hebraic.

Therefore it must remain highly doubtful whether Habermas has successfully shown that Ratzinger's alternative pre-modern model for the mediation of faith and reason is no longer critically viable. Is genuinely objective reason just a matter of conforming to pragmatically normative criteria for communication, as Habermas teaches? Or is our 'communication' of reason true to the degree that it participates in the infinite communication of the Logos by the divine Father who created finite reality, as Ratzinger suggests? There is great prima facie plausibility in the latter's claim that this idea alone rendered reason coterminous with being itself and suggested an unlimited diversity and scope for the reach of reason.

How ironic indeed that we are therefore faced with a debate between a religious rationalism arguing for the limitless sway of reason and a secular rationalism arguing for the limits of reason and yet a sublime respect for a faith that lies ineffably outside reason altogether! Is it the limitation and yet confinement of reason to formal checkability that guards against terror, or is it rather the advocacy of a generous extension of reason both in reach and kind?

I shall argue that the latter position of Ratzinger's is the right one and that it has a serious impact on the map sketched by Raymond Plant. In arguing this about Ratzinger, he is perhaps, as a German, somewhat unusual. But besides exhibiting many French influences in addition he draws upon longstanding traditions of German Catholic Romanticism that were deeply critical of Kant in the ultimate wake of the Lutheran pietists Jacobi and Hamann – who drew much inspiration from David Hume. For comprehending part of the reason why I have singled out Hume in this chapter, it is important to bear this 'Romanticism' of Ratzinger's in mind.

For what it implies is that it is not enough simply to try to 'reinstate' a pre-critical (pre-Scotist, pre-nominalist, pre-Kantian) outlook, since one has to ask just how it was possible for the latter to arise. What I think can be argued here is that the 'critical' view arose because of an increasing sundering of reason from the emotive and the aesthetic, and a corresponding sundering between reason and a will increasingly viewed as pure 'choice' and 'decision'. In order, therefore, to recover, as Ratzinger desires, a 'broader' reason, it is necessary to insist, in a 'Romantic' fashion, upon the embedding of reason in the emotive, the aesthetic, the linguistic, the social, the historical and the natural, far more explicitly than did even the 'high metaphysical' synthesis of faith and reason that preceded the Scotist rupture.

One can argue that the 'Romantic' current, far from being marginal (or dependent upon the Kantian shift) begins well back in the 'Enlightenment' or arguably the 'pre-Enlightenment', which already entertained doubts about both the consequences of the late medieval Christian legacy and the naturalist reaction against it. For example, with David Hume himself, whose inspiration of both German (Jacobi and Hamann) and French romanticism (Maine de Biran) was crucial.

As both Augustinian and Romantic Ratzinger differs markedly from Habermas's Jesuit Munich interlocutors, who are mostly themselves far too Kantian and try somewhat incoherently to combine Kant with pre-modern Catholic philosophy. However, the one non-Jesuit interlocutor in the collection – Michael Reder – makes important critical points (Reder, 2010: 36–50). These are threefold. Firstly, Habermas's rejection of religion's public right to speak in its own voice is a sub-category of Habermas's insistence that public virtue is a matter of Kantian *Moralität* and not Hegelian *Sittlichkeit*. In other words, he will not allow that there can be any publicly rational adjudication as to the common good and the shared ends of human flourishing. Reder rightly notes that this seems to take no account of the revival of the claims of virtue ethics. Secondly, Reder suggests that Habermas also ignores the idea that reason can speak negatively of the infinite by realizing that in the face of the infinite the usual logic of non-contradiction breaks down, as suggested by Nicholas of Cusa. Yet here Reder also presents Cusa anachronistically as a Kantian who asked epistemological questions about the possible reach of our intellect and so as articulating a sublime gulf between its positive finite and its negative infinite reach. But in reality Nicholas was still situating the human mind metaphysically within a finitude that he newly grasped as paradoxically extending of itself into the infinite. Accordingly, his idea of contradictory utterance does not express an impassable barrier so much as an analogical mediation that can be mystically traversed. He was more the Renaissance renewer of Neoplatonic tradition than an advance articulator of the post-metaphysical.[3] And were he but the latter then his example would be of little use in qualifying Habermas, because it would still leave reason sundered from faith. The former would merely sketch out a space for faith to fill with its own exclusive content.

Reder's third point is the most crucial: this is that, following Schleiermacher, we can understand 'feeling' as a category intermediate between faith and reason. Once more, however, Reder puts things in an overly negative 'critical' fashion, presenting Schleiermacher's 'feeling of absolute dependence' in terms of a failure of autonomous self-grounding reaching out to a Kantian sublime, rather than as a mode of cognitive relationship to the whole of immanent reality, as Schleiermacher actually articulated it. All the same it is true that Schleiermacher did not ultimately escape the Kantian lure, and so increasingly presented this experience of cosmic dependence and interdependence as specifically 'religious', rather than being the entire horizon of our human condition, both cognitive and practical, as the

---

[3] For an authentic reading of Cusa not through Idealist lenses, see Hoff, 2007.

On Religion: Speeches to Its Cultured Despisers originally intended (Schleiermacher, 1988). The trouble with Schleiermacher was that when he cleaved to this more interesting vision he lost the subjectively personal in the pantheistically immanent, but when he later confined feeling to 'a religious category' he lost the sense that all reason is a mode of feeling.

Reder is only able to put forward feeling as offering a kind of bridge to faith, in a manner that still leaves faith and reason profoundly divided. Beyond this we need to see how reason and faith are always thoroughly entangled and also provides a social model that allows for this entanglement. But before suggesting this, I shall try to suggest reasons why Habermas's notion of public discursive neutrality is philosophically incoherent.

Questioning discursive neutrality

As already stated, Habermas is acutely aware that we live in a period where the humanist consensus is being challenged both by naturalisms and by more militant forms of faith. In the face of this circumstance he proposes that we need to reinstate a firm Kantian distinction between what belongs to discursive reason, on the one hand, and to ineffable faith, on the other (Habermas, 2008). Discursive reason should recognize that it operates within strict limits and therefore is not competent to pronounce against either metaphysically naturalist or religious positions. Both must be allowed to speak in their own voices in the public domain (and one should welcome Habermas's step beyond Rawls in saying this) and yet – problematically from the point of view of democratic inclusion – official constitutional debate and decision-making must be conducted within the terms of 'neutral' discourse. The latter is notably an emotion-free discourse, following Kant's views about the moral law. For despite the contortions which Kant went through in relation to the role of feeling with respect to the ethical, this played for him either a negative role as the feeling of the emptily sublime ushering us into the presence of the moral law, or a subordinate role in terms of our 'feeling' that the moral should be harmonized with the sensorily pleasurable and the emotionally satisfying.[4]

---

[4] For my own understanding of Kant at this point see Milbank, 2003: 1–25.

It might be questioned, however, whether this adherence to a basic Kantian principle really does justice to the double novelty of the cultural situation in the twenty-first century of which Habermas is so acutely aware. Essentially there is nothing new about his Kantian proposal to sustain an agnostic neutrality in public discourse, free from metaphysical commitments of either a naturalistic or a spiritualistic kind. Such 'transcendentalist' neutrality was already often the norm (explicit or implicit) in the official assumptions of the preceding century. All that Habermas does, in effect, is to call defensively for the reiteration of a now threatened status quo. But this may be to underestimate the way in which the seemingly contradictory return of naturalism and religion at one and the same time puts both intellectual and sociological pressure upon the very possibility of a 'neutral' discursive space. In contrast to Habermas, the young French (and atheist) philosopher Quentin Meillassoux, whose work follows somewhat in the wake of that of Alain Badiou, has suggested two reasons for the current collapse of methodological agnosticism – reasons which it would be hard critically to surmount (Meillassoux, 2009).

The first reason is intellectual: the terms of 'transcendentalist' neutrality have been deconstructed within both Analytic and Continental philosophy, and therefore 'post-metaphysical' philosophy is collapsing – ironically because it has been exposed as the very consummation of the metaphysical as a supposedly autonomous and non-theological discourse about being. This is because the quest for certainty about being must inevitably collapse into the quest for certainty about knowledge and therefore a methodologically secular metaphysics mutates into a foundational epistemology. The latter relies upon showing how there is a proper fit between our minds, when critically regulated, and reality as it appears to our understanding. Yet it no longer seems plausible that there is a 'correlation' between the way our minds work and objectively given appearances. Instead, philosophy (again both Analytic and Continental) is proposing full-blooded accounts of nature which incorporate (with various degrees of reduction) an account of the human mind. Kantian anthropocentrism and finitism now appear to be unscientific and indeed to revert to the pre-Copernican. Conversely (one might add to Meillassoux), if one wishes to defend the spiritual character of mind, it is not possible to appeal to some supposedly 'given' transcendental circumstances; one would need instead a speculatively metaphysical account of the reality of mind and soul.

Hence if naturalism and religion are squeezing out the agnostic middle, this is not because the bounds of reason are being transgressed; it is rather because reason (with good reasons) no longer tends to credit such bounds, since if there is no demonstrable 'correlation' between intellectual category and phenomenal content, it is no longer possible to set the Kantian critical test of 'schematization' in order to distinguish between those concepts which do and those which do not violate our finitude.

Reason is being once more infinitized – but this occurs from two opposite directions: by either a naturalistic or a spiritualist metaphysics. In either case it is argued that a claim for limits is paradoxically self-refuting, as one must exceed a limit in order to know that it is absolute. In the naturalist case it is further suggested that our post-Cantorian ability to think the mathematically infinite suggests also an ability to think the natural infinite, if it is true that mathematics is the language of nature. In the spiritualist case it is suggested that since limits cannot be shown we must assume that a God-given soul can aspire somewhat outside their bounds. This does not at all mean, however, that such bold speculative programmes can be exhaustively justified from a rational point of view. To the contrary, their best practitioners admit that a certain stance of 'faith' is involved in their pursuit.

The second reason is sociological. Speculative metaphysics is not a leisurely pastime – rather, it is directly linked to people's pragmatic need to direct their life by certain definite beliefs about reality. Metaphysically agnostic philosophy, one can argue, has allowed religious extremism to fill a certain void. It fulfils a hunger that is as much one for a meaningfulness of reality as for an emotional and expressive dwelling within reality. Moreover, simply formal discursive conditions for politics and formal respect for rights does not deal with the fact that certain substantive choices and views have necessarily to prevail. Hence if one restricts reason to the formal and insists that it operates only within knowable boundaries, one will encourage entirely irrational and purely emotive political movements to take centre stage by exploiting procedurally rational norms against the intentions of those who set up those norms in the first place. This is what the Nazis did; Weimar was thoroughly 'Kantian' and Habermas repeats the error of Weimar even though he imagines that his philosophy guards against any repetition of totalitarianism. For the culture of Weimar was notoriously characterized by a drift of negative freedom towards decadence and nihilism. Nazism at once esoterically perpetuated this drift and exoterically put an end to it.

The sharp separation of reason and faith is dangerous for a politics that is 'liberal' in the sense of constitutional. It implies that faith at its core is 'non-rational' and beyond the reach of any sort of argument, while also implying that reason cannot really have a say on issues of crucial substantive preference. But in reality reason and faith are always intertwined in a beneficial way, even if this is hard to formulate theoretically. Reason has to make certain assumptions and has to trust in the reasonableness of the real – as indeed Kant himself acknowledged. Faith has continuously to think through the coherence of its own intuitions in a process that often modifies those intuitions themselves. So if critical faith has to become a more reflective mode of feeling, then reason has always to some degree to feel its ways forward. What reason at first seeks to know, it already knows obscurely, as Plato taught in the *Meno* – which is to say that it feels it: Plato says through the reach of *eros*.

The mediating role of feeling gives the lie to the Habermasian idea that one requires a content-neutral formal framework in order that arguments between apparently incommensurable positions may take place. For all arguments short of tautology have to assume an area of given agreement in a merely ad hoc fashion, and to win an argument usually means (following Socrates) that one shows someone that something he imagines he thinks contradicts something which he thinks more habitually and fundamentally. Outside a horizon of shared faith no arguments would get off the ground and shared faith means something like 'common feeling'.

From Kant to Hume: the alternative mediation of feeling

The Kantian agnostic notion of public space is feeling-neutral, yet this is not the only 'enlightened' model to hand. Both the Scottish and the Italian Enlightenment saw the public sphere as primarily one of 'sympathy' (Bruni and Zamagni, 2007: 77–122). Often this just meant imaginative projection or animal instinct and this predominantly Stoic perspective tended to neglect questions of teleology or of shared 'ends' and shared attitudes as to substantive human goods. Such a pluralism of emotion would seem to suggest that the play of sympathy still requires a formal regulation, or else publicly relevant sympathy must be restricted to a utilitarian concern for the maximization of sensory pleasure and the diminution of sensory pain. For this reason the lingering Roman cast of much eighteenth-century ethical thought inevitably drifted towards subjective rights in one direction and towards utilitarianism in the other. But where this is the case then 'the feeling of sympathy' provides no real alternative to formalist neutrality save in terms of a crudely materialist reduction that would simply deny the pertinence of all faith commitments, of whatever kind.

Here, though, one can argue that David Hume was (to some degree) an exception and that the centrality of sympathy in his thought is somewhat guarded against a displacement in primacy by subjective right and egoistic happiness. The key to this difference is a certain marrying of sympathy with teleology. For in the case of Hume, in the long-term wake of Benjamin Whichcote through the Earl of Shaftesbury, 'sympathy' at times seems to be a self-grounding end in itself and the sympathetic links between people to be something that reason itself cannot really grasp. While we are to 'sympathize' with public 'utility', the 'public' is itself only composed through the reciprocal bonds of sympathy, which are irreducible to any mere 'original instincts of the human mind', or, in other words, any projected egoism (Hume, 1978: III.III.vi, 619; 618–21). Hence Hume's human 'sympathy' remains (extraordinarily enough) a kind of 'occult' sympathy, in continuity with the inscrutable binding powers within nature: 'the coherence and apparent sympathy in all the parts of this world' (Hume, 1948: XII, 86; VI, 42). (By historical derivation 'sympathy' in Platonic, Stoic and Hermetic thought meant the secret power that binds together the cosmos, the body and human society.)[5]

One can link this with the entire nature of Hume's philosophy and suggest that our current situation is 'Humean' and not Kantian, both in intellectual and sociological terms. But in order to make this claim, and fully to show how sympathy as irreducible goal is consonant with Hume's entire philosophy, one must briefly sketch out a revisionist account of the nature of this philosophy, which rescues it from the usual empiricist, egocentric and materialistic construals.

---

[5] The idea of 'cosmic sympathy' associated with the notion of a universal 'world-fire' is thought by many commentators to have originated with the Stoic philosopher Posidonius of Rhodes. For a summary of the influence of the notion up to medieval times, see Magdalino and Mavroudi, 2008: ch. 2.

Intellectually speaking, Hume, unlike Kant, attempted a full-blooded 'experimentalist' approach to human nature and the human mind. This meant that he was prepared to account for human thinking in terms of pre-human natural processes. At the same time, he was prepared to think nominalism, with which much of modern science had long been linked, through to its very limits.

It might be thought that Hume's naturalism is in natural harmony with his nominalism. However, this turns out not to be the case, for in order to explain human nature scientifically he must do so in terms of 'atomic' individual substances and efficient causality. Yet Hume shows that nominalism is as fatal for individual substance and efficient causality as it is for universals, for genus, species and real relation as it is for formal, teleological and material cause. In this way he turns Ockham's minimizing rationalist instrument against Aristotle, against even Ockham's legacy itself. Hence he says that there are, rationally speaking, only bundles of qualities and no 'substance', and that any inherent 'link' between cause and effect is just as occult and merely nominal as scholastic ideas of specific form which had frequently been derided as obscurely tautologous (a tree is a tree because it has the form of a tree, etc.) ever since the seventeenth century.

Given this circumstance, Hume has been read in three different ways: (1) as a positivist, who reduces science to observation of constant conjuncture; (2) as someone implicitly calling for a Kantian transcendentalist solution; (3) as someone so ultra-modern that he indicates a new 'nocturnal', proto-Romantic entry to a traditional realist metaphysics. For this third and highly revisionary perspective it is as if he knocked over all the furniture inside the Western intellectual house and then exited into the sunlight through a front door marked 'reason' with a triumphantly complacent sceptical smirk on his face, but then, when no one was looking, sneaked round to the back where the garden lay in shadows, and was conducted by a Jacobite servant through a back door marked 'feeling' and then proceeded to put back in place at least some of the furniture he had earlier abused.[6] In fact, on this view,

---

[6] We know that when he was in France Hume was regarded as a crypto-Jacobite and even occasionally crypto-papist opponent of Voltaire's 'Whiggish' view of English history in favour of a defence of the Catholic deep past (including Thomas More) and the Stuart recent past; that Catholic apologists sometimes returned the compliment of Hume's covert deployment of the Catholic sceptics; and finally that Hume's political thought continued to inspire the thought of the

Hume rescues modern scientific rationality only through linking it once more (albeit obscurely) to a traditional metaphysic by ascribing a new disclosive role to 'feeling'.

The first two views assume that Hume was only a sceptical rationalist. The third claims that he advanced beyond scepticism in the name of feeling and the view that feeling, not reason (reason being but a variant of feeling) is what *truly* discloses to us the real. We require politically this irreducibility of feeling if we are not once more to surrender to either a formalism of reason or a reductionism of the senses – neither of which will be hospitable to the presence of religious or even substantively ideal reasonings within the public realm.

Any truly attentive reading of Hume suggests strongly that the third reading is the correct one.[7] The positivist reading is false because Hume is clear that even constant conjuncture is something ineffably felt and established according to habitual imagination and not something rationally known. This mode of empirical connection is for him in the end extra-rational. It is 'felt' and not merely 'imagined', precisely because the imagination performs a mysterious work in excess of rational probability by assuming that an absolutely novel instance will fall into the same 'historical' sequence of cause and effect as instances have been taken to so fall in the past: thus we 'feel' the link of cause and effect and do not merely 'speculate' that what is constantly conjoined might be in some way connected.[8]

---

traditionalists in France up to and beyond the French Revolution. This all casts serious doubt on MacIntyre's ascription to Hume of an 'Anglicising subversion'. See Bongie, 1965 and MacIntyre, 1988: 281–99. MacIntyre's reading of Hume is accurately criticized by Donald W. Livingston: see subsequent note. It may well be that Hume is in a certain fashion *nearer* to Aristotle than is Francis Hutcheson, whereas MacIntyre has this the other way round.

[7] A variant of such a reading (which I can do little more than roughly sketch in this chapter) is upheld by the greatest living Hume scholar, Donald W. Livingston, who has made the sadly rare attempt to read all of Hume's works (including the historical ones) together in the round. In his two crucial studies of the Scottish philosopher, Livingston validly compares him to Vico, in so far as both thinkers point out, and draw back from, the existential and political consequences of living according to pure reason and suggest that, by contrast, the emotions and the imagination may have an irreducible role in the discerning of truth. See Livingston, 1984 and 1998.

[8] This is why feeling tends to be always blended with the imagination in Hume. See Hume, 1978: I.I.v, 12–13: 'cohesion' amongst ideas is 'a kind of ATTRACTION, which in the mental world will be found to have as extraordinary effects as in the natural'.

It is of course this sense of a 'connection' that Kant elaborated into a rationale a priori, and yet the Kantian rendering of Hume is also false because there is simply no warrant to suppose that the biases of our mind are anything other than natural, or that the phenomena we know are not the things themselves – as they explicitly are for Hume. 'Correlationism' in Kant between rational category and sensory information remains a mode of pre-established harmony, and the unsophisticated core of Kant's (astonishing) surface sophistication is that it is only his own variant on a speculative monadology that contradictorily permits the 'banishing' of speculation (Milbank, 1997: 7–35). This is because one requires the idea of a noumenal (monadically spiritual) realm in order firstly to be able to declare that phenomena do not disclose noumena ('things in themselves') and secondly to be able to suppose that the human spirit, as noumenally self-determining beyond the sphere of natural causality, can stand outside and so perceive the 'bounds' of the phenomenal and the categories supposed to apply only to the phenomenal.

Hume, by contrast, never denies the full ontological ('noumenal' as well as 'phenomenal') reality of causation, substance, personal identity or the soul:[9] he doubts them all, but in the end finds a new way to affirm them. In a Baconian tradition he sees knowledge as to do with experience and making, but insists (in a Socratic-Platonic lineage, as he indicates) that what we most experience and make is ourselves.[10] Even though he takes it that we are but part of a chain of natural causation,[11] he says that the best clue to the nature of the latter lies within our own self-experience. But within ourselves the experience of our own consecutive causal action is a matter of feeling, habit and

[9] I disagree with Edward Caird that Hume's prime target is the *imago dei* in human beings. Caird bases this claim on the view that Hume attacks deductive reasoning as linked to notions of direct spiritual insight and the notion of reason as a divine spark. It is true that Hume adopts the model of Baconian inductive reason, but he also subverts it by (a) saying that the empirical knowledge of other things depends upon 'Socratic' self-knowledge and (b) saying that our self-experience is of fathomless processes. Moreover, in the *Dialogues Concerning Natural Religion* Hume is prepared equivalently to reconceptualize *God*, following Plotinus, as supra-intellectual. See note 11 below and Caird, 1987: 69–130.

[10] Hume sees his relationship to Bacon as like that of Socrates to Thales: Hume, 1978: Introduction, xvi–xvii.

[11] Hume, 1978: I.IV.v, 248: 'motion ... is the cause of thought and perception'.

imagination. One might say that 'we are led according to a consistent pattern to make ourselves up'.

In one place in the *Treatise* Hume indicates quite clearly that we have to assume that causality in nature is something analogous to this human process:

> I do not ascribe to the will that unintelligible necessity which is suppos'd to lie in matter. But I ascribe to matter, that intelligible quality, call it necessity or not, which the most rigorous orthodoxy must or does allow to belong to the will. I change nothing, therefore, in the receiv'd systems with regard to the will, but only with regard to material objects. (Hume, 1978: II.III.ii, 410)

In other words, Hume insists in an 'intellectualist' manner that the will never exercises pure 'free choice' but is always in some fashion 'compelled'. Yet this cannot mean that he reduces the will to determination by efficient causality, because he has already deconstructed the latter. So even though he is arguing for a naturalistic account of willing, it is still in terms of our experience of willing that we must try to decipher causality and not vice versa. Therefore he is a revisionist *not* with respect to orthodox psychology, but with respect to the philosophy of nature: in nature herself there must reside something analogous to 'will'. It follows that the primacy of feeling in Hume entails also a species of vitalism, as the *Dialogues Concerning Natural Religion* in several places indicate.[12]

This therefore reverses not only his scepticism as regards causation but also as regards constitutive relation. Reason can only make sense of individual items that are shifting and unstable but utterly isolated, and in no way intrinsically connected with anything else. The same must be true, rationally speaking, of our 'impressions'; yet we 'feel' certain unshakeable links between them in various ways. The feeling of association that sustains the link between cause and effect in our experience of thoughts then leads to a legitimate projection of intrinsic association also into the world of things, since we are otherwise unable to make sense of our experience of causality and the way in which its

---

[12] Hume, 1948: VI, 42. Hume's alter ego Philo (as he surely is, by and large – and note the Platonic name!) is happy to entertain the notion that the world is like 'an animal or organized body' and seems 'actuated with a like principle of life and motion' which is a kind of world-soul.

constantly conjoined elements seem to involve an emotive coinherence that is in excess of rational constant conjuncture, as already explained (Habermas, 2008). Hence while the denial of internal relation lies at the heart of Hume's thought in so far as it is a merely rational empiricism, a certain 'internal' (or better, 'constitutive') relation returns within his thought in so far as it is an extra-sceptical empiricism of feeling that even points us back towards a metaphysical realism in the broad sense of affirming a structure to objective reality that is independent of our perceptions of that reality.[13] Significant in this respect is the fact that Hume declares that the crucial difference between mere fictions, apparitions, dreams and reality is nothing other than the strength of feeling we have in the face of the real, despite the fact that every experience of the real is only conveyed by a series of impressions that we *imaginatively* put together.[14] It is as if Hume is saying that reality is simply a very convincing and continuous story that frames all the other stories because we feel it does with an unshakeable degree of intensity. A story that we have to take to be true, like Vico's *vera narratio*.[15]

Hume, then, is saying that all thought is feeling (and reason is tempered feeling); that we must trust at least some of our most constant feelings and that there may be something 'like' feeling already in pre-human nature. (This concurs with the fact that he affirms and does not at all deny 'design' in nature, while seeing this as far more immanent than did the Paleyite approach: Hume, 1948: VI–VIII, 42–56; XII, 94.) Clearly Hume parted company with rationalism by empirically observing that reflection cannot seriously break with habit and that even the most basic assumed stabilities (substance, the self, causation) depend upon habit and not upon sheer intuited 'givenness'. But

---

[13] I prefer the term 'constitutive' to the term 'internal' relation, because the former implies a relation that enters into the very substance of a thing (and is not therefore merely accidental and 'external') without implying that its *relata* can be logically deduced from the nature of the thing after the fashion of idealism. For if there is *no* element of external contingency in a relation then all relations are in the end internal to the one monad of all reality and relationality is after all abolished.

[14] Hume, 1978: Appendix, 623–9; 'An idea assented to *feels* different from a fictitious idea, that the fancy alone presents to us' (629); I.III.viii, 98–106; I.IV. ii, 193–218.

[15] Indeed Hume's historicism is more thoroughgoing than Hegel's or Marx's because he denies that there is any reality beneath established habitual fiction – whether composed by nature or by humanity. In terms of human history there can therefore be no social order outside a continued allegiance to such fictions.

he also began to break with empiricism by allowing (albeit in a highly reserved fashion) that, in being slaves to habit, human beings must acknowledge the workings of a natural power constituted through time that *exceeds* our capacity to observe it.[16]

Within the terms of this genuinely Humean perspective (properly developed in terms of a Jacobian-Biranian hybrid) one can see how 'feeling' operates as the crucial third term in two respects. First, between matter in motion and mind that experiences 'meanings'. It is not that mind 'represents' an external world; it is rather that natural habits in us turn reflective, more intense and more adaptable. In a footnote on the second page of the *Treatise*, Hume actually *rejects* Lockean 'ideas' and his favoured term 'impression' for patterned or structured cognitive content is initially agnostic about the origins of these impressions.[17] They are *not* sense impressions nor representations, even though they are assumed to be of sensory origin: they are rather more like 'phenomena' in Husserl's sense though without his subjectivism, since they are not sharply distinguished from external 'objects'. (Indeed it was the influence of Hume which allowed Husserl to break with neo-Kantianism.)

In this context, Jerry Fodor's neo-positivist use of Hume to support a 'representationalism' of the brain is completely erroneous and shamelessly deploys only the first part of the *Treatise* (Fodor, 2003). For Hume is *not* a sceptic about metaphysics and a dogmatician about morals. Instead he is a sceptic concerning reason in both domains, but a trusting affirmer of feeling and 'sympathy' in both domains also. Sympathy retains for him both Stoic and Platonic connotations and we fail to note that he was a self-declared 'academic sceptic' like Cicero – this means a sceptic *of the Platonic school*. A kind of incredibly apophatic Platonist, one might almost say.[18] Hence

---

[16] Clare Carlisle and Mark Sinclair well describe this sequence regarding habit that passes from Cartesian rationalist scepticism through empiricist scepticism to conclude in affirmed vitalism. However, they fail to allow that the inklings of the third 'ontological' move are already there in Hume. See their 'Editors' Introduction' to Ravaisson, 2008: 7, and also their 'Editors' Commentary', 111–12.

[17] Hume, 1978: I.I.i, 2 n. 1; I.III.x, 106. Edward Caird rightly insists on this point. See Caird, 1987, 69–130.

[18] Besides Hume's citing of Plotinus in the *Dialogues*, his use of the Platonic-Ciceronian dialogue form and his speaking through the mouth of 'Philo', one can cite his approving mention of the Origenist, Platonist,

in his account of philosophies which is clearly *in order of merit*, Hume put scepticism at the top followed by Platonism and then Stoicism, with Epicureanism at the bottom.[19] Like Vico and Doria in Naples, he incorporates elements of Hobbes and so of Epicurus, but finally rejects this mode of materialism as 'uncivil' – as too linked with a selfish individualism.[20]

This academic scepticism has its political equivalent in his 'speculative Toryism' and support for the ancient if not the modern House of Stuart. Hume thought that human society only exists through the ability of monarchic or aristocratic families to combine particular with general sympathy – otherwise the range of human sympathy is too restricted to accommodate justice (Hume, 1978: III.II.vii–x, 534–67). Hence Hume, unlike Locke, Rousseau or Kant, considers that the core of political society is a matter of substantive feeling – no mere formality could ever at bottom move human beings to collective action. It follows that a Humean response to Habermas would include the point that political order depends always less on any formal procedure than on a 'political class' however constituted or to whatever degree dispersed – that is, a class of people able to link their personal destinies with the destiny of the whole of their society: local, national or global.

For Hume's rejection of contract theory entails the view that any merely procedural set of norms, such as Habermas's protocols of free communication and tacit aiming towards publicly recognizable truth, provides no basis on which the necessary content of such communication and truth-proposing can arise. Equally, it provides no guarantee that human beings, normally bound within local circles of prejudice, will in fact embrace such protocols. To mend these lacunae, from a Humean perspective, one must invoke sympathy twice over. Firstly, a shared sympathetic horizon must arise, whose substantive content will

Freemason and Catholic convert, his fellow Scot the Chevalier Andrew Michael Ramsey in a footnote to *The Natural History of Religion*. See Hume, 1948 and 1993: 190–3 n. 1.

[19] Hume, 1987: XV, XVI, XVII, XVIII, 'The Epicurean', 'The Stoic', 'The Platonist', 'The Sceptic', 138–80.

[20] Although he breaks important new ground in his systematic comparison of the Edinburgh and Neapolitan Enlightenments, and specifically of Hume and Vico, John Robertson wrongly assimilates Vico to Hume's supposedly more explicit Epicureanism, instead of assimilating Hume to Vico's clearly more explicit Platonism. See Robertson, 2005.

alone provide an adequate framework of binding social norms, even though it cannot be established through the formal rules of communicative action. Secondly, such a horizon can only merge if a group of people (however small or large) are able imaginatively to extend their immediate sympathies towards a much larger social group.

In this way Hume – in a no doubt over-Stoicized fashion – still retains an antique and 'aristocratic' virtue perspective upon the political which Kant abandons.

Feeling is in the second place a middle term between reason and faith. Hume the defender of church establishment took it that the unity of interest between monarch and people has to have sacred sanction if people are really to feel its force.[21] Likewise, in his ethics the comparison of promise as fiction to transubstantiation as fiction (he actually says that the latter is a *more* rational notion as less 'warped' by the exigencies of perpetual public interest) is not meant merely sceptically (Hume, 1978: III.II.v, 524–5). Rather, by carrying the sceptical critique of religion in a proto-Nietzschean fashion through also to ethics and to aspects of our belief in cause and substantial unity, Hume is at once chastening all our all-too-human assumptions and yet at the same time indicating how religion as 'natural' is in continuity with the rest of human natural and cultural existence. It secures our sense of the diversity, unity, order and mystery of life in terms of the polytheistic, the monotheistic, the extra-humanly designed and the apophatic – all of which aspects of religiosity Hume explicitly affirms.[22]

Feeling against fanaticism

It follows from the above that the Humean view that what binds us together is shared sympathy cannot possibly make any easy discriminations (à la Habermas) between what belongs to the realm of reason and what belongs to the realm of faith. For just as, in some sense, political society at its core must always be monarchic/aristocratic, so, also, religion must always be established: in Europe we disallow

---

[21] Hume, 1987: VII, VIII and XI: 'Whether the British Government inclines more to Absolute Monarchy or to a Republic', 'Of Parties in general' and 'Of the Parties of Great Britain', 47–72.

[22] Hume, 1993: *passim*. Religion, for Hume, secures our sense of the diversity, unity, order and mystery of life in terms of the polytheistic, the monotheistic, the extra-humanly designed and the apophatic.

public bloody sacrifice and we tend to ban Scientological offers of high-cost chemical salvation not simply because we are 'enlightened', but because at bottom our mode of 'enlightenment' still retains a Christian colouring.

If the risk then seems to appear that fanaticism could win through the democratic process if the latter is not 'transcendentally' bound to the formal use of reason, then one needs to reflect further. Firstly, how could one ever legislate for this without in reality suppressing freedom of speech, and forever excluding those perfectly rational voices who do not accept the Kantian terms of settlement? Although Habermas talks in the voice of dry reason, he actually puts forward the outrageously provincial view that the basis for global human association forthwith must be universal acceptance of the Kantian critique of metaphysics! Quite apart from the intuitively unjust character of this proposal, how does it make pragmatic sense of the fact that Habermas can enjoy a respectful conversation with Joseph Ratzinger, even though the latter (unrepentedly wedded to a pre-Kantian metaphysical synthesis of faith and reason) does not accept the only basis upon which, according to Habermas, they can be having a proper conversation!

Secondly, and more crucially, I have already pointed out how formalism gives substantive claims the licence to be unreasonable and unaccountable, precisely because something substantial *always* rules in the end. In this way Habermas encourages rather than guards against a dangerous positivity. Faith placed behind an impassable sublime barrier is encouraged to be dangerous faith – as much to be fanaticism as to be a Wittgensteinian fideism or an Iris Murdoch-style agnosticism, and for just the same reason, which is that its claims have been declared to be utterly ineffable from the point of view of public, philosophical reason.

Habermas indeed allows that religious claims can be 'translated' into public terms, but few religious people will accept the adequacy of such translation, since it leaves the rational aspect of specifically religious content redundant and suggests that faith makes no difference at all to the shape of genuine human action. (It is of course no accident that one exception here might be certain currents of German Lutheranism which reduce the religious sense to an inner feeling of assurance of extrinsic justification.) However, if religious people are not encouraged to explicate their own specific faith-based logic in the public domain, then their sense that their faith makes 'all the difference' may take on a virulently fideistic and fundamentalist form.

Moreover, if 'translation' means merely into the terms of the norms governing fair communicative discourse, this translation must always mean the loss of substantive 'ethical' content as well as of religiosity. And it remains patronizing to both religious *and* secular people to say that the only humanly 'shareable' aspect of religious truths must be a non-religious one – as if, for example, an agnostic could have *no sense whatsoever* of the specific mode of solidarity generated by the eucharist and the idea of 'the body of Christ'. It is simply not the case that people of other faiths or of none can only embrace the insights of, say, Judaism in a purely non-religious guise. This disallows the fact that they might well allow certain intimations of transcendence to be involved in their act of partial appropriation.

For to define reason quite apart from faith is to place it also quite apart from feeling, since it can be convincingly argued after Hume that reason, as much as faith, arises only as a specific variant upon the experience of feeling which is always to do with reciprocal recognition of an 'other'. If this is the case, then reason partakes of the obscurity as well as the clarity that is always involved in any experience of emotion. The latter presents itself as a horizon to be explored and as something which has to be reflexively sifted in terms of how far it is to be trusted. Reason cannot therefore escape being situated within a prospective horizon nor be exempted from the requirements of trust and risk that require a certain exercise of faith, as Jacobi argued. Because discursiveness is always inextricably bound up with emotions and is not austerely trapped within a series of apprehensible procedural criteria (Habermas cleaves all too closely to Weber here) there can be *partial* degrees of assent as to religious perspectives: for example, in terms of the feeling that 'the good' is rather more than a mere human fiction. Many people both feel and articulate a sense inherited from both Platonic and biblical tradition that 'goodness' is a reality not reducible to the natural and yet not simply another 'thing' in the way that a stone or a building is a thing. At the same time they draw back (inconsistently or otherwise) from the full affirmation of a transcendent or supernatural realm.

Of course the kind of Humean perspective which I am suggesting nonetheless *can* favour naturalism as much as it can favour religion. The habituated and the vital might be sheerly immanent, somehow not requiring grace. This means that, if transcendentalism is both false and dangerous, we must now accept that the public space is one of a clash of rival metaphysics and not one of polite agnostic neutrality and humanism undergirded by transcendental philosophy. We live now in the era of Dawkins versus Ratzinger, not of agnostics and clerics equally savouring the novels of Iris Murdoch, nor of a continued Teutonic compromise (ever since Kant and Hegel) between the legacy of the French Revolution and the spirit of Christianity.

However, this does not condemn us to a future of unmediated violence, and I have already offered arguments as to why the return of metaphysics can temper violence on the side of religion, since it requires the worldviews of faith also to express themselves as worldviews of reason – a possibility that Habermas *dangerously* disallows. But the reason for optimism is also because the shared horizon of feeling with its inherent fluidity permits of many substantive shared outlooks and actually fosters *less* conflict than a situation where we will endlessly debate (as in the history of the United States) whether formal barriers between faith and reason have been transgressed or not.[23] In the face of the arrival in the West of Islam we now see far more clearly how our shared modern Western ethos is both an extension of a Christian ethos besides being a radical departure from it. The horror of Muslim critics of the West is often a horror at both these aspects. Thus we cannot have a genuine debate with Islam unless we allow the porosity of faith and reason and try to assess the ways in which Islamic faith and reason both is and is not compatible with Western faith and reason or ways in which it might become more so.

The elevation of the natural

To these sociological considerations one can add psychological ones. Here also I would argue that Habermas's strictures on both naturalism and metaphysics are somewhat misplaced and that both can offer a better barrier against terror than the humanistic critical philosophy which he persists in promoting.

---

[23] Just as, for Hume, human beings as creatures of feeling do not really know quite how atheistic or theistic they are, so also they never really know how far they are in the domain of esoteric faith and how far in that of exoteric reason.

In certain ways (going completely counter to Habermas and his Munich Jesuit interlocutors) naturalism is less problematic for religion than is transcendentalism. For the a priori categories of understanding can in principle be themselves psychologized with the advance of brain science – especially if they have been *already* pragmatized, as by Rawls or Habermas.[24] The norms of communicative action can thereby be reduced to evolutionary purposiveness. All that would then hold out against such reduction is the issue of freedom: the freedom of human discourse to construct the language that denies even the force of the evidence that the human person is pre-determined; the freedom of the 'last experimenter' upon the human brain whose own decision to experiment can never be neurologically explained without an infinite series of experiments being carried out. These arguments defending freedom are valid, but all they defend is a freedom to experiment or a bare freedom to refuse the force of the evidence (the freedom of the crank which nonetheless oddly auto-validates his crankiness) without any practical upshot that would incarnate freedom itself as something that makes a real difference in the 'real' realm of matter in motion.

Therefore no truly substantive freedom, linked to the reality of a wide range of human emotional and ethical categories, is here established. This is because rationalism, of which transcendentalism is a mode, is unable to attribute any teleology to the will other than bare self-assertion. No choosing, outside the range of formal reason, can be defined by that reason as anything other than mere subjective predilection. Thus in relation to neural science all it can do is indicate a bare and contentless transcendence of the brain by a supposed human mind.

As to both formal and instrumental reasons themselves, precisely because they can be publicly and exhaustively expressed in linguistic structures, they are somewhat subject to a reductionist view as regards consciousness because we could imagine all instrumental and cooperative uses of reason as taking place unconsciously. It is at this point that the quasi-transcendental status of governing pragmatic norms (like Habermas's rules for a perfect speech community, or Rawls's

---

[24] On the relationship between transcendentalism and pragmatism in both Habermas and Karl-Otto Apel, see Ferry, 1994. For a scintillating account of the way in which John Rawls's pragmatizing of Kant's transcendentalism creates fatal problems for his account of justice, see Sandel, 1982: 15–65.

'neutral' principles of justice derived from the supposition of the 'veil of ignorance') slide back towards mere empirical generalization, in such a way that they no longer protect the dignity of human freedom as such and become instead mere utilitarian accounts of how to coordinate the clash of inevitably differing animal perspectives. Hence within the bounds of mere rationalism one can propose, with more or less plausibility, that consciousness is mere epiphenomenon or even, in some sense, illusion.

If the quasi-spiritualism of the transcendental approach is subject to such reduction, then conversely it is possible for naturalism to undergo a perfectly coherent elevation.

For if we acknowledge 'feelings' in Hume's sense as always accompanying 'impressions' and supplying them with their relative weight and significance, then we do not have any 'bare consciousness' with which one could possibly dispense – in the way that a camera does not need to be conscious in order to take a picture. When emotion is brought into consideration then consciousness is always rather a 'modification of consciousness' in such a way that its qualia belong to a 'language' (external as well as internal) that is entirely incommensurable with the discourse of firing neurons. Even the bare experience of consciousness is thus incommensurable,[25] but in the case of feelings one has more than an irreducible spectator, but rather an entirely irreducible realm of 'actors' who are emotionally inflected and active states of mind which find expression in the evaluative register of human discourse.

So far was Hume from pointing in the direction of the reduction of mind to brain that he actually says that purely physical explanations of feelings should *only* be invoked when these feelings are pathological (Hume, 1978: I.II.v, 60–1). This means that he sustained not only the soul, but also a certain teleology of the soul. Even though he could give no rational defence of subjective unity, his affirmation of this inexplicable unity in terms of feeling involves far more of a narrative and teleological register than the Cartesian or the Kantian model of self-awareness.[26] Indeed for Hume we make ourselves up as fictions, but since he denies the reality of any purely self-sustained

---

[25] As is rightly argued by Colin McGinn in McGinn, 1999.

[26] Hume: 1978: I.I.vi, 261: 'our identity with regard to the passions serves to corroborate that with regard to the imagination, by making our distant perceptions influence each other, and by giving us a present concern for our past or future pains or pleasures'. Hume has just – like Plato – compared

will, it follows that for him we are obscurely compelled within our very own fictioning towards certain ends, such that we are also 'made up' by forces not under our command. Nor is freedom here quite denied, because will is for Hume but a more intense manifestation of the adaptability of natural habit which at bottom he appears to see as a kind of spontaneity (Hume, 1978: II.III.i–iii, 399–418).

Feelings, for Hume, are in some sense and to a crucial degree trustworthy: we can distil true from false feeling through long processes of experience, comparison, interacting and rational analysis – which is yet itself for Hume but a further feeling about feeling, since he sees ideas as merely reflectively doubled impressions, intensifying their crucially accompanying emotions (Hume, 1978: I.I.i, 1–7). And as trustworthy, we can say, they are therefore not reducible to brain-processes. But this does not mean that they are 'yet more interior' than the brain itself. To the contrary, since feelings are for Hume prior to identity – identity being a kind of patterning of feelings – they at first impinge from 'without', or rather they impinge as our insertion within the very stream of passing reality.

In this way Hume concurs in advance with the views of modern philosophers who claim that we think with our bodies and even our whole natural and social environment rather than with our brains alone (Clark, 2008; Noë, 2009; Tye, 2009). For to imagine, with Fodor, that we think only with our brains is to remain the victim of the Lockean 'mirror of nature'. It is to think of the brain as a repository of representing ideas or 'evidences' of things, just as Locke thought of the mind as 'taking pictures' of things rather in the way that the eye reflects visible realities. This is oddly to 'anthropomorphize' the brain, which is only a physical organ! All the brain does is encode signals from the senses and the body in neurological connections. Hence the reason why researchers discover that there is never any perfectly predictable one-to-one correlation between thoughts and observably firing neurons and that the networks of neurons seem spontaneously to reorder themselves in parallel to thoughts is that what goes on in the brain is

the human psyche to a 'republic' containing several members who are synchronically speaking *hierarchically* arranged in 'reciprocal ties' and diachronically speaking connected by sequences of cause and effect. The self is thus both a drama and a narrative and its only substantial identity lies in this continuity, not, as for Locke, in any 'punctuality'. And see again Livingston, 1984: 91–111.

not the only, nor even the prime material instantiation of thinking. For
if thoughts as feelings and reflected feelings are in any sense real, the
brain can only be the *occasion* for the arising of these things, which
we should more properly say are caused by our entire insertion in
our environment and our active reception of this environment – just
as every physical reality constitutes a 'prehensive' active reception of
its temporal antecedents and spatial surroundings (Whitehead, 1978:
19–20). Because neither the brain nor the mind primarily 'mirrors', we
can see how the crucial aspect of thought is to do with 'feeling' other
realities in such a way that one is both responding to them and assert-
ing oneself in relation to them   in terms of a rather more ecstatically
inflected version of Spinoza's *Conatus*. Thought is reciprocal – it estab-
lishes a real relation, precisely because it is a species of feeling.

And far from this being an 'irrational' conclusion, it is in fact what
alone saves metaphysical realism and a realist basis for science. For
in terms of pure reason it is impossible, as Hume saw, to understand
why there are regular links within nature, and hence one will tend to
become sceptical about their reality. Moreover, the reduction of the
mind to brain-processes must invite scepticism as to whether the brain
truly mirrors anything objective and scepticism as to the very existence
of reason itself or the rationality of reality, once reason has been so
denatured that one no longer considers it to be a spiritual category.

It is perfectly possible and indeed more logical for naturalism to
entertain the view that we do not think merely with our brains but
also with our bodies and with our environment. However, if consciousness somehow 'reaches out to things' in this rather Aristotelian way,
then does one not have to speak of some sort of 'spiritual exchange'
between action and response taking place, however rooted this may be
in materiality? Is not me thinking the tree as the tree where the tree is,
also me being really moved by the tree in an ontological dimension of
emotion in which the tree is situated alongside myself? Would not this
be the precondition of the idea that meaning is 'out there' in things as
John McDowell has suggested (McDowell, 1994:108–26)?[27] Otherwise
one would have to espouse the 'direct realism' of the Franciscan Peter
John Olivi as revived by Thomas Reid: but as explicitly with Reid,

---

[27] McDowell refuses, however, to make the ontological moves which would
accommodate his insights about meaning in terms of allowing an ontology of
nature in excess of the conclusions of natural science.

this involves a vicious mode of correlationism that necessitates some sort of pre-established harmony. Actually Hume is curiously nearer to Aristotle, as Ravaisson eventually (in effect) realized: his 'feelings' which seem to migrate from things in order to shape 'selves' can, not implausibly, be seen to play in a more affective mode the rational role of Aristotelian species which is abstracted from the hylomorphic compound to become pure form within human cognition.[28]

This defence of the 'outwardness' of cognition and meaning in terms of the priority of feeling can also readily concur with the advocacy of panpsychism by various recent analytic philosophers (Skrbina, 2005: 249–69). If other things besides ourselves belong within the space of meaning, then, in order to avoid idealism, this will be because something already approximating to mutual feeling (without necessarily being fully conscious as we experience consciousness) exists within the physical world and is indeed its most primary ontological characteristic – responsible for shaping the sedimented habits that then constitute the regular shape of the universe, and with which human 'culture' is in essential continuity. This 'culture' *is* our nature, because the more variegated character of human habit is only possible through an equally heightened consistency of habit that is both the manifestation of, and the condition of possibility for, the exercise of 'free will'. Both the variety and the consistency are but an intensification of the very nature of habit that one can take to be the heart of the natural order.

In the light of these considerations one can see how the clash of naturalistic and religious visions is a clash that is amply capable of mediation.

For the fact is that *a certain Enlightenment* (and indeed the most sophisticated and crucial one; the one that engendered political economy) – however ultimately unsatisfactory it may be from a Christian perspective – was already concerned to restore that supra-political space which had been 'the church' under the new name of 'civil society'. And its goal of binding together in 'sympathy' was at least a distorted echo of the earlier binding together in charity (eschewing any merely

---

[28] 'Hylomorphic' alludes to the Aristotelian view that every terrestrial reality is composed of 'form' and 'matter', which as unformed is in itself a mysterious negativity. Aristotle also thought that in the process of knowledge the form appears in the space of comprehending mind as still the 'same' form, but now abstracted from matter. Hence this is generally known as a theory of 'knowledge by identity'.

unilateral gesture). Once one has grasped this double point one can then see that Habermas's alternative between the post-metaphysical and the metaphysical, and between the modern secular and the post-modern 'freely theocratic',[29] is not an exclusive one after all, even for genuinely modern times.

For the idea of a 'community of feeling', extended from society to nature and back to society, is both a Christian and a post-Christian one. Indeed it is our most crucial European legacy – that lies in essential continuity with the trajectory of Plato, Aristotle, Augustine and Aquinas, rather than the deviant paths of Scotus, Luther and Kant – which we must now both defend and elaborate. This is central if we are to revive genuinely post-metaphysical theo-political discourse.

References

Bongie, L. L. 1965. *David Hume: Prophet of the Counter-Revolution*. Oxford University Press.

Bruni, L. and Zamagni, S. 2007. *Civil Economy*. Oxford: Peter Lang.

Caird, E. 1987. *The Mind of God and the Works of Man*. Cambridge University Press.

Clark, A. 2008. *Supersizing the Mind*. Oxford University Press.

Ferry, J.-M. 1994. *Philosophie de la communication I*. Paris: Cerf.

Fodor, J. 2003. *Hume Variations*. Oxford University Press.

Habermas, J. 2008. *Between Naturalism and Religion: Philosophical Essays*, trans. Ciaran Cronin. Cambridge: Polity Press.

    2010a. 'An Awareness of What is Missing', in J. Habermas, N. Brieskorn, M. Reder, F. Ricken, and J. Schmidt, *An Awareness of What is Missing: Faith and Reason in a Post-Secular Age*, trans. C. Cronin. Cambridge: Polity Press, 15–23.

    2010b. 'A Reply', in Habermas *et al.*, 72–83.

Habermas, J., Brieskorn, N., Reder, M., Ricken, F. and Schmidt, J. 2010. *An Awareness of What is Missing: Faith and Reason in a Post-Secular Age*, trans. C. Cronin. Cambridge: Polity Press.

Habermas, J. and Ratzinger, J. 2006. *The Dialectics of Secularization: On Reason and Religion*. San Francisco: Ignatius Press.

---

[29] See Soloviev, 2008: 53–4. Soloviev explained that 'free theocracy' means that 'the Church as such does not interfere in governmental and economic matters, but provides for the government and district council [!] a higher purpose and absolute norm for their activities'.

Hoff, J. 2007. *Kontingenz, Berührung, Überschreitung: zur philosophischen Propädeutik christlicher Mystik nach Nikolaus von Kues*. Freiburg and Munich: Karl Alber.

Honnefelder, L. 2002. *La métaphysique comme science transcendentale*. Paris: Presses Universitaires de France.

Hume, D. 1948. *Dialogues Concerning Natural Religion*. New York: Hafner.

    1978. *A Treatise of Human Nature*. Oxford University Press.

    1987. *Essays Moral, Political and Literary*. Indianapolis: Liberty Fund.

    1993. *The Natural History of Religion*. Oxford University Press.

Livingston, D. W. 1984. *Hume's Philosophy of Common Life*. University of Chicago Press.

    1998. *Philosophical Melancholy and Delirium: Hume's Pathology of Philosophy*. University of Chicago Press.

McDowell, J. 1994. *Mind and World*. Cambridge, MA: Harvard University Press.

McGinn, C. 1999. *The Mysterious Flame: Conscious Minds in a Material World*. New York: Basic Books.

MacIntyre, A. 1988. *Whose Justice? Which Rationality?* London: Duckworth.

Magdalino, P. and Mavroudi, M. 2008. *The Occult Sciences in Byzantium*. London: La Pomme d'Or.

Meillassoux, Q. 2009. *After Finitude: An Essay on the Necessity of Contingency*, trans. Ray Brassier. London: Continuum.

Milbank, J. 1997. *The Word Made Strange*. Oxford: Blackwell.

    2003. *Being Reconciled: Ontology and Pardon*. London: Routledge.

Noë, A. 2009. *Out of our Heads*. New York: Hill and Wang.

Ravaisson, F. 2008. *Of Habit*, trans. C. Carlisle and M. Sinclair. London: Continuum.

Reder, M. 2010. 'How Far Can Faith and Reason be Distinguished? Remarks on Ethics and the Philosophy of Religion', in J. Habermas, N. Brieskorn, M. Reder, F. Ricken, and J. Schmidt, *An Awareness of What is Missing: Faith and Reason in a Post-Secular Age*, trans. C. Cronin. Cambridge: Polity Press, 36–50.

Robertson, J. 2005. *The Case for Enlightenment: Scotland and Naples 1680–1760*. Cambridge University Press.

Rowland, T. 2010. *Benedict XVI: A Guide for the Perplexed*. London: T&T Clark.

Sandel, M. 1982. *Liberalism and the Limits of Justice*. Cambridge University Press.

Schleiermacher, F. 1988. *On Religion: Speeches to its Cultured Despisers*, trans. Richard Crouter. Cambridge University Press.

Skrbina, D. 2005. *Panpsychism and the West*. Cambridge, MA: MIT Press.
Soloviev, V. 2008. *The Philosophical Principles of Integral Knowledge*, trans. Valeria Z. Nollan. Grand Rapids, MI: Eerdmans.
Tye, M. 2009. *Consciousness Revisited*. Cambridge, MA: MIT Press.
Whitehead, A. N. 1978. *Process and Reality*. New York: Free Press.

Arguing out of bounds: Christian eloquence and the end of Johannine liberalism

JOHN PERRY

In his contribution to this volume, Raymond Plant explores what justification liberalism can offer for itself to those who, in one way or another, have reasons not to affirm it. Putting the question even more pointedly, we might ask, can political liberalism justify itself to religious citizens for whom the claims of the state and the commands of God might be in tension? Whatever answers we might have offered in the past, Plant believes that the situation is increasingly problematic due, in part, to policies such as the Human Rights Act 1998 and the Equality Act 2010. He argues that these have replaced a vague 'ethos' of liberalism – one that can be fudged and glossed over in the face of tension – with quite explicit rules and principles that admit no fudging or glossing.

Under such a regime, the picture that emerges is one that resonates with what Leo Strauss called the theo-political problem: the Philosopher, the Jew and the Christian will sometimes find themselves subject to multiple loyalties that admit of no harmonization. For Strauss, this threat is best captured in the death of Socrates. The leaders of Athens thought that Socrates' teaching threatened the common good, but Socrates' loyalty was to the pursuit of truth. That was his calling and, whatever the consequences for the city, Socrates could do no other. In such cases, we can find ourselves cast in the unwelcome role of Antigone, caught between loyalty to her city and its ruler, on the one hand, and her brother and her gods, on the other. Although Strauss got to this conclusion as a philosopher indebted to Plato, and also as a Jew, the picture is also a deeply Christian one – or at least one with which Christians find much resonance. The theologian Oliver O'Donovan, himself indirectly influenced by Strauss, summarizes this well:

[Antigone] represents the 'dilemma' of which I speak: the Christian sense that the most authentic relation of truth to the public realm is that which issues in martyrdom. Christians, whose understanding of the world starts from the crucifixion of Jesus, have this much in common with Plato reflecting on the death of Socrates: they perceive the inevitability of tension between a transcendent moral truth and the good of any public order. (O'Donovan, 1984: 4)

For those who would seek to justify liberalism to religious believers, and Christians in particular, it is hard to imagine a less optimistic starting point. But it is a fitting one. The early modern world that gave birth to liberalism was filled with such stark dilemmas. It was a world in which whether one kneeled for communion, what catechism one's children received, what vestments the priest wore – all of these were, for some, matters of life and death, as grave as whether Antigone could bury her brother.

If this picture rightly describes liberalism's early modern origins then it follows that liberalism's goal was to create a world in which there would be no more Antigones. If one's political and theological views could be reinterpreted or reinvented *just so*, then all one's loyalties would be in harmony. In such a world, either it would be obvious to Creon that his law violated Antigone's freedom of conscience, or it would be obvious to Antigone that her conscience must defer to national security. But in any event, in this world there will be no tragic conflict.

This vision held secure for past centuries, but we now have reason to doubt whether it is quite the neat-and-easy solution that the early liberals claimed. What we see today is that liberalism's reworked political theory and political theology, which sought to provide all this, involved a great deal of fudging and glossing. With increased moral and religious pluralism, we realize that what had, in the heady days of the Enlightenment, looked like a once-and-for-all solution to such dilemmas was in fact only a temporary solution. In the words of one writer, it '*finessed* as many problems as it attempted to solve' (Mittleman, 2003: 16).

This tension can take many forms – debates about religious attire in France and Christian hoteliers refusing rooms to homosexuals have been in the news recently – but the particular source of tension on which I will focus concerns what sorts of reasons ought to be offered in public debate. The view that such arguments must be phrased in the language of public reason has dominated of late: this is the view of

John Rawls and Jürgen Habermas. While there are important differences between Rawls's and Habermas's positions, for present purposes what they share is more important than where they differ. Both require public discourse, at least some of the time, to be limited in ways that some religious people may have good reasons to oppose. This fits exactly the question posed by Raymond Plant: can liberalism persuade Christians not to offer distinctively Christian reasons in political debates, even when those are the actual reasons for which they hold or advocate a given position? In stating the question in these terms, I am self-consciously limiting my scope to one particular religion. I will be pleased if followers of other faiths find analogues in their traditions to Christianity's reckoning with public reason, but I do not want to assume that the problem, or the solution, is the same for all.[1]

My goal in what follows is to describe the state of the debate about religious reasons in public, at least how that debate appears from within theology. I begin by identifying the historical roots of this debate in classical and contemporary liberalism, especially in John Rawls's notion of public reason. I will argue that we have reason to reject Rawls's restrictions on public discourse and, furthermore, a consensus is now forming to this effect. The inadequacies of this position are well captured in an exchange between the philosophers Richard Rorty and Nicholas Wolterstorff, where Rorty begins by advocating Rawlsian public reason but then abandons it. I conclude by arguing that although public discourse should not be guided by neutral principles, this does not mean it should be unguided by anything at all. One place that Christians in particular might look for guidance is classical and Christian rhetoric, in which public speech is a *moral practice*. As such, some contributions are better or worse than others. That is, they excel in rhetorical excellence; what Christian rhetoricians called *eloquence*.

This provides grounds for moral evaluation of acts of discourse, but not evaluation of the sort advocated by Rawlsian liberalism – which, as we shall see, is tied to a suspicion of rhetoric rooted in rationalism. In particular, I will advocate the concept of *decorum*. It runs throughout

---

[1] Indeed, it may be one of the recurring problems of this debate that religion is assumed to be a unitary concept. Speaking of 'the problem of religion' is about as oversimplified as speaking of 'the problem of sport'. We would need to know what sport we're talking about, just as we often need to know whether we're concerned with Christianity or Judaism or Hinduism or Mormonism.

classical, Christian and Renaissance rhetoric and seeks to guide discourse not via neutral principles, but by an appreciative understanding of one's audience.

Johannine liberalism: 'settle the just bounds'

Regardless of whether liberalism is, as Plant asks, an ethos or legal dogma, we cannot study it without specifying our target more precisely. I will focus on the liberal trajectory that connects the work of John Locke and John Rawls, which I call Johannine liberalism.[2] Of course, this means there are other liberal trajectories that I intentionally leave aside. For example, Martha Nussbaum prefers a trajectory concluding with Rawls but beginning with Roger Williams rather than with Locke (Nussbaum, 2008). And the legal scholar John Witte is sympathetic to Locke so long as we see Locke as a contributor to the Calvinist tradition culminating in Abraham Kuyper rather than leading to Rawls (Witte, 2000). So while the Locke–Rawls connection is separable, the thread that joins them is my focus. The criticisms that I am about to offer may or may not apply to those alternative liberalisms.

Two features of the Locke–Rawls liberal trajectory are significant for our topic. First, the governing metaphor invoked by Johannine liberalism to adjudicate conflicts between religious and civic duty is the image of borders or boundaries. This is clear from the start in the *Letter Concerning Toleration*: 'I esteem it above all things necessary to distinguish exactly the business of civil government from that of religion and to settle the *just bounds* that lie between the one and the other' (Locke, 1983: 26). Some moral and legal conflicts are well described using this image. For example, if the city of Oxford and the county of Oxfordshire disagree about what speed drivers ought to travel on their roads, I am right to expect a jurisdictional solution resolving which authority I must obey. But the problems of religion and public life are often not like such border disputes. Rather, they are like Antigone's dilemma. The Jewish teenager cannot draw a line between those daily tasks for which he is loyal to the God of Abraham, Isaac and Jacob and those for which he is loyal to the Republic of France. Nor could the Mennonite schoolchildren, who refused to recite the

[2] I take the phrase from my former teacher, the late Philip Quinn. See Quinn, 2005: 249.

Pledge of Allegiance to the flag, draw a line between their solidarity with fellow Mennonites and with their fellow American citizens. So too for the Catholic pharmacist who conscientiously objects to filling prescriptions for abortifacients, or the Sikh whose turban prevents him from wearing the traditional uniform of the Royal Canadian Mounted Police. In such cases, carving up jurisdictions so that this duty fits here and that duty fits there will not work. No amount of fine-tuning the underlying principles will do.

Rawls takes Locke's vision to its logical conclusion in a variety of ways. For one, a more religiously and morally pluralistic society requires, in Rawls's words, a higher level of abstraction (Rawls, 1999b: 10). While Locke required toleration of other Protestant denominations, Rawls extends this to requiring abstract respect for a much broader range of diversity, including members of other faiths entirely or those of no faith – and then beyond the realm of religious faith, to neutrality on essentially any trait, practice or moral conviction. It is the heart of Rawls's theory that the government takes no sides on contested moral questions, at least not on constitutional matters. In his words, 'Features relating to social position, native endowment, and historical accident, as well as to the contents of persons' determinate conception of the good, are irrelevant, politically speaking, and hence placed behind the veil of ignorance' (Rawls, 1996: 79). This serves to fortify the jurisdictional boundaries between 'determinative conceptions of the good', on the one hand, and 'civil concernment', on the other.

The other way that Rawls takes Locke to his logical conclusion is by recognizing that, in a condition of moral and religious pluralism, these 'just bounds' must apply not only to actions, but to discourse as well. It is not only that laws should not embody determinative conceptions of the good, but that the reasons offered for or against laws must not either. This is what Rawls calls public reason. While Locke never fully articulated a concept of public reason, he endorses it implicitly, in so far as he thinks certain sorts of reasons count in public debate and others do not. Rawls limits public reason to argumentation that is based on 'political values'; Locke advocates a similar limit via his recurring phrase, 'lawful in the ordinary course of life' (Locke, 1983: 25). So, for example, he writes:

Is it permitted to speak Latin in the market-place? Let those that have a mind to it be permitted to do it also in the Church. Is it lawful for any man in his own house to kneel, stand, sit, or use any other posture; and to clothe himself in white or black, in short or in long garments? Let it not be made unlawful to eat bread, drink wine, or wash with water in the Church. (Locke, 1983: 39)

Here Locke has restated all of the key controversies of his day in the language of public reason, with reference to political values. If these are 'lawful in the ordinary course of life', then they cannot be made unlawful due to objections arising from what Rawls would later call comprehensive doctrines. Notice that not only is Locke explicitly arguing for tolerating these particular practices, he is implicitly shaping what counts as a valid reason in the debate itself. Other commentators have often failed to see the analogy between these two claims, between public reason in Rawls and secular justification of laws in Locke. Part of my argument is that we will fail to understand liberalism unless we see the fundamental similarity of these moves, rooted as these both are in a problematic metaphor of boundary-keeping.

This brings us to the second feature of the Locke–Rawls trajectory relevant for our topic. Both use heuristic devices to generate the foundational principles of their respective political theories: Locke's state of nature and Rawls's original position. What links these is the priority they place on specifying principles *in advance*, principles that constrain one who assents to them even against his or her interests in a given case. Their motivation for this is fairly obvious: if we don't establish the rules for our game *in advance* of particular controversies, then when conflicts do arise, we will each support self-interested (and thus unfair) rules. This was well captured by my five-year-old daughter Hannah. Noticing that there was only one Popsicle remaining in the freezer, she turned to the rest of us and, without a hint of irony, proposed the followed rule: 'The Popsicle belongs to whoever was born in June.' On its surface, birth-month is as fair a way as any to decide who gets the Popsicle – except that Hannah already knew which month she was born in. If she didn't, if she was behind a veil of ignorance vis-à-vis her birthday, then it would be a viable principle.

This lies at the very centre of Rawls's project, though he is not always as forthcoming about this as he might have been. In an essay published in the same year as *A Theory of Justice*, he is perfectly clear. There he uses neither 'original position' nor 'veil of ignorance'. Instead, he imagines a group of people with complaints against some institution.

'They do not begin by complaining', he says, 'they begin instead by establishing the criteria by which a complaint is to be counted legitimate' (Rawls, 1999a: 200). We do this so as to prevent manipulation of the principles and so that everyone will be obliged to adhere to principles when it violates their self-interest – even when they won't get the Popsicle because they weren't born in June.

The rules about complaining are not a passing example for Rawls; it is the core of his theory and his view of ethics generally. He says, 'A person's having a morality is analogous to having made a firm commitment in advance to acknowledge principles having these consequences for one's own conduct. A man whose moral judgments always coincided with his interests could be suspected of having no morality at all' (Rawls, 1999a: 200). So for Rawls, having a morality *simply means* assenting and adhering to principles of that sort formulated in this way. This is not merely a claim for the general value of principles but a stronger claim that principles of a certain sort define morality.

This arises in both Rawls and Locke from a deep distrust of the give-and-take of political debate, of conclusions that emerge 'in the heat of the battle', as it were. This is most obvious in Rawls, where the express purpose of the original position is to segregate as clearly as possible considerations of justice from concrete controversies. 'No one [should] be given the opportunity to tailor the canons of a legitimate complaint to fit his own special conditions, and then to discard them when they no longer suit his purpose.' To this he attaches a footnote: 'Thus everyone is, so far as possible, prevented from acting on the kind of advice which Aristotle summarizes in the *Rhetoric*', where Aristotle shows that which argument one uses depends on one's persuasive intent. But this strikes Rawls as disingenuous, and he appeals to 'Smith's and Hume's idea of an impartial spectator', which he sees as 'derived from the conception of a person so placed that he has no incentive to make these manoeuvres'.[3]

Locke also distrusts the concrete give-and-take of political debate. This is especially clear in his early work, where he opposed toleration. His reason mirrors Rawls's concern. We cannot tolerate until we have

---

[3] Rawls, 1999a: 200–1. Though Rawls would like to see his view of impartiality as originating with Smith and Hume, Amartya Sen contrasts the two. He argues (in a book dedicated to Rawls) for the superiority of Smithean 'open' impartiality over Rawlsian 'closed' impartiality (Sen, 2009: ch. 6).

a clear, formally neutral principle specified in advance to delineate its limits. Initially, he thought such a principle was impossible and therefore he opposed toleration.[4] Though he later changed his mind about whether the principle was possible, he never abandoned his view that it was necessary. What he feared was that if rulers or judges ever made exceptions for religious reasons to generally applicable laws, there would be no end to the exceptions. So if a pacifist is allowed alternatives to compulsory military service because he believes God forbids war, we will soon have people claiming conscientious exemptions from anything they find inconvenient. Locke asks rhetorically, under such a regime 'who would pay taxes?' (Locke, 1997: 22). No one, of course. We would all conveniently conclude that Her Majesty's Treasury is an abomination in the eyes of the Lord.

This was why Locke initially opposed toleration, and knowing this helps us understand why his metaphor of 'just bounds' is so prominent in his later, pro-tolerationist work. Liberal toleration as we have inherited it – that is, Johannine liberalism – originates in a suspicion of toleration and a specific overcoming of that suspicion. Had he not been so suspicious, Locke could have allowed magistrates to decide such matters on a case-by-case basis. Obviously, some conscientious claims are spurious, some are sincere, and it is not always easy to tell the difference. But Locke is unwilling to allow this case-by-case analysis because he so deeply distrusts anything that is not a clear principle specified in advance, immune from manipulation – just as in Rawls's original position. There may be, as I have said, situations for which such neutral principles are the best solution, for which the metaphor of just bounds is appropriate, but political discourse – which is so unavoidably shaped by ongoing give-and-take – is not one of them.

The pitfalls of this approach are best captured by an exchange between Richard Rorty and Nicholas Wolterstorff. They arrive at the position that I think Rawls ought to have arrived at, had he accounted for these criticisms. I think a consensus is forming to this effect; if it is not, it ought to be.

---

[4] This was Locke's view in the 'First Tract on Government', which he wrote (though never published) against his Christ Church colleague, Edward Bagshaw, who was an advocate of broader toleration (Locke, 1997). On this see Perry, 2011, ch. 3.

Rorty and Wolterstorff on religious reasons

Rorty and Wolterstorff's exchange actually originated in 1993 with Stephen Carter's book *The Culture of Disbelief*, which advocated a greater public role for religion. In response, Rorty – American philosophy's great high priest of secular, democratic pragmatism – wrote a harshly critical review, arguing that Carter's vision threatened the great compromise that lies at the heart of liberalism: religious believers agree to privatize their faith in exchange for being tolerated. To convey the way in which he saw religion as marginalized and trivialized in American public life, Carter had written:

One good way to end a conversation – or to start an argument – is to tell a group of well-educated professionals that you hold a political position (preferably a controversial one, such as being against abortion or pornography) because it is required by your understanding of God's will.

To which Rorty responds:

Saying this is far more likely to end a conversation than to start an argument. The same goes for telling the group 'I would never have an abortion' or 'Reading pornography is about the only pleasure I get out of life these days.' In these examples, as in Carter's, the ensuing silence masks the group's inclination to say: So what? We weren't discussing your private life; we were discussing public policy. Don't bother us with matters that are not our concern.

Rorty concludes: 'The main reason religion needs to be privatized is that, in political discussion with those outside the relevant religious community, it is a conversation-stopper' (Rorty, 1999: 171). Throughout his review of Carter's book, Rorty offers an impassioned and persuasive defence of the view that public arguments must be limited to secular reasons of the sort that could persuade all reasonable people. He cites both Rawls and Habermas, but it is a view shared widely throughout American and British society and defended by other philosophers, such as Bruce Ackerman, Robert Audi and Ronald Dworkin.

In 2003, Rorty revisited the issue in an exchange with Nicholas Wolterstorff and, as it happens, was persuaded by Wolterstorff to abandon his earlier view (Rorty, 2003). What persuaded him, and the view he came to embrace, captures nicely the current state of debate on this topic. Wolterstorff asks (Wolterstorff, 2003: 132ff.), is religion really a conversation-stopper? It needn't be. If someone invokes God's will or the Qur'an or the Bible in a political debate, must we simply throw up our hands and abandon the conversation? Of course not. As in any conversation, we use our interlocutor's statement as a launching point. We might try, 'How did you come to see that as God's will?' Or, 'Why should the Qur'an's statement be authoritative for law in our country?' Or, 'Are you sure that's what the Bible says? What about this other passage over here?' To any of these statements, our interlocutor may have better or worse replies, but in most conversations we can move some way to better understanding – sometimes even convincing – each other. Eventually the conversation will stop, but that is a feature of all conversations, not just ones involving religion. So, religion is not necessarily a conversation-stopper in the way that Rorty claimed. In the meantime, everyone should offer whatever reasons they want to offer in public. We may not convince one another, and we may end up disagreeing with one another and putting the matter to a vote – but that is how disagreements are supposed to be settled in a democracy.

Rorty was not one to change his mind easily, but on this question, that is exactly what he did. He writes: '[Wolterstorff] has convinced me that my response to Carter was hasty and insufficiently thoughtful ... So I shall offer a chastened, and more cautious, restatement of my anti-clerical views.' The chastened view is no less secular or anti-clerical, but it is, I think, much more consistent. The first feature of his new view is that his real target is not congregational-level religion but what he calls 'ecclesiastical organizations'. It is 'only the latter', he writes, 'that are the target of secularists like myself'.

Our anti-clericalism is aimed at the Catholic bishops, the Mormon General Authorities, the televangelists, and all the other religious professionals who devote themselves not to pastoral care but to promulgating orthodoxy and acquiring economic and political clout. We think that it is mostly religion above the parish level that does the damage ...

So we secularists have come to think that the best society would be one in which political action conducted in the name of religious belief is treated as a ladder up which our ancestors climbed, but one that now should be thrown away. We grant that ecclesiastical organizations have sometimes been on the right side, but we think that the occasional Gustavo Guttierez or Martin Luther King does not compensate for the ubiquitous Joseph Ratzingers and Jerry Falwells. (Rorty, 2003: 141)

The second feature of Rorty's new view is that there is no available principle or rule to distinguish an allowable class of reasons from a non-allowable class. Rorty concedes that Wolterstorff should be free, if he so chooses, to cite Psalm 72 in support of social welfare legislation. He concedes this because, he says:

I can think of no law or custom that would hinder [Wolterstorff] from doing so that would not hinder me from citing passages in John Stuart Mill in justification of the same legislation. The fact that Psalm 72 belongs to a set of Scriptures claimed by various ecclesiastical organizations which I regard as politically dangerous is not a good reason to hinder Wolterstorff from citing this Psalm, any more than the fact that many people regard Mill's utilitarianism as morally dangerous is a good reason to stop me citing *On Liberty*. Neither law nor custom should stop either of us from bringing our favorite texts with us into the public square. (Rorty, 2003: 143)

Thus Rorty abandons his attempt to distinguish allowable and non-allowable reasons in public. But what if, rather than advocating redistributionist taxation, someone supports a law restricting the rights of homosexuals by citing the usual verses from Leviticus or St Paul? Rorty responds: 'Here I cannot help feeling that, though the law should not forbid someone from citing such texts in support of a political position, custom *should* forbid it.'

People who quote Leviticus 18:22 with approval should be shunned and despised. Our attitude to them should be the same as that toward people who remark that, though of course Hitler was a bad thing, it cannot be denied that the Jews *did* kill Christ – or, to vary the example, people who urge that, although the lynch mobs went too far, it is a truly terrible thing for a white women to have sex with a black man. (Rorty, 2003: 143)

Rorty's position here is so ideologically loaded it is hard to know where to go next. What *should* guide our public speech? Here comes Rorty's punch-line. Rorty realizes this is ideologically loaded and, in fact, embraces it. He writes:

It would be nice if I could appeal to a principle which differentiated between citing Psalm 72 in favor of government-financed health insurance and citing Leviticus 18 in opposition to changes in the law that would make life in the U.S. more bearable for gays and lesbians. But I do not have one. I wholeheartedly believe that religious people should trim their utterances to suit my utilitarian views ... But I do not know how to make either of these propositions plausible to them. (Rorty, 2003: 143–4)

That is more or less where Rorty leaves it. It was one of his last published articles; he died four years later in 2007.

Rorty's change of mind on this question can serve as a picture of the larger debate as a whole. His early view held and continues to hold massive sway in society at large, the halls of government and throughout university departments of philosophy, politics, religion and law. But in light of the critique represented by Wolterstorff, I believe a consensus has now formed among some that this is misguided, and it is misguided along precisely the lines that Rorty comes to realize. In particular, public speech cannot be regulated by neutral rules specified in advance. When explaining our views to our fellow citizens, or seeking to persuade them, we should each offer whatever reasons we think best, whether that be in the form of a logical syllogism or a poem, whether it be drawn from a sacred text, a philosopher or our favourite film. This consensus may not yet have reached disciplines outside liberal political theory (where it emerged), and I have yet to see it in the opinion pages of the *Guardian*, but nonetheless it can be called a solidly emerging consensus.

We see this in the academic world in the work of wise and careful scholars such as William Galston (himself a student of the aforementioned Leo Strauss), Michael Sandel, Chris Eberle and Kwame Appiah – as well as more brash and less careful scholars such as Stanley Fish.[5] What they share is a realization that narrowly procedural conceptions of justice are inadequate. Limits on public reason based on such a conception are bound to be unfair, excluding reasons purely because they are contested, and often excluding reasons that we have good reason to endorse. For example, they show that the limits by which Rawls seeks to exclude certain arguments against abortion would have excluded the most important arguments for the abolition of slavery (see Galston, 1991: 274; Sandel, 1996: 21–3). But we also see hints of this consensus outside the academic world, at least anecdotally. For example, a recent pamphlet widely discussed in the British media, *Citizen Ethics in a Time of Crisis*, included contributions not

---

[5] See Appiah, 2005; Eberle, 2002; Fish, 1999; Galston, 1991; Sandel, 1996.

only from Sandel, John Milbank, Rowan Williams and Nigel Biggar, but also from Philip Pullman and Polly Toynbee. What the contributors seem to share is a sense that speaking of moral goods in a non-neutral way – that is *advocating* concrete goods – is essential. This is not identical to actually rejecting Rawlsian public reason, but it certainly shows growing discontent with the underlying perspective that made limits on public reason plausible in the first place.

What Rorty comes to realize when he abandons his earlier view is that there simply are no neutral principles to guide public discourse, at least not principles that could be specified in advance of the concrete give-and-take of an actual conversation. He wishes there were a principled way to admit arguments from Mill the utilitarian while excluding Micah the prophet – 'It would be nice if I could appeal to a principle which differentiated [these]', he says – but he admits, 'I do not have one'. So that is the state of the debate. As far as Raymond Plant's question goes, I do not think Johannine liberalism is capable of justifying itself to religious citizens who would experience such linguistic limits us burdensome, unfair and conceptually problematic.

Can rhetoric be a better guide?

But if this signals the beginning of the end of Johannine liberal public reason, where should we go next? We could abandon the effort to guide public discourse in any way and let it be a free-for-all, but this is unattractive precisely because so much of what Rorty says about Christians is *correct*. Much Christian political discourse is appallingly bad (though so is much secular discourse). Rorty's objection is partly sociological: the Ratzingers will always outnumber the Martin Luther Kings (how one would verify that empirically, I am not sure), but the deeper problem with simply making public discourse a free-for-all is that this cedes communication itself to the realm of amorality. But Christians in particular have reason to deny this: speech is a morally laden activity, such that there are more or less excellent acts of speech; speech can be more or less *morally worthy*.

We all know the usual horror stories that Rorty has in mind, and which he wants to exclude as valid public discourse in a pluralistic liberal society. Consider, for example, the mother who was denied visitation rights to her daughter because, in the words of the judge, 'she is … a lesbian living a life of abomination' (quoted in Levinson, 1997: 81).

That was in 1992. The only support the judge offered for his verdict were two parentheses containing the words 'Leviticus 18:22'. But if Rorty has abandoned the Johannine way of distinguishing allowable and unallowable reasons, it is not entirely clear what *is* wrong with the judge's ruling.[6] The appeal to the Bible cannot be the problem, because Rorty says explicitly that 'neither law nor custom should stop either of us from bringing our favorite texts with us into the public square'.

Suppose we described this scenario to classical philosophers, medieval theologians or Renaissance humanists. I suspect that almost every one of them would give the same answer: the standard that Rorty is reaching for, but unable quite to grasp hold of, is *rhetoric*. Rhetoric not in the pejorative sense as manipulative speech – the object of ridicule in Plato's *Gorgias* – but rhetoric as an art or practice of effectively communicating truth through an appreciative understanding of one's audience. If that is our standard then what is wrong with the judge's appeal to Leviticus is not that it violates some Rawlsian or Jeffersonian principle, but that it is a bad argument *given the audience's starting point*. It fails as an act of persuasion, which is the *telos* of rhetorical acts. It fails to display eloquence, which is what a rhetorically excellent act achieves. The judge is offering reasons for why this woman may not visit her daughter; he thinks the woman's sexual orientation is a good reason not to allow visitation. But whether that reason persuades his audience of the conclusion depends on whether the audience shares the judge's premise that those with a certain sexual orientation are unfit parents. As this is the point of dispute in the case, we can be fairly sure that the audience does not share that premise. Adding a parenthetical reference to Leviticus only further obscures the matter, for only an audience that accepts Leviticus as a reliable moral authority would find this persuasive.

If this is so, then the problem with the judge's argument is not captured by the filter of Johannine or Rawlsian public reason, but it might be by the prudential norms of rhetoric. In the remainder of this chapter I will list three ways in which the classical or Renaissance rhetorical tradition could help guide public reason. Note that I do not see

---

[6] There is obviously something legally wrong with the verdict, but let us set aside for present purposes that this arose in the context of a judicial ruling. My question is how we can identify what is wrong with this as a communicative act.

myself merely as replacing one set of rhetorical norms (Rawlsian) with another set (classical), for it is part of my argument that Johannine liberalism's approach to public reason is an *abdication* of rhetoric. Locke and Rawls seek not persuasion but deductive, rationalist proofs that make persuasion unnecessary – hence their shared suspicion of the give-and-take of political conversation and their confidence in neutral principles. Locke's opposition to rhetoric is well known (he calls it 'that powerful instrument of error and deceit'), and William Galston has argued effectively that especially Rawls's later work collapses the distinction between classical political philosophy and rhetoric in problematic ways (Galston, 1989: 722). Similarly Descartes, against Vico, sees reason as *replacing* rhetoric (Herrick, 2008: 183). Locke's rejection of rhetoric is especially telling if we recall what he identifies as its crucial fault: it uses figural language, which is subject to multiple meanings. 'All the ... figurative application of Words Eloquence hath invented ... are [a] perfect cheat' (Locke, 1975: 3:10.34). The contrast with the Christian rhetorical tradition could not be clearer. 'For Augustine, it is precisely the capacity of figurative language to express multiple meanings simultaneously that makes it ideal as a medium for communicating the nature of true justice' (Dodaro, 2004: 122). Ironically, the Johannine abdication of rhetoric exacerbates the very problem it sets out to solve. In the following pages, I briefly consider three possible aspects that are worthy of recovery.

Rhetoric as a practice

First, the tradition of rhetoric helps us conceive of communication as a moral practice. This point was best made by the twentieth-century rhetorician Thomas Farrell. He notes that despite 'a widespread revival of Aristotelian *ethical* and *political* philosophy, [this] has thus far not been accompanied by any great interest in a renewal of the Aristotelian *rhetorical* tradition' (Farrell, 1991: 184). Farrell has in mind his fellow rhetoricians, but theologians and philosophers will most associate the recovery of Aristotle with Alasdair MacIntyre. *After Virtue* begins by describing a collapse of moral *language*, a *linguistic* apocalypse, from which Aristotle (and Aquinas) can save us. But then why not turn to Aristotle's *Rhetoric* first of all?

Farrell was clearly thinking along similar lines, because what he advocates is rhetoric conceived as a *practice* in the MacIntyrian sense, which he uses to distinguish rhetoric as virtuous activity from rhetoric as 'pragmatic exertion of power through discourse' (Farrell, 1991: 185). Recall that MacIntyre's notion of a practice distinguishes internal and external goods. That is, between goods that are contingently related to a practice and goods that are fundamental and integral to its mastery. Persuasion is a goal at which one aims in rhetoric, just as – in MacIntyre's famous example – checkmate is the goal of chess. However, one does not engage in these practices only to win (or persuade), but because 'with the acquisition of skill, there comes an appreciation for the well-played match, regardless of results'. In MacIntyre's example, if we are rewarding a child with candy for winning at chess, then

so long as it is the candy alone which provides the child with a good reason for playing chess, the child has no reason not to cheat and every reason to cheat, provided he or she can do so successfully. But, so we may hope, there will come a time when the child will find in those goods specific to chess, in the achievement of a certain highly particular kind of analytical skill, strategic imagination and competitive intensity, a new set of reasons, reasons now not just for winning on a particular occasion, but for trying to excel in whatever way the game of chess demands. Now if the child cheats, he or she will be defeating not me but himself or herself. (MacIntyre, 2007: 188)

So too for rhetoric. One can cheat at rhetoric just as one can cheat at chess. But this does not mean Plato's critique of rhetoric in the *Gorgias* is right, any more than cheaters at chess make that a corrupt pursuit.

Augustine makes this point effectively where he contrasts St Paul's two admonitions 'contest not in words' (on the one hand) and 'exhort in sound doctrine' (on the other). The former pursues mere 'rhetorical' victory, while the latter pursues truth. 'For to contend in words is not to care how error is overcome by truth, but how your speech is preferred to that of another.' He who avoids contending with words 'so acts with words that the truth becomes clear, that the truth is pleasing, and the truth moves' (Augustine, 1958: 4.61).

Conceiving of rhetoric as a moral practice ought to be especially attractive for Christians, given rhetoric's prominence throughout church history. This is true chiefly of Augustine, and Augustine's appropriation of Cicero, though this was controversial at the time for being too sympathetic to pagan philosophy. Even Augustine himself had qualms, especially in the years immediately following his conversion.

Yet his humanism ultimately won out, and this legacy of learning from Scripture alongside the humanities lasted to the early modern period, notably in writers like Erasmus. In fact, some have argued that Christian humanism gave birth to a notion of toleration that could have, and perhaps should have, stood as a counter-tradition to the liberal toleration that soon surpassed it. Aubrey's *Brief Lives* tells the remarkable story of how Hobbes was initially fascinated by rhetoric, but abandoned this in a sudden, and what turned out to be fateful, moment. 'Being in a Gentleman's Library', Hobbes noticed Euclid's *Elements* lying open on the table. He read it through and never looked back. 'This made him in love with Geometry' (quoted in Remer, 1996: 177). Hence his political work became a quest for a science of politics – that is, one that (because it is a closed system, as geometry) is exempt from the need for rhetorical persuasion. Locke shared Hobbes's aversion to rhetoric and, like Hobbes, saw ethics as a closed, mathematical system. What we now call toleration is primarily the Hobbesian-Lockean variety, which (though indebted to humanism at points) is largely distinct from it. What separates the two is their contrasting views of rhetoric. We, and Locke and Rawls, are heirs to the tradition that rejected rhetoric. So much the worse for them – and us.

Decorum

By far the most widely discussed concept in all of classical rhetoric is decorum, sometimes called literary decorum or literary propriety. This concept runs throughout all classical work on rhetoric, and it is also central for what guidance rhetoric could offer to Christians seeking to speak well in public. Writing of Augustine's use of the concept, Robert Dodaro describes it best:

Literary decorum has its source in ancient Greek and Latin rhetorical precepts governing the determination of what is suitable and fitting in discourse (*to proton, aptum*) and is thus concerned with linguistic or literary congruence ... Cicero, who influences Augustine in this regard, followed Aristotle in locating the central task in establishing a balanced mean or harmony between different elements within a discourse. (Dodaro, 2001: 70)

Decorum is concerned with what is *apt*, primarily defining apt *with regard to one's audience*. Dodaro's example of Augustinian decorum (or lack of it) is a priest making a crude joke during a funeral sermon (Dodaro, 2001: 70). That is actually closer to capturing what is wrong with the judge's appeal to Leviticus against the lesbian mother. Both fail to be eloquent not because of some external standard that exists apart from the speaker–audience exchange. Rather, the standards exist within the speaker–audience relation and thus arise from them. This dependence on audience is what distinguishes the standard of decorum from the fixation on principles of Johannine liberalism.

But the contrast with the norms of liberal public reason is greater still, for it differs not only in the focus on the audience but in (characteristically) denying that the 'fit' between speaker and audience can be determined in advance by principles. One becomes decorous, and ultimately eloquent, by practising speaking. It is not the sort of thing one can learn from a book. 'It thus becomes – and clearly was for classical education – not only a rhetorical criterion but a general test of basic acculturation. To know how to establish the decorum of a particular occasion meant you had, as a child or a foreigner might, learned to find your footing in that culture' (Lanham, 1991: 46). It is this lack of footing in the culture that most strongly tells against so much Christian political speech currently. It simply fails to account for the audience's starting point, and thus fails as an act of persuasion.

Some recent theologians have spent their careers worrying about Christians finding too sure a cultural footing. Certainly Stanley Hauerwas and to a lesser extent William Cavanaugh see it as theologically problematic to be too sure of one's footing in a liberal society given that they perceive tensions between liberal and Christian politics and ethics. This is an important critique, for which I have much sympathy, but I do not think it should dissuade us here. Hauerwas's concern is better understood as a twentieth-century recurrence of Jerome's nightmare. Jerome, too, feared loving rhetoric too much.

In mid-Lent 374 the scholarly Saint Jerome, who delighted in reading ancient authors, had a dream in which he was hauled before a divine tribunal and asked what he was. 'A Christian,' Jerome replied. 'You lie,' the judge responded. 'You are a Ciceronian, not a Christian. For your heart is where your treasure is.' In his dream Jerome was then flogged, after which he repented and acknowledged that to read 'worldly books' is indeed to deny Christ. (Sloane, 2004: 112)

In Hauerwas's nightmare the judge declares, instead, 'You are a liberal, not a Christian', but the lesson is the same. The problem is that Christian tradition has essentially rejected Jerome's dream as the product of an over-scrupulous conscience. Reading 'worldly books' – even Locke and Rawls – is not, on further reflection, 'to deny Christ'.

Yet I remain sympathetic to the concern underlying Hauerwas's objection to over-easy acculturation. Hauerwas's dependence on MacIntyre leads me to the belief that had MacIntyre *not* ignored Aristotle's *Rhetoric*, perhaps Hauerwas would not find it so hard to know what to say, as a Christian, in public.

Prudential, not deductive

This process of finding one's rhetorical footing in a culture, as with children, is not learned via rules, even if there are rules of thumb to guide it. Augustine mentions repeatedly that a speaker cannot speak eloquently and think of the rules at the same time (like learning to ride a bike while thinking about how to ride a bike). He writes, 'in the speeches and sayings of the eloquent, the precepts of eloquence are found to have been fulfilled, although the speakers did not think of them in order to be eloquent ... They fulfilled them because they were eloquent; they did not apply them that they might be eloquent' (Augustine, 1958: 1.4). Thus decorum, which is necessary for the expression of eloquence, must be learned in the concrete, and it is for this reason that the Johannine commitment to ideal principles simply reinforces its suspicion of rhetoric. 'Literary decorum requires subtle and *subjective* judgments by the author' (Dodaro, 2004: 137). Recall Rorty's initial example of unacceptable Christian speech, of reasons that ought not to be allowed.

'[Imagine you] tell a group of well-educated professionals that you hold a political position (preferably a controversial one, such as being against abortion or pornography) because it is required by your understanding of God's will.' ... [T]he ensuing silence masks the group's inclination to say: So what? We weren't discussing your private life; we were discussing public policy. Don't bother us with matters that are not our concern.

We can read between the lines easily enough: the thinly veiled subtext is that this is some naïve, uneducated Christian who sidles up to a group

of intellectuals at a cocktail party where she really does not belong –
drinks in the Senior Common Room, say. Now contrast Rorty's image
with the following, offered by the literary theorist Kenneth Burke:

Imagine that you enter a parlor. You come late. When you arrive, others
have long preceded you, and they are engaged in a heated discussion, a discussion too heated for them to pause and tell you exactly what it is about.
In fact, the discussion had already begun long before any of them got there,
so that no one present is qualified to retrace for you all the steps that had
gone before. You listen for a while, until you decide that you have caught
the tenor of the argument; then you put in your oar. Someone answers; you
answer him; another comes to your defense; another aligns himself against
you, to either the embarrassment or gratification of your opponent, depending upon the quality of your ally's assistance. However, the discussion is
interminable. The hour grows late, you must depart. And you do depart,
with the discussion vigorously in progress. (Burke, 1973: 110)

That is decorum. 'We may as well put in our oars like everyone else'
(Cunningham, 1991: 2). The difference between Burke's parlour and
Rorty's cocktail party (and Rawls's original position) is stark. The
'well-educated professionals' of Rorty's example know in advance
what they will allow in their conversation and what they won't. And
the newcomer hasn't bothered to listen for long enough to find her
footing. This captures both what is wrong with Rawls's exclusion of
religious reasons, and what is wrong with so much Christian political
discourse: the arrogant assumption by some that they have been there
from the beginning and therefore control the terms of discussion, as
well as the foolishness of the newcomer who doesn't wait and listen
for long enough to hear what the argument is about.

Part of what makes acquiring the virtues of rhetoric so challenging
today is that there is a diversity of audiences, and audience presuppositions, unanticipated by the classical rhetoricians. We enter one
parlour one day, and another quite different parlour the next – each
with its own ongoing, initially impenetrable, conversations. There is
one, perhaps unlikely, early modern thinker that contemporary rhetoricians have found helpful on this point: Jane Austen; in particular, her
novel *Persuasion*. 'Austen differs from her predecessors in this volume
by construing rhetorical communities as plural. Whereas Aristotle,
Cicero, and the others base rhetorical arguments on the beliefs of a
single polis, republic, or political commonwealth, Austen traces the

different ends and discourses that shape a diversity of social milieux in early nineteenth-century England' (Olmsted, 2006: 97). In the novel, Anne Elliot becomes unable to converse with her father and sister, for their rhetorical world 'is organized around ends and values that she does not embrace' (Olmsted, 2006: 98). Like the person who wanders into Burke's parlour – and unlike the Christian interrupting Rorty's cocktail party – Anne realizes this and aspires to the virtue of decorum. As Austen describes her, Anne found it '"to be very fitting that every little social commonwealth should dictate its own matters of discourse; and hoped, ere long, to become a not unworthy member of the one she was now transported to"' (Olmsted, 2006: 97). As she does this, the tension with her family's world, with its quite different ends and values, is heightened.

Austen's skill in defining those ends and values can be understood in terms of the classical (Aristotelian and Ciceronian) emphasis on common beliefs as the premises for rhetorical arguments. While Aristotle emphasises rhetoric depends on 'generally accepted opinion' or 'what seems true to people of a certain sort'; Austen shows this varies between discursive communities. (Olmsted, 2006: 98)

Austen also shows, and could perhaps therefore accommodate, concerns such as Hauerwas's that 'becoming a not unworthy member' of various 'social commonwealths' is not without its cost, as it is not for Anne. It also reinforces why a single, unified public reason is not the solution for a pluralist society. There is no available *lingua franca* with which Anne can bridge the diverse linguistic communities she encounters.

Conclusion: arguing offside

I have argued that the metaphor of just bounds – so central for Johannine liberalism – is problematic, especially when applied to setting borders between allowable and unacceptable classes of speech. Various critics of Rawls have made a case for this, and even some former supporters of Rawls, such as Rorty, have been persuaded by these criticisms. I therefore suggested that a consensus was now forming that we abandon our attempt to restrict speech via neutral principles specified in advance. Such principles are grounded in a suspicion of rhetoric and a confidence in rationalism that we now have reason to doubt. Reasons deriving from comprehensive doctrines, including distinctively religious reasons, must be welcomed in public.

But I did not want to leave us without any guidance, and therefore suggested the classical rhetorical tradition has something to offer that will guide public speech without the pitfalls of Johannine public reason. To this end, I suggested (1) that rhetoric helps us see public speech as a moral practice, (2) that we promote the norm of decorum, which values persuading others of the truth via an appreciative understanding of one's audience and (3) that decorum requires prudence, not technical skill. It is an art, not a science, as conveyed by the example of Burke's parlour and Anne Elliot's inculcation into diverse rhetorical communities.

I close with one final example, taken from the world of sport, which conveys the contrast between the rhetorical approach that I propose and the principled approach that I attribute to Johannine liberalism. In some sports, like ice hockey, there is a fixed line painted on the playing surface indicating where offside offences can occur. If you cross that offside line without possession of the hockey puck, you are offside. But the line itself never moves. This is not how offside works in soccer, that is, European football. In football there is no fixed offside line; instead the 'line' moves as your opponent moves and the most skilled attackers in the game know how to work this to their advantage. They dance over and back, over and back, as their opponents move, always looking for the greatest advantage without being whistled for an offence.[7]

The boundary-marking approach espoused by Johannine liberals is analogous to hockey: they want a line, fixed once and for all. Mention the Bible or Qur'an? That crosses the line. (But Mill is still onside.) Mention personhood or the human good or flourishing? The whistle blows. If you claim that the social institution of marriage exists to promote friendship and loyalty between two people, or that the purposes of the social institution of private property is to meet the needs of the poor, then again – you have crossed the line. But this is wrong: what I should say in public, whether as a Christian or not, *varies* just like the offside line in football.

---

[7] The analogy is based on an idea suggested to me by the Rev. Steve Hellyer, St Matthew's Church, Oxford.

Christians in particular have much to learn if they are to dance effectively along the offside line. They need to become skilled in the practical art of rhetoric. It is the absence of this skill that most harms the church's moral witness and, ironically, emboldens the cry for fixed Johannine limits. Martin Luther King, William Wilberforce – they knew how to dance along the offside line. This does not mean they never crossed the line, for they often did. But their skill was in knowing how to cross the line at just the right moment, so that their audience raced along with them to join the cause – and thereby shifted where the offside line falls. Thus it *used to be* offside to affirm the moral equality of blacks and whites, because this was thought to be a peculiar and contentious claim, one rooted in a comprehensive doctrine that many reasonable people rejected. But the claim is no longer offside; if anything, our thinking on racial equality has shifted so dramatically in the past century that it is now the other way round: denying equality is offside. But this can only be true if the offside line moves, if we are playing football and not hockey.

Augustine was aware of a final pitfall: a too-great confidence in the power of speech to persuade. As a professor of rhetoric who resigned his post after converting to Christianity, he knew that persuasion sometimes requires no words at all. According to Augustine we should aspire to speak both wisely and eloquently. But if someone cannot, if he can only do one or the other, he 'should [speak] wisely … rather than say eloquently what he says foolishly'. And if he is capable of neither, 'let him so order his life … that he offers an example to others and his *way of living* may be, as it were, an eloquent speech' (Augustine, 1958: 4.61).

References

Appiah, K. A. 2005. *The Ethics of Identity*. Princeton University Press.

Augustine. 1958. *On Christian Doctrine*, trans. D. W. Robertson. Upper Saddle River, NJ: Prentice Hall.

Burke, K. 1973. *The Philosophy of Literary Form: Studies in Symbolic Action*. Berkeley and Los Angeles: University of California Press.

Carter, S. L. 1993. *The Culture of Disbelief: How American Law and Politics Trivialize Religious Devotion*. New York: Anchor Books.

Cunningham, D. 1991. *Faithful Persuasion: In Aid of a Rhetoric of Christian Theology*. University of Notre Dame Press.

Dodaro, R. 2001. 'The Theologian as Grammarian: Literary Decorum in Augustine's Defense of Orthodox Discourse', in M. F. Wiles and M. J. Yarnold, eds., *Studia Patristica* 38. Leuven: Peeters, 70–83.

2004. *Christ and the Just Society in the Thought of Augustine*. Cambridge University Press.

Eberle, C. J. 2002. *Religious Conviction in Liberal Politics*. Cambridge University Press.

Farrell, T. 1991. 'Practicing the Arts of Rhetoric: Tradition and Invention', *Philosophy and Rhetoric*, 24, 3, 183–212.

Fish, S. 1999. *The Trouble with Principle*. Cambridge, MA: Harvard University Press.

Galston, W. 1989. 'Pluralism and Social Unity', *Ethics*, 99, 711–26.

1991. *Liberal Purposes: Goods, Virtues, and Diversity in the Liberal State*. Cambridge University Press.

Herrick, J. 2008. *The History and Theory of Rhetoric*. Boston: Allyn & Bacon.

Lanham, R. 1991. *A Handlist of Rhetorical Terms*. Berkeley and Los Angeles: University of California Press.

Levinson, S. 1997. Abstinence and Exclusion: What Does Liberalism Demand of the Religiously Oriented (Would-Be) Judge?', in P. J. Weithman, ed., *Religion and Contemporary Liberalism*. University of Notre Dame Press, 233–55.

Locke, J. 1975. *An Essay Concerning Human Understanding*, ed. Peter H. Nidditch. Oxford: Clarendon Press.

1983. *A Letter Concerning Toleration*, ed. James H. Tully. Indianapolis: Hackett Publishing.

1997. 'First Tract on Government', in *Political Essays*, ed. Mark Goldie. Cambridge University Press, 3–53.

MacIntyre, A. 2007. *After Virtue*. University of Notre Dame Press.

Mittleman, A., ed. 2003. *Religion as a Public Good: Jews and Other Americans on Religion in the Public Square*. Oxford: Rowman & Littlefield.

Nussbaum, M. 2008. *Liberty of Conscience: In Defense of America's Tradition of Religious Liberty*. New York: Basic Books.

O'Donovan, O. 1984. 'Principles in the Public Realm. The Dilemma of Christian Moral Witness'. An Inaugural Lecture Delivered before the University of Oxford on 24 May 1983. Oxford: Clarendon Press.

Olmsted, W. 2006. *Rhetoric: An Historical Introduction*. Oxford: Blackwell.

Perry, J. 2011. *The Pretenses of Loyalty: Locke, Liberal Theory, and American Political Theology*. Oxford University Press.

Quinn, P. 2005. 'Can Good Christians Be Good Liberals?', in Andrew Chignell and Andrew Dole, eds., *God and the Ethics of Belief: New Essays in Philosophy of Religion*. Cambridge University Press, 248–76.

Rawls, J. 1996. *Political Liberalism*. New York: Columbia University Press.
  1999a. *Collected Papers*, ed. Samuel Freeman. Cambridge, MA: Harvard University Press.
  1999b. *A Theory of Justice*. Cambridge, MA: Belknap Press of Harvard University Press.

Remer, G. 1996. *Humanism and the Rhetoric of Toleration*. University Park: Pennsylvania State University Press.

Rorty, R. 1999. 'Religion as Conversation-Stopper', in *Philosophy and Social Hope*. New York: Penguin, 168–74.
  2003. 'Religion in the Public Square: A Reconsideration', *Journal of Religious Ethics*, 31, 1, 141–9.

Sandel, M. 1996. *Democracy's Discontent*. Cambridge, MA: Belknap Press of Harvard University Press.

Sen, A. 2009. *The Idea of Justice*. Cambridge, MA: Belknap Press of Harvard University Press.

Sloane, T. 2004. 'Rhetorical Selfhood in Erasmus and Milton', in Wendy Olmsted and Walter Jost, eds., *A Companion to Rhetoric and Rhetorical Criticism*. Oxford: Blackwell, 112–27.

Witte, J. 2000. 'The Biology and Biography of Liberty: Abraham Kuyper and the American Experiment', in Luis Lugo, ed., *Religion, Pluralism, and Public Life: Abraham Kuyper's Legacy for the Twenty-First Century*. Grand Rapids, MI: Eerdmans, 243–62.

Wolterstorff, N. 2003. 'An Engagement with Rorty', *Journal of Religious Ethics*, 31, 1, 129–39.

Index

Made in the USA
Monee, IL
24 December 2021